PHILOSOPHY/SOCIOLOGY

International
Library of the
Philosophy of
Education

Beyond the Present and
the Particular

International
Library of the
Philosophy of
Education

General Editor

R. S. Peters

Professor of Philosophy of Education
Institute of Education
University of London

Beyond the Present and the Particular:

A Theory of Liberal Education

Charles Bailey

Department of Education
Homerton College, Cambridge

Routledge & Kegan Paul

London, Boston, Melbourne and Henley

First published in 1984
by Routledge & Kegan Paul plc

14 Leicester Square, London WC2H 7PH, England

9 Park Street, Boston, Mass. 02108, USA

464 St Kilda Road, Melbourne,
Victoria 3004, Australia and

Broadway House, Newtown Road,
Henley-on-Thames, Oxon RG9 1EN, England

Set in Press Roman 10 on 11pt
by Columns of Reading
and printed in Great Britain
by St Edmundsbury Press Ltd,
Bury St Edmunds, Suffolk

Library of Congress Cataloging in Publication Data

Bailey, Charles, 1924-

Beyond the present and the particular.
(International library of the philosophy of education)
Bibliography; p.
Includes index.
1. Education, Humanistic—Philosophy.   I. Title.
II. Series.
LC1011.B27   1984   370.11'2   84-4882
British Library CIP data also available

ISBN 0-7100-9897-9 (c)

This work is dedicated with affection and respect to my colleagues, past and present, in the Education Department, at Homerton College, Cambridge.

Contents

Contents

Epigraph

This is what generalising and talking about the past have in common; they are both departures from that which is present and particular. This common feature is what links them with rationality. The idea of rationality is that of the ability, given certain present and particular data, to unite or relate them with other data in certain appropriate ways. This is the Kantian idea of concepts as unifiers, binders together, creators of a *multum in parvo*.

Jonathan Bennet, Rationality

In the first place, reasonableness is not exhausted in the exercise of reasoning. A rational man may well be an intellectual, but he will not be an intellectualist, if this means that he retreats into his own corner and contents himself with spinning webs. Indeed, to try to squeeze a normal man into a tiny bed of his own cognitive faculty, and then lop off whatever will not fit into it, is to stunt him and indeed to kill him . . .

Secondly, rationality has a far larger field than that of propositions and concepts. It is as truly at work in judgments of better and worse, of right and wrong, as in those judgments of analytic necessity to which a narrow convention would confine the name of reason. It may exhibit itself, for example, in the sanity and good sense with which one appraises the types of human experience . . .

Thirdly, rationality extends to reasonableness in conduct. A man would not in our present sense deserve the name, no matter how clever he was, or how judicious in problems of value, who was incapable of translating his insights into action.

Brand Blanshard on the rational temper, in Reason and Goodness

Acknowledgments

This attempt to write a modern characterization and defence of liberal education has been provoked and stimulated by many encounters over the last two decades. Particularly in conferences and in-service courses with teachers I have frequently been asked to spell out the overall view of education in which were lodged my particular views on moral education, the curriculum, appropriate teacher strategies and attitudes, and so on; and this has always been difficult to do in any brief but satisfactory way. Without these repeated challenges the book might never have been written.

A second provocation has been the succession of suggestions from politicians and others in recent years that seem to me to threaten what is most valuable in education. It has become increasingly necessary for me to make clear to myself why I see certain educational content and method to be valuable, and the exact nature of the forces and arguments threatening these values.

In this undertaking my greatest debt is to those who have wrestled with these problems before me in recent times, especially Paul Hirst, Philip Phenix and John White, all of whom have had the courage and wisdom, against the spirit of the age, to address the right fundamental questions and problems. My criticisms of these three writers, liberal educators all, will, I hope, be seen as a mark of respect for their endeavours rather than the reverse.

I have been helped and encouraged by many friends and colleagues in conversations directly and indirectly related to what I have written. I would particularly like to mention Paul Hirst, who kindly read the first four chapters and encouraged me to continue; Michael Bonnett, David Bridges, Ray Dalton, Patrick Heffernan and Terry McLaughlin, who were kind enough to comment on parts of Chapter 6 for me; and John Beck who gave me much wise advice and also read and commented on Chapters 9 and 10. For this and a great deal else I am grateful to my Cambridge colleagues. They are not, of course, to blame for what I have done with, or in spite of, their advice.

I am indebted to the Principal, the Trustees and the Academic Board of Homerton College for releasing me from my teaching duties for one term in 1982 and another in 1983. Without this generous release, and the readiness of colleagues to undertake some of my duties, I could not have produced the book.

I am grateful to the following publishers for permission to use the extensive quotations from their copyright works in my Chapter 6: Routledge & Kegan Paul for quotations from Paul Hirst's 'Knowledge and the Curriculum', and for quotations from John White's 'Towards a Compulsory Curriculum'; McGraw-Hill for quotations from Philip Phenix's 'Realms of Meaning'.

1 Introduction – Theory and education

Since the aim of this work is to present a comprehensive and coherent *theory* of liberal education it is important to be clear in what sense I am talking about theory.

The word 'theory', like many other useful words in our language, has more than one meaning. Some of these meanings are plainly derogatory. For example 'theory' can mean 'an unproved assumption' or a 'mere idea', and there could be little to say about theory if this was all there was about it. We do not have to look far, however, to see that when we talk about bodies of ideas like the wave theory of light, the theory of radioactive decay, or the special theory of relativity, although there is a sense in which we are talking about assumptions, we are certainly not talking about *mere* ideas or lightly held assumptions. We are talking rather about carefully worked out and internally coherent bodies of ideas that seem to explain observed phenomena over a wide range of experiences. Although not verified beyond any peradventure of doubt, these theories enable us to make reasonable predictions and have not been refuted, though critically probed in many ways.

There are two important points to note about these scientific or explanatory theories. Firstly, they are not, as is sometimes supposed, derived from some piling up of observations until a theory emerges. They are, instead, the result of imaginative and creative ideas on the part of a Newton, a Rutherford or an Einstein about how things might be. Only then can propositions be deduced from the theories which we might try, as Karl Popper[1] has indicated, to refute. The theory stands as an explanation in so far as we fail to refute it. The theory is, to use Popper's language, the unrefuted conjecture.

The second point to notice about scientific theories of this kind is that it would be arrant nonsense to say of such a theory, 'It is all right in theory but not in practice.' This would be nonsense because a failure in practice would amount to refutation. Einstein's general theory of relativity, for example, provided propositions about the motion of the perihelion of Mercury, about the deflection of light in a gravitational field and about the displacement of spectral lines towards the red, all of which provided opportunities for refutation. Had the propositions not been found to fit practice in the sense of practical observation, then the theory would not have been all right but would have been discarded, however elegant the internal coherence of the mathematics might have been.

I do not want to claim that an educational theory, least of all the theory of liberal education to be advanced in this work, is a scientific theory in this sense. All I am concerned to show at the moment is that here is one quite respectable sense of 'theory' which anchors it securely alongside a particular kind of practice.

Another sense of 'theory' sees it as related to practice in another way, and since this is the sense in which I am using the term 'theory' in the expression 'a theory of liberal education' I must try to spell it out as carefully as possible. The sense I have in mind is a combination of the two following meanings from 'Webster's International Dictionary':

(i) the body of generalisations and principles developed in association with practice in a field of activity, and
(ii) a belief, policy or procedure proposed or followed as the basis of action.

It will be seen that both of these meanings attach theory clearly to practice and action and that two complementary ideas are blended together. In the first the idea is that of principles or rules developed *together with* the practice of an activity, say medicine, jurisprudence or education; and in the second there is the idea of the body of beliefs or principles *guiding* the practice or action. The two ideas are superficially contradictory in that one seems to derive theory *from* the practice whilst the other might be seen as imposing theory *on* the practice. This would be to oversimplify, however, since reflection does show that the two ideas appear to co-exist in theories of practice. In medicine, for example, the actual practice produces knowledge about the body, about disease, the effect of drugs and surgical practice and technique. Reflection on the practice raises problems, not only those requiring laboratory-based research but also those of an ethical or valuative kind not susceptible to scientific enquiry. The body of knowledge and valuative attitudes so gained in turn guides practice and can be studied by student practitioners. Not all of the rules and principles so studied are of a factual, cause-effect kind, though in medicine many of them are. The important point is that there is an inter-play of practice and reflection upon the practice, with the reflection becoming more structured, systematic and sophisticated as the body of knowledge, and the literature in which it is embodied, grows.

Theory in this sense is not so much explanatory, as in the case of scientific theory, rather it is systematic reflection for a purpose, the continual characterization, delineation and guidance of a practical activity. The idea that theory, especially educational theory, has a guiding function, has of course been indicated by others. Paul Hirst, for example, in a well known paper has written:

> Educational theory, like political theory or engineering, is not concerned simply with collecting knowledge about certain practical affairs. The whole point is the use of this knowledge to determine what should be done in educational practice.[2]

Later he says of theory of education:

> It is the theory in which principles, stating what ought to be done in a range of practical activities, are formulated and justified.[3]

What has *not* been so commonly noted is that such a reflective theory of practice from time to time re-defines, re-characterizes, the practice itself. This is certainly true of educational theory, where what *counts* as education, or what makes a practice educational rather than non-educational is one of the questions continually reflected upon and calling for imaginative conjecture. People like Froebel, John Dewey and A.S. Neill do not simply perceptively describe the existing educational practice of their time, nor yet do they merely inform and guide such practice, what they do is to set out to recast that practice, reformulate it along more justifiable lines. Such thinkers have not just told teachers how they might better achieve agreed ends, they have questioned the ends and proposed different ones.

Educational theory, then, in the sense used here, is inescapably linked with practice. It cannot be the case that the theory is all right only to fail in practice since the proper relationship to practice is the test on which the theory stands or falls. It is very important, however, that the relationship of such a theory to practice is not misunderstood and some possible (indeed common) misunderstandings must be noted.

(i) It does not follow from the idea that theory must properly relate to practice that a theory is false or bad if it cannot be implemented without disturbing in some way *present* practice. Mixed-ability grouping, for example, is not shown to be a false or bad theoretical idea simply because it cannot be effectively managed with normal methods of class teaching, since the theory normally carried the accompanying idea that existing methods of teaching *should* be disturbed. All this is a consequence of the guiding and/or re-defining nature of educational theory. As mentioned above, educational theory might tell us how better to achieve ends already agreed upon, but it might also tell us what is wrong with the ends we are setting and why and how they might be bettered. There is much confusion in the interpretation of educational research because of a failure to distinguish between arguments as to ends and arguments as to means. Relatively straightforward experimental techniques and correlation studies can usefully inform us about preferable methods *if* the desired end is clear and agreed, and *if* the desired end does not change as the method changes, and *if* non-relevant variables can be avoided in the experimental comparisons. This essential clarity is rarely met with in educational research, however, partly because of the difficulty of controlling variables, but more importantly because there is nearly always a different attitude to ends implicit in the adoption of different methods. Consider, for example, the following pairs of contrasts:

comprehensive organization	selective organization
setting by ability	mixed-ability grouping
traditional mathematics	modern mathematics
formal teaching	informal teaching
differentiated subject curriculum	integrated curriculum

Any teacher familiar with these juxtapositions will know that they involve not only differing methodologies, arrangements and techniques, but differing views or conceptions of what the enterprise is supposed to be about. Setting and mixed-ability grouping, for example, are not just two opposed ways of achieving the same end, where one might be shown experimentally to be the better; they are two different conceptions of what should be going on in the education of children and young people. The issue between them is not therefore to be determined solely, or even perhaps at all, by experimental and statistical methods of investigation, but by a much more complex comparison of valuative positions backed by some kind of philosophical – ethical, conceptual, logical – argument.

Where a theory, in this sense, characterizes or re-characterizes a practice, then by implication it defines or re-defines what is to count as a skill or a successful method within the practice. The test is still in the practice, but not necessarily in the *existing* practice.

(ii) It does not follow from the idea that theory must properly relate to practice that the substance of the theory, and changes to the substance of the theory, must only derive from inside the practice itself. There is no reason why ideas influencing the practice should not come from outside the practice, from any appropriate bodies of disciplined thought or even from other practices. Of course such an influential idea, discovery or argument *can* come from within the practice upon which it bears, but it does not have to. A doctor in general practice *can* have such an idea or make such a discovery, but so can a bio-chemist or even a metallurgist. A teacher *can* have an idea influencing educational theory and thereby educational practice, but so can a philosopher or a psychologist. Ad hominem arguments against a theoretical point on grounds of the inadequacy of the protagonist's teaching experience are common in the educational world, as is the ad populum argument that something should be done because it is fashionable. Both are clearly fallacious. All that should count is that the theory should be clear as to the *kind* of propositions being urged: whether they are, for example, conceptual or ethical recommendations or scientific, and, further, that the appropriate kind of justificatory argument should be offered or relevant criteria of falsifiability should be indicated where the claims are allegedly scientific.

(iii) It does not follow from the idea that theory must properly relate to practice that the *only* appropriate tests of a theory are those seeking to refute it in practice. Such tests *are* appropriate for theories or parts of theories claiming to be scientific, that is, theories claiming to state how things are. Examples of such theories, not necessarily true, would be:

(a) Children are encouraged to learn by the promise of extrinsic rewards.
(b) Punishment has an alienating effect, especially on adolescents.
(c) Clever pupils make slower progress in mixed-ability groups than equally clever pupils in groups of relatively similar ability.

Such tests are not appropriate, however, for claims seeking to guide or re-define practice which make no claim to be scientific. Claims like:

(d) Liberal education should involve the development of the rational mind in whatever form it freely takes.
(e) Education should always involve initiation into what is worthwhile and be concerned with knowledge and understanding.
(f) Teachers should respect their pupils as persons.

It is clear that (a), (b) and (c) differ from (d), (e) and (f) in that the first three claim to state what *is* the case, whilst the second three are all about what ought to be the case. Both kinds of claim or theory guide practice but they do this in two different ways.

The kind of facts claimed in the first three examples guide practice by telling us (if true) what happens if we do certain things. They do not tell us, of course, that we *have* to do that thing. To know that children are encouraged to learn by the promise of extrinsic reward, for example, does not in itself mean that I should, as a teacher, promise my pupils extrinsic rewards. There might well be other considerations. It does not even tell me that I should promise extrinsic rewards to my pupils if I want them to learn, since there may be other, more desirable ways of encouraging my pupils to learn. There are, therefore, two appropriate considerations about factual claims, or what we might call *fact* theories: firstly, how can they be tested for falsity and, secondly, in what way should they influence my action? Educational research has tended to be dominated by the methodology of statistics and experimentation necessary for answering the first question, and all too little attention has been given to the important but quite different requirements of the second question.

The second question, indeed, moves into the area of the type of theory exemplified by (d), (e) and (f) above: the type of claims, or *value* theories, as to what ought to be, or should be, done. It is this type of theory that cannot be tested by the statistical and experimental techniques appropriate to scientific or factual claims. This type of theory is about what is to be held important, significant and valuable; about what we *should* do, not in the sense of what *causes* us to do things, but in the sense of what reasons we present to ourselves as justification for doing things. There is a sense in which all such theories are ultimately moral in nature. A theory of liberal education, for example and to anticipate what is to follow, must make and justify a number of valuative claims before it can get anywhere near seeking factual theories to help it. We need to claim, for example:

(i) children *should* be liberally educated, and
(ii) liberal education *should* take such and such a form, have such and such aims, satisfy such and such criteria,

and to argue such claims, justify such claims, *before* we are in a position to see what factual information or claims may or may not be relevant.

Such arguments will of necessity be conceptual, logical and philosophical. A theory of this kind can only be tested by its internal coherence and consistency and by its coherence with other values we accept, especially those about persons characterized as creatures who reason and value coherence, consistency and justification. I do not believe myself that this makes such theories mere matters of opinion when compared with the theories susceptible to statistical and experimental testing. Critical probing for coherence and logical consistency is a rigorous, rule-governed activity. Some theoretical structures and prescriptions *are* more coherent than others and can be shown to be so. In any case, there would appear to be no other grounds on which we can rationally choose between one value theory and another, between one advocated course of action and another. If fact theories, as I have claimed, can never in themselves tell us what to do in education, and if value theories are to be thought of as merely arbitrary acts of commitment, then however much the statistics and experiments are multiplied, our acts and decisions would be ultimately non-rational.

I have tried to indicate in this section that a theory of liberal education can be a rationally justifiable theory, but that to be such it must be a *critical value theory* whose appropriate tests are those of coherence and consistency. Theories of this kind relate to practice, and would be worthless without such a relationship, but they relate to it in a special kind of way.

There is perhaps one other point that needs to be made about theories claiming to guide action and practice before leaving this introduction. Action-guiding theories do not have to be proven with the certainty attributed to, say, mathematics, and I have already said that in large part they are not to be tested for truth or falsity in the same way as scientific theories. In seeking to be guided by the most consistent and coherent justificatory framework the rational temper requires that we hold our views at any one time critically, that is, subject to change if we can better them in terms of consistency and coherence; but the rational temper also requires that at any given time we are prepared to *act* on the justifications or reasons that present themselves to us at that time as the best. The twin dangers are, on the one hand, ceasing to care about justification and only valuing decisive action, and, on the other, losing the will to act in a vain search for the perfect justification. It sounds like a clever philosophical trick to say that anyone who asks, 'Why bother about justification?' is already bothered about justification, but it is nevertheless a profound truth. One can, of course, simply not bother about justification, but you cannot *argue* for such a happy abandonment. Similarly, one can, as a matter of fact, not bother about consistency and coherence, but you cannot *argue* for such a rejection. To attempt to argue either of these positions is already to play the justificatory game where the necessary ground rules *are* consistency and coherence. Rationality does not require, then, that in practical matters like education we act only on theories held to be completely proven, whatever that might mean; but rationality does require that we act on a systematically related body of beliefs justified by us as the most consistent and coherent we can arrive at. Indeed, at any given time we might not even be able to act directly or properly on the basis of an accepted theory because many things have to be changed to make such direct action in accord with the theory possible. Our theory is like an ideal. It directs us in our resisting and in our cooperating; and how anyone knows quite what to resist and what to support without such an ideal or theory puzzles me greatly.

Teachers, then, if they see themselves as general and liberal educators, rather than the hired instructors of specific and limited vested interests based on economics or politics, have need of a theory of liberal education of this critical value kind. The rest of this work seeks to construct such a theory.

Justification of Liberal Education

part I

2

Education and its justification

2.1 The nature of justification

Justification is part of the rational life. I *can* hold beliefs and perform actions without seeking to justify either. What I cannot do is *argue* that I should not justify my beliefs or my actions, for the simple but important reason that to *argue is* to seek appropriate justifications for beliefs, assertions or actions. Those unbothered about justification must be unbothered about convincing others by argument. It is worth pondering this basic claim about justification for in a theory of liberal education much can be made to depend upon it.

The point made here is a logical one, but our valuation of justification is also clearly exemplified in practice. All research, discussion, investigation, debate and decision-making techniques would be pointless without their underlying assumption of the need for justification. It might even be claimed that one of the major distinguishing characteristics of human beings in their fully developed state is their ability and disposition to persuade one another to belief and action by means of justificatory argument. We consider that we are falling short of our most commendable characteristic when we resort to other techniques of persuasion, like force, threats, irrational emotional appeals, manipulatory conditioning and other influences below the level of consciousness.

Justification, then, is producing reasons for beliefs and actions. This can be at the level of reasons for a single belief or single act, or at increasingly complex levels of reasons for complicated sets of beliefs and actions. Justifying education is clearly an example of an extremely complex kind of justification.

2.2 Justification and majority opinion

Each of us is rational to the extent that our beliefs and actions are justifiable. As Anthony Quinton has pointed out,[1] this is quite separate from any merely psychological feeling of the indubitability of our beliefs. Similarly, at a social level, an institutional framework like a system of education can be said to be rational to the extent that it is justifiable in some sense that goes beyond majority approval.

This, again, is an important point that is easy to be confused about. To say that to implement an educational ideal in a democracy you must convince a sufficient number of others, possibly a majority of others, about the ideal, is probably correct. But to say that the *justification* of an educational ideal rests upon the number of those convinced about it is clearly not correct.

Thus to determine educational policy by a collection of opinions, seeking an existing consensus or majority view as to what we ought to do, is an incorrect basis for policy because it reduces the complexity of justification to the simplicity of head-counting. What must be done is to convince enough people of the consistency, coherence and validity of an argued framework of claims and beliefs constituting a justificatory theory. One's democratic commitment is satisfied by the recognition that implementation will need some kind of majority acceptance. Such a commitment does not have to suppose that the will of the majority is the determinant of what is right.

Indeed, there is a close connection between rationality, democracy and justification. Democracy, it has well been argued,[2] is the name of those forms of government least offensive to the rational person. The rational person supports democracy mainly because it provides the greatest hope that what is reasonable will prevail. When the majority becomes tyrannical, when it ignores minorities, when the actions of the majority become irrational, then the spirit of democracy has gone. Democracy is not synonymous with majority dominance, and it is one of the fallacies of our age to suppose that it is.

Justification, then, is the production of reasons for beliefs and actions, not the collection of supporters; it is a matter of reason rather than rhetoric, of conviction rather than persuasion. Justification is required as a feature of the attempt to make human life rational, to make our activities and beliefs part of an intelligible and coherent whole, to understand what we are about.

2.3 Justification and respect for persons

To respect someone as a person is, primarily, to acknowledge that human being as a centre of rational purpose and intention, a reasoning being, worthy of being treated accordingly. There are many implications of this but the point I wish to draw attention to here is the relationship between the idea of person, characterized as a reasoning being, and that of justification characterized as the reasoned support of belief and action. The connection lies, on the one hand, in the fact that persons are creatures for whom justification matters, and, on the other, in the fact that justification is a unique institution of persons.

This network of ideas needs further consideration, both because of its intrinsic importance and because it will perform considerable service in the arguments of this book. To start with, there is the strange idea, strange but true, that the person for whom justification is important is both bound and free, as Kant pointed out long ago.[3] Justification binds because reasoned support for beliefs or actions cannot be made up of any old ideas that come to mind. Reason must *be* reason. Reason is subject to certain rules of coherence and logic in order to be reason at all. But reason in the form of justification frees or liberates because in presenting to himself data from beyond the present and the particular man frees himself from the restrictions of immediate response to stimuli, the restrictions which appear to govern the actions of the rest of the animal kingdom. Man uses stored knowledge, both from his own memory and from all the books and other artefacts constituting Karl Popper's 'third world',[4] and this, together with his imaginative conjectures and hypotheses about how things *might* be, liberates him from the tyranny of the immediate present. He also uses rules, laws, principles, concepts and classifications which enable him to transcend the meaningless barrage of isolated particulars. In referring to these extending facilities of the mind, reflecting as it were, man engages in the characteristically human activity of reasoning about his beliefs and actions. He justifies his beliefs and actions; and in doing what is justifiable and believing what is justifiable he both binds himself and exercises his freedom.

The idea of justification enters, of course, into the consideration of how persons should treat persons, and this in two ways. The first is reasonably obvious, namely, that the treatment of persons by persons always calls for justification. Within the limits imposed by the necessities of the material world I can do what I like to things, but I cannot do what I like to persons. I have to justify what I do to persons and perhaps also what I do to creatures like animals who are nearer to being humans than mere things, or at least can be seen as sharing some important characteristics like susceptibility to pain. Education, at the very least, involves doing things to persons, influencing their behaviour and beliefs, and thus involves actions calling for justification. If this is reasonably obvious the second way in which justification is connected with the treatment of persons is rather more involved. This consideration derives from the fact that persons are reasoners and justifiers and this has to be borne in mind in persons' treatment of persons. This can be seen, I think, if we compare the treatment of persons by persons with the treatment of animals by persons, or at least our normal moral consideration of such treatment.

Because animals can suffer pain, and because persons know that animals can suffer pain, persons have moral scruples about their treatment of animals which involve ideas like not causing unnecessary suffering to animals. We do not, however, have the same scruples about failing to reason with animals or failing to explain things to them, basically because we do not believe that animals can reason or understand explanations. In short, our moral attitude to animals is determined by what we believe to be the case about them, by our conceptualization of them. We distinguish living things from non-living things; among living things we distinguish between those we believe to be sensitive and those not; and our moral attitudes towards these creatures is very largely determined by these conceptualizations.

What persons know about persons, however, is very complex. We know that persons are living beings and can suffer pain, so some of the same scruples that arise in regard to our treatment of animals arise also in regard to our treatment of one another. Additionally we know that persons are reasoners and justifiers, and we have moral scruples about failing to treat persons *as* reasoners and justifiers. Respecting persons involves justifying our treatment of them, as does respecting animals, but no treatment that failed to recognize persons as actual or potential reasoners and justifiers would *be* justifiable. Justification thus enters into the idea of respect of persons in two ways with a complex relationship.

This idea relates importantly to the justification of educational practices and policies. Education involves the influencing of some people by others and therefore calls for justification; but, because the subjects of education are persons, no educational practice will be justifiable that fails to recognize these subjects as actual or potential reasoners and justifiers. Much of what follows will be an expansion of this one idea.

2.4 The justification of education

We can talk meaningfully about the justification of education, ask meaningful questions about how education is to be justified, because in its most central usage the word 'education' picks out the influence of one or more persons upon one or more other persons. It is true that we talk about self-education, and we also talk about the educative effects of non-persons like natural scenery or works of art. These usages, however, surely would not have gained meaning without being analogical extensions of the central case. I know what is meant by 'educated by nature' because, and only because, I know what it is to be educated by another person. Any attempt to be clear about education, then, should not be led astray by analogical extensions, but keep to the central case and normal usage of the word.

At the very least, to educate someone is to influence them in some kind of way, to change the person's behaviour or belief or state of mind.

We can push this analysis a little further by claiming, as Richard Peters has done,[5] that an influence characterized as educational is always valuable or worthwhile in some sense, or at least supposed to be so by the educator. For the educator to say of the same circumstances, 'I am educating this person but what I am doing is not valuable or worthwhile,' would sound to most of us downright contradictory. Peters has also argued, though somewhat more prescriptively and controversially, that an influence characterized as educational must involve knowledge and understanding in some sense. This, I believe, is to confuse an important part of the characterization and justification of *one* kind of education with the basic characterization of *any* kind of education. *All* usages of 'education' seem to involve worthwhile or valuable influence upon behaviour and belief, or, in some still more basic instances, upon nurture and growth; but knowledge and understanding in the honorific senses that Peters wants to attribute to them are not necessarily involved in all these instances and usages.

What *is* brought out by the claim that educational influences must be valuable or worthwhile is the important idea that they must be justifiable, and it makes discussion of the justification of education clearer if we accept from the start that there might be more than one kind of justification for more than one kind of education, rather than a kind of blanket or monolithic justification for all kinds of education whatever.

That there are different kinds of education is manifested by the variety of practices we call educational and the variety of institutions in which such practices take place. The 'Oxford English Dictionary' notes that the word 'education' is often used 'with limiting words denoting the nature or the predominant subject of the instruction or kind of life for which it prepares, as classical, legal, medical, technical, commercial, art education'. We can add to this list, of course, the widely held idea of a liberal education which we shall want to explore in some detail. It seems from all this that the *only* point of any substance that can be made conceptually about the idea of educating is that education is always connected with something held to be valuable or worthwhile in some kind of way, and that quite separate issues of justification are raised by each separate claim that something is worthwhile and therefore can provide the basis for an education. In spite of all that has been written about it to seek a justification for education as such is a bit like seeking a justification for 'living' or for 'development' when these are uncharacterized or unqualified in any way.

The attempts of R.S. Peters to provide both an analysis of the concept of education and a justification for education are instructive here. Peters has always been attracted to the idea of an honorific conception of education, characterized in terms of both worthwhileness and knowledge and understanding and justified by its connection with the good and civilized life. Critics were quick to point out that the analysis itself was unduly prescriptive, that whilst it might well be argued that this is what education *ought* to be like it was quite another thing to claim that this was how the word 'education' was commonly used, for patently it was not. Peters then accepted that there was a more general concept of education connected with any kind of basic child-rearing, but claimed that the more honorific concept of 'the educated man' emerged in the nineteenth century and that this was his main concern.[6]

These attempts have generated much criticism and debate,[7] with the basic difficulty lying in the attempt to delineate different concepts of education. Surely these problems can be avoided, and the more substantial problems more clearly displayed, if we accept that the concept of education, *when unqualified*, does simply pick out the idea of the rearing and developing of young persons. The 'Oxford English Dictionary' notes that the purely physical connotation 'to rear, bring up children or animals by supply of food and attention to physical wants' is now obsolete, and we can accept that. The next meaning given, however, 'To bring up young persons from childhood so as to form their habits, manners, intellectual and physical aptitudes', allows for both the general and the large number of specific cases and also allows us to characterize the particular kind of 'bringing up' we wish to justify.

To sum up the connection between justification and education, then, we must note that it is never education as such that needs justifying, but always some particularly characterized kind of education. To put this another way, we might say that education, in its most general sense, can be taken to mean something like developing young people in some worthwhile way. What then needs showing is that any particular kind of development we have in mind *is* worthwhile, that is, that it *is* justifiable. Of course we might want to say that some kinds of development are *more* worthwhile than others, as indeed they are; but there is no need to do this by attempting to monopolize the term 'education' for such developments only, for we can do all we need in our justificatory arguments.

In the next chapter I shall attempt to characterize a general liberal education before returning to the problem of justifying it in Chapter 4.

3   Types of education

3.1 Introduction

If education in its broadest and least controversial sense is to be thought of as facilitating the development of others, usually the young, in some worthwhile way, as I have claimed, then clearly there can be many kinds of assisted development all quite properly called education in some qualified way. I want to claim that a liberal general education is a special kind of education having characteristics and justifications of its own which distinguish it from all other kinds of education. I shall not in this chapter spell out all these characteristics, justifications and distinctions, for all that will occupy several chapters. I must say enough here, however, to separate the idea of a liberal general education from all other kinds of education. The basis of the division is clear and simple; it is the implications that are complicated and will need expansion and explanation in further chapters.

3.2 Instrumentality and utility

We speak of one thing or action being instrumental to something else when we use the thing or action to produce something else that we value. Most people do not value washing machines, for example, in themselves, but rather because they value the saved time, or the more efficiently washed clothes. There are great numbers of things we try to possess and things we try to do that are valued instrumentally, that is, valued not for themselves but for what we can do with them, what they lead on to, what they are useful for or have utility for.

Things we can learn can clearly be like this. I can learn:

to fill out an income-tax form
to focus a microscope
to use an index
to calculate
to mount a butterfly
to read

to write
to start a motor-cycle
and so on.

All these are useful things to be able to do. More correctly they *can* be useful under certain circumstances, and this is an important character-istic of all instrumentality. To say of A that it is instrumental to B is also to say that we only value A *if* we value B. Focusing a microscope is of no use to me unless I want to examine micro-objects. Mounting butterflies is not a useful skill to one uninterested in collecting dead butterflies. We sometimes say that the value of instrumental things or activities is *extrinsic* to the thing or activity, as contrasted with the *intrinsic* value of some thing or activity we value for itself rather than for a purpose extra to it.

If the extrinsic value of instrumental things or activities is one characteristic of importance to note about them another is that instrumentality or usefulness can be very specific and limited or it can be very general and wide. Compare, for example, knowing how to mount a butterfly with knowing how to read, or knowing how to focus a microscope with knowing how to write. Some things are useful in a very limited context, and one would want to be quite sure of the need before making the effort to acquire the skill. Other things, like reading, writing, looking after one's own health, communicating with others, whilst still instrumental, are of such widespread and multi-various utility as to appear like necessities for all human beings, and present no difficulties about predicting future usefulness. Any instru-mental learning can be considered under the aspect of the specificity or generality of its utility. One important characteristic of a general liberal education, to be explored more fully later, is that it should always be concerned with the more generally useful rather than the less.

Not only particular items of learning but whole educational enter-prises can be considered from the point of view of utility or instru-mental value. I mean such things as legal education, medical education, the education and training of teachers or the education and training of army officers. Any kind of specific vocational preparation could fall under this classification and can be marked clearly off from that of a general liberal education.

Little needs to be said about the justification of these essentially vocational forms of education. The justifications would derive from the acknowledged usefulness of, say, the law, medicine or teaching and some assurance of the non-harmfulness of the vocation in a social or moral sense. Some additional comments, however, might anticipate future arguments.

Vocational preparation must always be connected with factual knowledge about the likely need for such vocations. The younger the person being considered for vocational preparation the more difficult it is to predict the usefulness of that preparation for *that* person for any continuous stretch of that persons's life. Even if it can be shown that there will be a social need for *some people* to practise a given vocation it does not follow that all people will need to practise it, and the direction of young people into such vocational preparation becomes unjustifiable.

Another point that is sometimes made about directly vocational education is that most examples of such education contain highly generalizable elements, some elements of science in medical education for example, or the psychological studies undertaken by most preparing teachers. Whilst it is true that such generalizable elements undoubtedly appear in otherwise specific training programmes, it does not follow that vocational education can be an appropriate 'vehicle of general education', to use the language of the Newsom Report.[1] This is partly because the general elements are normally eclipsed actually and in the minds of students by the directly specific requirements, but also and more importantly because the general elements are always considered with reference to the specifically vocational demands of the course. Indeed, teachers and lecturers on vocational courses are sometimes criticized when the teaching goes beyond the directly relevant. That an example of vocational education contains within itself one or more elements of learning that are very general in their utility does not, therefore, provide in itself a justification for including such a vocational course in general or liberal education.

3.3 General liberal education

A general liberal education stands in contrast to all kinds of vocational education, but not in quite as simple a way as is sometimes claimed. It is not simply the case that vocational education is concerned with the useful and general liberal education is not; that vocational education has extrinsic value whilst the value of general liberal education is intrinsic, or that vocational education is concerned with means and general liberal education is concerned with ends. To make any or all these claims would be near the truth, certainly, but would fail to make a number of important qualifications and reservations and thereby confuse the argument.

Let me try to characterize what I mean by a general liberal education without submitting to the stranglehold of a definition or, at the moment, considering problems of justification.

A general liberal education is characterized most centrally by its liberating aspect indicated by the word 'liberal'. First and foremost a general and liberal education must be aimed at liberating the person who receives it. What it liberates the person from is the limitations of the present and the particular. The liberally educated person is capable of responding to the stimuli of his present and particular environment in a way that stands in the starkest possible contrast to animal reaction. Most human beings become capable of some escape from the tyranny of the present and the particular, but the extent of this escape is the measure of the liberal education they have received.

The liberating elements of such an education are characterized by fundamentality and an associated generality. The intuitive idea here is that the more fundamental is an aspect of knowledge and under-standing I have, the more general are its applications and the more liberated I am in terms of choices I can make and perspectives I can bring to bear. All this, of course, needs expansion and illustration but I am trying here to provide a sketch before making blueprints.

As well as its concern for the fundamental and the general a general liberal education is also concerned to locate activities in aspects of knowledge and understanding which can become ends in themselves; activities and aspects of knowledge and understanding, that is, likely to have intrinsic value rather than *only* capable of serving as means to other ends.

Lastly, but perhaps most profoundly, a general liberal education can only achieve these characteristics of liberation, fundamentality, generality and concern for intrinsically valued ends, I believe, if it is concerned with involvement in a life of reason. The connection here, I hope to be able to show, is not a contingent one but a necessary one. A general liberal education is necesssarily what Professor Hirst has called the development of the rational mind[2] simply because nothing else could be so liberating, fundamental or general.

Even this brief sketch should reveal why the distinction between vocational and liberal education, clear and important though it is, should not be oversimplified. Part of what is being said about a general liberal education, for example, is that in a special sense it must be *more* useful than any specific vocational education that can be given. Some expansion of this brief sketch is now called for.

3.3.1 *Liberation*

The idea of a liberal education has always been associated with the notion of freedom or liberty in some sense or another of those much abused terms. It is not clear, however, that the sense has always been the one used here. Aristotle, to take a famous example, distinguished the education fit for free men from that fit for slaves and artisans. Professor

Hirst has pointed out, rightly I think, that in spite of the distant social setting of Aristotle's remarks they pointed to four characteristics of a liberal education in some universal sense: the non-mechanical nature of such an education and the demand for the exercise of man's higher intellectual abilities; the non-utilitarian significance; the breadth or absence of narrow specialization; and the intrinsic motivation of the studies. Aristotle, however, seemed to see all this as characterizing an education *fit for* free men, rather than as helping young persons, as yet restricted, to *become* free.[3]

Few today would want to defend a special kind of education for some who are alleged to be free and another kind for those who are in some sense unfree, though certain aspects of the grammar-school and secondary-modern school division dominant in England in the 1950s and 1960s were seen by some as approaching this kind of dichotomy. The kind of connection I see as existing between freedom and a liberal education is quite different. This can be spelled out in two different but related ways.

Firstly, all children are born into specific and limited circumstances of geography, economy, social class and personal encounter and relationship. There is a great deal of evidence from psychologists and sociologists to show how profound are the influences of these special circumstances. I shall return to a consideration of some of these influences later. The point here is a simpler one, namely that education can obviously be of a kind that will entrap or confirm a young person in the limiting circumstances of his birth, *or* it can be of a kind that will widen his horizons, increase his awareness of choice, reveal his prejudices and superstitions as such and multiply his points of reference and comparison. Whether or not an education or part of an education is to be judged as general and liberal can be determined in a rough kind of way by its likelihood of having the second rather than the first of these consequences. This is one meaning of what it is to liberate a person, by means of education, from the restrictions of the present and the particular.

The second way in which the connection between liberty and a liberal education can be described is at once more complicated and more profound and far-reaching in its implications. It is concerned more with what the liberally educated person is released *for,* as contrasted with the sense just described, which emphasizes what such a person is released from. What the liberally educated person is released *for* is a kind of intellectual and moral autonomy, the capacity to become a free chooser of what is to be believed and what is to be done, a free chooser of beliefs and actions — in a word, a free moral agent, the kind of entity a fully-fledged human being is supposed to be and which all too few are! The word 'autonomy' is not lightly chosen here. The idea is one of self-*government*, not romantic anarchy. The supposition is that by knowledge and reason one can come increasingly to understand the forces acting upon one both inside the psyche and outside in the social framework and thereby make oneself independent of them. We do not *have* to be determined in our actions and our beliefs by our social-class origins, the introjected perversities of our super-egos or by social or individual conditioning of whatsoever irrational form. We can break what Erich Fromm[4] was pleased to call the incestuous ties of clan and soil.

Stated like this, of course, the idea is a mere assertion of faith in an ideal. An ideal at that which many see as an outmoded attachment to eighteenth-century enlightenment, blind to the romantic reaction, the insights of depth-psychology, the revelations of two world wars, rampaging and alienating technological growth and the power of social and political pressure and change. Whether in all this welter of ideas we have ever succeeded in replacing the ideal of the free and rational moral agent by anything better is most doubtful. Whether anything else can stand in the stead of reason as an anchor point for a theory of liberal education we have yet to examine. For the present I am saying that a liberal education liberates *from* the tyranny of the present and the particular and liberates *for* the ideal of the autonomous, rational, moral agent. What all that fully means and implies I have yet to spell out. I am not claiming that this is an ideal that all will fully realize, even if to *fully* realize rational autonomy made any sense. What is important is to know which way to go.

3.3.2 *Fundamentality and generality*

The knowledge and understanding to be gained in a liberal education must be as fundamental as possible in order to have the generality of application that is more rather than less liberating. The term 'fundamental' is used here in the sense of necessary foundation, and stands opposed to particular items of knowledge that might be useful in themselves but upon which nothing or not much can be built. The idea is perhaps more easily seen by example. Pupils might learn how to make toffee using a prespecified recipe and with exact instructions about what to do; but they might, alternatively, learn by experimenting the properties of sugar when heated to different temperatures. The latter knowledge is more fundamental, underlies more possibilities of application and is therefore more generalizable and more liberating than the former which, though pleasant to know, is very particular and limited in application to mere repetitions. Again, pupils might learn by specific but unreasoned instruction to open doors for other people; but they might, instead, learn by reason and discussion general principles of helpfulness and cooperation. The latter is more fundamental than the former or any particular instruction of that kind. Principles are more fundamental than the particulars subsumed under them, though the principles may, in some cases, have to be arrived at by a study of particular cases; and those general clusters of rules and principles which we refer to as disciplines are more fundamental than any isolated facts or items of knowledge unrelated to anything else.

I shall, in due course, need to outline in some detail what content we might give to liberal education in order to satisfy this criterion of fundamentality. My concern at the moment is simply and briefly to characterize the idea. One reservation, however, needs to be made. Fundamentality does not have much to do with what is sometimes called 'the basics'. People who use this phrase seem usually to mean something like basic arithmetic and basic literacy. Now it is true that these *are* of fundamental value and wide generality of application and would certainly be part of a liberal education – but they would only be a part of it. There are many other fundamental aspects of knowledge and understanding, some of them scorned by those who would urge the 'basics' upon us, for which we shall want to justify a ·place in our account of liberal education.

3.3.3 *Intrinsically valued ends*

Ours seems to be an instrument-dominated society. The point is often made that we talk continually of technological growth, of increasing wealth and of a raised standard of living without much accompanying discussion of what criteria govern the acceptability of technology, what the wealth is to be for, and what is to measure a standard of living in terms other than per capita income or gross national product in money terms. Instruments serve ends; for wealth or technology to become ends in themselves is clearly a perversion of human endeavour. In earlier times, with relatively limited technologies, perhaps this was easier to realize, at least for some, but the prevalence of poverty and the capacity of technology to relieve it meant that technological advance was eagerly sought and the concept of progress became elevated to an almost unchallengeable position. This idea is now being questioned by a variety of people, not only in western societies but in less developed countries less sure than they were that to attain western technology is an unmixed blessing.

Education occupies a peculiar position in these debates. On the one hand education can clearly be viewed instrumentally on a small or grand scale. It is fashionable at this time in England to point to the part education can play in the wealth creation process, by familiarizing pupils with technology, helping them understand and to be favourably disposed towards industry and to appreciate the importance of wealth creation. Teachers are sometimes blamed for not inducing more able pupils to take up the study of science rather than of the arts. All this is to view education as instrumental. Educators, however, have long seen their task as not solely concerned with these instrumentalities but also with things worthwhile in some way in themselves, with the intrinsically worthwhile. These kinds of things are most readily to be seen in the arts: listening to and creating music, enjoying and creating works of art and literature, engaging in physical and aesthetic activities. But inquiry and discovery in the sciences can also be intrinsically worthwhile if it is concerned with the search to know and to understand for the sake of knowing and understanding and not necessarily for utilitarian application. Certainly there is a danger of oversimplifying this distinction, as R.S. Peters has pointed out,[5] but the distinction is nevertheless there, characterizing perhaps more the attitude with which studies are approached than simply the content of studies. One of the things that wealth can do in a society is to make these intrinsically valuable delights, creations and discoveries possible for all. Liberal education, in the sense of its concern for the intrinsically worthwhile, can only become available for all in a relatively wealthy society, that is true, but if a society becomes solely concerned with wealth production and no longer sees education as concerned with ends, then all becomes caught up in a pointless and particularly vicious and alienating circle.

A liberal education, then, will be characterized by its capacity to liberate pupils from the pressures of the present and the particular, and it will do this by its concentration upon what is fundamental and generalizable. It will also embody a concern for activities, both mental and physical, that are valued ends rather than, or at least as well as, valued instruments.

3.3.4 *Reason*

My final assertion, in a sketch of a liberal general education, was that all of the above is best facilitated by a central concern with reason, by what Professor Hirst has called 'the development of the rational mind'.[6] One can accept Professor Hirst's general point here without necessarily wanting to agree with all that he makes follow from this, or, indeed, to agree entirely with his account of what constitutes having a rational mind.

Part of the general point is that it is *only* reason that can liberate one from the present and the particular. There is a sense in which to be able to refer some immediate stimulus to memory, to imagination, to anticipation of consequences, to relevant rules and principles and information that can be brought to mind and *then* decide how to respond, is both to be rational and to be liberated from the restrictions of immediate stimulus-response reactions. To point this up by contrast this is just what feelings and allied affective states cannot do. To act on feeling alone is to *react*: to be trapped in a particular response immediately following a particular feeling. The intuitive ideas that we are *swept* by emotion, that we *lose* our temper, are *overcome* by feeling, and so on are all indications of the idea that it is only reason that can free us from the compulsion of immediate reaction if it is sufficiently developed.[7]

There is a peculiarity about reason that is associated with the idea of autonomy. For me to act on reason or to hold a belief on reason, that is to act or believe rationally, the reason must be my own. I must come to see for myself *why* it is right to believe this or do that. On the other hand, for me to believe or act on reason is not simply to do or believe what I like. The oddity here is that reason must originate and operate in individual minds yet also operate on rules and principles that go beyond individual minds because they are publicly shared. To be rational is partly to operate an individual skill or corpus of skills, but also partly and importantly to become initiated into public bodies of knowledge in which statements gain meaning by their location within clusters of other statements related in publicly organized ways and tested for truth in publicly organized ways.

This is the other part of the general point made by Professor Hirst that one is bound to agree with. To develop a rational mind is to come to be able to reason, to know and to understand, within a limited number of different ways in which true propositions can be publicly articulated. Hirst has suggested the forms that these different ways of knowing might take, but the significance of his general thesis can be accepted without necessarily agreeing with his specific suggestions. The point I want to stress here is that there is a strange public-private link in the life of reason and both poles have to be developed in a liberal education. There is reason to believe that the public side of knowledge has been overemphasized in both theoretical writing and in the practical activities of schools, whilst what I am calling the private side, the side of the individual knower or reasoner, has been neglected. We must return to this, but at this stage of the argument at least one can agree wholeheartedly with Hirst when he says:

> to characterize the objectives of education in relation to the develop-
> ment of rationality is certainly to put at the very centre of what is
> pursued those forms of knowledge and belief in which we make
> sense of our experience. It is necessarily by means of knowledge, if
> not by knowledge alone, that fancy gives place to a recognition of

fact, that irrational wishes give place to reasonable wants, and that emotional reactions give place to justifiable actions.[8]

Liberal education, then, achieves through the development of reason the liberation from the present and the particular; it focuses upon the fundamental and the generalizable; and it has concern for the intrinsically worthwhile rather than for the solely utilitarian.

4 The justification of liberal education

4.1 Introduction

In Chapter 2 it was argued that it did not make sense to talk of justifying education as such, partly because we already build into the notion of education the idea of some worthwhile, that is to say justifiable, influence being exerted upon someone's behaviour and beliefs. There is something odd about seeking a justification for exerting a justifiable influence! Nevertheless, it was also argued that when we claim that an influence is worthwhile we need to show that it *is* worthwhile, and this is where justification comes in. Thus justifications will vary according to the kinds of worthwhile influences that are embodied in various kinds of education. In particular justifications called for in education of a vocational, utility or instrumental type will differ, not only one from another, but collectively from the justification required for a liberal general education.

Justifications for any kind of instrumental education will be of three kinds: firstly, the justification of the end to which the instrumentality is directed; secondly, a demonstration of the efficiency or effectiveness of the proposed education in preparing people for the justified activity, profession or whatever; and thirdly, some consideration of the likelihood of the person being prepared actually ever engaging in the justified activity, profession or whatever it is that he is being prepared for. For example, I justify engaging John Brown in a particular form of medical education if I can show:

(a) the general desirability of practising medicine;
(b) that this particular form of education will effectively prepare someone to practise medicine; and
(c) John Brown is likely to practise medicine if successfully medically educated.

I propose to say no more about justifying instrumental education here except to note that one of the main reasons for *not* engaging pupils in ordinary schools in vocational education is the difficulty of satisfying the third condition of justification. We just do not know, in most cases, what type of vocational preparation any one pupil really needs. This is a simple, but vitally important, consideration if we are not to engage in a shocking waste of pupils' time and a deplorable betrayal of wrongly engendered expectations.

4.2 General liberal education

Justifying a liberal general education occupies a different framework altogether. Why should we engage children and young people in the type of education briefly characterized in the previous chapter, and which I am referring to as a liberal general education? We cannot justify this type of education by reference to something else that it is instrumental to in any specific sense, because it does not have this kind of specific instrumentality. This is not to say that a liberal general education is not useful in any sense at all. I shall want to argue, *inter alia,* that it is precisely its *general and fundamental utility* that provides part of the justification for a liberal general education. A second justification comes from the way in which a liberal general education, as described here, is related to the very conception of justification itself. This is the justification used by Professor Hirst, but he deals with it rather briefly and it is an important enough argument to warrant rather more extended consideration. Thirdly, I believe there to be powerful moral reasons why a state wealthy enough to do so should extend to all its young subjects an involvement in liberal general education.

These justifications, as I explained in Chapter 2, constitute reasons for believing that we should provide a liberal general education for our young people and, of course, reasons for actually doing so. They are justifications in the area of practical reason, and, like other reasons for action, they have to be seen as making a package of reasons for doing something that is a better package than any that can be assembled for doing something different within the same area of choice. The arguments to be offered, then, support the assertion that if a universal compulsory education service is maintained by the adults of a national community for their young the education provided for all within it should be of the liberal general type. Schools might, of course, offer additional types of education for some or all pupils, but this would be based on quite separate arguments that would have to be provided and not confused with the overriding arguments for a liberal general education.

Before engaging in the three main sets of justificatory argument it is perhaps worth listing again in summary form the characteristics of a liberal general education in the form argued for here. A liberal general education is to be characterized in four ways:

(i) By its capacity to liberate a person from the restrictions of the present and the particular – it is *liberal*.
(ii) By its involvement of pupils in what is most fundamental and general – it is *fundamental and general*.
(iii) By its involvement of pupils in intrinsically worthwhile ends and not only means. Intrinsically worthwhile activities may turn out to be useful for other purposes, but they are not entered into for that purpose – it is *intrinsically worthwhile*.
(iv) By its involvement of pupils in reason and the development of the rational mind – it is *rational*.

Why, then, should we involve pupils in any education so characterized?

4.3 The general utility justification

To offer as a justification for a liberal general education that it has the most general usefulness of any education that could be provided sounds odd for an education that we are claiming is to be concerned with the intrinsically worthwhile. This is especially so in the light of the contrast that has been drawn between a basically non-instrumental education on the one hand and a variety of specifically instrumental educations on the other. Nevertheless, I believe the justification can be made and is an important one.

The first point to be made is that the general utility of a liberal general education is not sought or intended but is rather a logically necessary consequence of an education having the characteristics described above. This is because of the characteristic of fundamentality. The more successful we are in involving pupils in knowledge and understanding that is genuinely fundamental the more generally useful this will be because what it *means* for the knowledge and understanding to be fundamental is precisely that it underlies all more particular choices and decisions. The argument would be that we involve pupils in what is fundamental because fundamental understanding of human experience is intrinsically worthwhile, but in doing this we are necessarily providing pupils with the knowledge and understanding that has the most general relevance and utility for anything they are likely to want to do.

Two questions now arise: why should I claim that fundamental knowledge and understanding is intrinsically worthwhile, and, secondly, is it possible to show more concretely the relationships between fundamental knowledge and understanding and the possible particular choices and activities that it underlies? The first is difficult to answer fully without involving justifications yet to be discussed, and the second is difficult without an account of the content and substance of a liberal general education to be dealt with in Chapter 7. Nevertheless some attempt must be made to give at least preliminary answers to these questions. The reader is reminded once again that we are gathering together a package of supported reasons and ideas, not trying to assemble an inappropriately watertight proof.

The answer to the first question, then, is to do with what persons ought to value as the ends to which all usefulness is directed. It is suggested that among those ends, importantly, should figure the most fundamental knowledge and understanding of the possibilities of human action in, and experience of, the world persons find themselves in. One cannot avoid a concern for ends since all instrumentalities are meaningless without a consideration of how they lead to valued ends. One cannot, as it were, simply engage in useful activities, since activities can only *be* useful or not in relation to some valued end. It is probably true that in the early history of mankind knowledge and understanding were purely instrumental to very basic and primitive ends like survival, food, sex, shelter and power over others. It is also true that these are still powerfully valued ends at the present time. In some parts of the world at the time of writing survival, food and shelter are still not securely realized for untold numbers of people. It would be ridiculous to claim that such people should concern themselves with knowledge and understanding as intrinsically valuable. Nevertheless, one of the very reasons for holding such a state of affairs to be deplorable is the idea that civilization enables man to transcend these primitive ends and to add more sophisticated valued ends that include enquiry for its own sake. People might start out studying the stars to help with the growing of crops, but they end up trying to understand the universe simply because that understanding is intrinsically valued. Very much to the point of what is being argued in this section, too, is the fact that where societies have been able to escape from the subordination of all thought and action to the struggle to survive they have in fact vastly speeded up their technical advance and raised the standard of living of their peoples. In world history, as I am claiming in education, knowledge and understanding sought for their intrinsic worthwhileness can have a general and powerful utility precisely because they are not trapped in response to the present and the particular. Those who naggingly urge that our education should be more relevant to the needs of an industrial society seek to trap people rather than to liberate them. They seek to make their responses always to the present and the particular rather than to the general and the universalizable. As in research, however, so in education, the greater utility comes from not deliberately seeking it.

Brand Blanshard, the American philospher, puts our point very well when he is discussing the appropriate selection of knowledge that the rational temper needs to make:

> We say selection. The other theories say that too, as all theories
> must. Where, then, do we differ from them? In this: whereas they
> say that selection must be made with an eye to utility, or to class-
> less society, or to conformity with faith, or what not, we say that
> the selection must be made with an eye to understanding what the
> world is like. Such understanding is the goal that the impulse to
> know is seeking from its inception. It is the only end that leaves the
> mind free; it is therefore the natural end of what we call 'liberal'
> education.[1]

Blanshard here hits the nail on the head. There is an unavoidable
connection between the valuation of liberty and the valuation of
knowledge and understanding for their own sake — 'the only end that
leaves the mind free' — and we find Professor Hirst striking the same
note when he urges that liberal education should be considered as the
development of the rational mind in whatever form that freely takes.[2]

The second question as to the connection between fundamental
knowledge and understanding and particular choices and activities
that it might underlie is perhaps best answered with some examples.
I shall give four brief examples in an attempt to mark the distinction
and the relationship.

Example (i) Cookery and science
Cookery is often taught as a system of careful adherence to recipe
specifications. Ingredients and procedures are carefully laid out and
conformity is strictly required. Experiment is not fostered and success
is judged by the production of a good cake, pastry or whatever. This
mode of instruction fosters a dependence upon collections of recipes
(cookery books) for the rest of the person's life. It is not only in
cookery that one sees this particular approach to content and method.
A 'cook book' approach can also be seen in some schoolwork in needlework, craftwork, and even in subjects like mathematics or badly taught
science. The alternative, liberal education approach, would be the
avoidance of specific and recipe-based work in favour of an attempt to
promote understanding of underlying principles of nutrition, human
biology, available food materials and the various ways in which they
respond to heat, liquid immersion, and so on. These underlying principles, worthwhile knowing in themselves as part of a general understanding of ourselves and our world, also have the greater utility, the
more universal utility, because they underlie *all* the particular exercises of cookery in which we might engage. They also, of course,
fundamentally underpin the rational exercise of many other activities
like choosing meals in restaurants, planning one's activities in relation

to eating, even if one never cooks a meal at all.

Example (ii) Rote drill and general principles

Max Wertheimer gave an example many years ago of the advantages of
an approach through general principles over that of specifically learned
formulae.[3] His example was in teaching procedures for finding the area
of a parallelogram. Two classes were compared, both of whom had
previously learned that the area of a rectangle can be arrived at by
multiplying the length of the rectangle by its breadth. The first class
were simply told that to find the area of a parallelogram the base is
multiplied by the perpendicular height. The pupils were required to
remember this and use the information to find the area of a number of
parallelograms of different sizes. The second class were required to find
out for themselves how the area of a parallelogram might be calculated,
using their previous knowledge about rectangles, and using scissors,
pencils, rulers and protractors. Wertheimer describes how many of the
pupils in the second group discovered that a parallelogram can be
converted to a rectangle of the same area by drawing vertical lines,
cutting the parallelogram and then reassembling it as in Figure 4.1.
Having made this discovery the pupils then quickly moved to the idea
that base multiplied by perpendicular height would give the area of the
parallelogram.

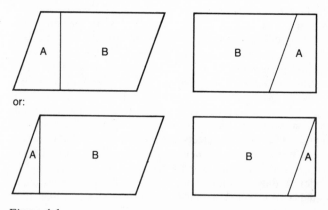

or:

Figure 4.1

More significant was what happened when each class was asked to
find the areas not only of parallelograms of different sizes, but also
of shapes such as those in Figure 4.2. Shape 1, of course, is simply a
parallelogram drawn in another position, but even here some of the
group taught by rote formula had difficulty in seeing that the formula

applied to this shape as well. Most of the 'discovery' group, however, made ready application of what they had discovered, not only to shape 1, but also to shapes like 2 and 3 which are clearly subject to the same fundamental principle.

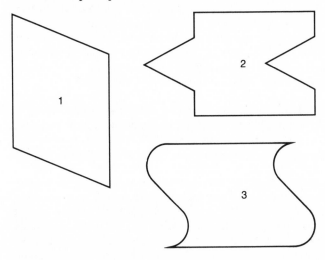

Figure 4.2

What had happened here was that whilst the first group had learned a specific rule applicable to very specific content, or at least perceived as so limited, the second had learned a principle of some generality applicable to a wider range of content. In being more fundamental the principle was more useful, more general than the specific rule. Principles are higher level rules of greater generality of application than the rules subsumed under them. Principles help to gather masses of specific detail and example into graspable and manageable clusters of thought. In a word, principles help us to understand. To learn by learning principles is not just to learn the same content by a different method, it is actually to learn a different content for a different purpose. To learn principles is directed to the end of understanding the human situation for basically no other reason than the worthwhileness of understanding as against not understanding. Once again we meet the idea that aiming for the intrinsically worthwhile rather than the more immediately useful nevertheless gives us the greater utility.

Different approaches to moral education point to the same contrast between rules and principles. One can be taught a strict code of rules, something like the ten commandments, only to find that one cannot apply them to all circumstances without contradiction. Understanding normative interpersonal relationships and human action in terms of more general principles, however, like respecting persons or loving one's neighbour, enables more flexible responses and a greater framework of understanding at the same time. Again this is a matter of content and method together; and, again, what is intrinsically worthwhile, understanding persons and their relationships, turns out to have the widest and most general relevance and utility. As Brand Blanshard has pointed out, moral principles turn out to have a much more universal usage and validity than relativists like Westermarck, who concentrated on diversity of rules and customs, could have supposed.[4]

Example (iii) Mathematical understanding and drill computation
There is little doubt in most people's minds that some ability at basic mathematical computation is highly generalizable, useful in a wide range of contexts. Up to a point this is probably still true but it is dependent upon a social context that changes faster than teachers sometimes realize. Most of the specific calculations in old English weights and measures that I was drilled in at school I have never executed thereafter. The specific necessities I was being trained to face have not turned out to be necessities after all, they were simply *too* specific. On the other hand, *some* of the mathematics I learned did generate a basic understanding of the calculable and the measurable way of making sense of things that has been widely relevant. Some attempt to educate children mathematically in this more general sense, without trying to predict future needs in any specific sense is to be seen in recent mathematical syllabuses. Like all educational innovations, their success depends upon how teachers use them, but the emphasis on understanding, on principles, on coherence and generality of utility, as against the rote learning of isolated facts and skills, is a liberal education emphasis as against a narrow utility approach. A pupil cannot master at school all the mathematical, logical, measuring or symbolizing skills he *might* need. A liberal education must therefore involve pupils in a more fundamental and flexible mathematical understanding which, whilst providing a form of understanding of the world worthwhile in itself, lays a foundation on which any of a great variety of mathematically specific skills can be based. Trying to educate pupils in what is intrinsically worthwhile is the opposite of trying to anticipate and meet specific utility needs; but it is compatible with a wider utility if properly understood.

Example (iv) Aesthetic appreciation and received views
To some, of course, the mere presence of aesthetic elements in a general education is sufficient to show a concern for liberal rather than utilitarian education. Once again, however, it all depends on what

is going on under the name of aesthetic education. If there is a genuine attempt to differentiate aesthetic understandings from other forms of understanding, to help pupils make their own justifiable aesthetic judgments and perhaps embody those judgments in creative activities, then once again we have a liberal education approach concerning an understanding that is intrinsically worthwhile, as all discriminably distinct forms of human understanding are, and which is, at the same time, universally relevant because it underlies all particular exercises of aesthetic judgment of skill. Attempts, on the other hand, either to cover all particular manifestations of aesthetic skill (painting, pottery, weaving, music, dancing, etc.), or to treat aesthetic judgments as collections of information to be passed on from teacher to pupil in order to pass career-assisting examinations, is to drop into the utility form again.

These sketchy examples are offered only to begin to fill out the idea of the intrinsically worthwhile, engaged in with no view of utility, nevertheless having a wide and fundamental utility. To make this point is sometimes seen as a betrayal of the argument justifying liberal education by its concern for the intrinsically worthwhile, but I cannot see why this should be so. Because we say that what is intrinsically worthwhile is *not done* for any specific purpose beyond itself, we do not have to argue further that it *cannot* have any use whatever itself. A developed aesthetic taste might well help me to choose curtains or plan my garden; but it does not follow from this that I acquired aesthetic taste and judgment *in order* to choose curtains or plan my garden, since I *might* have had nothing to do with either of these activities.

It must not be imagined that these four examples delineate in any way a content for a liberal education. This task comes later. The present point is simply that educational tasks approached with intrinsic worthwhileness in mind can nevertheless have a most general utility, especially when the intrinsic worthwhileness is that connected with man's discriminably different and most fundamental ways of understanding, giving sense to, his experiences.

The first justification for engaging people in a liberal general education as characterized here, then, is that its very rejection of *specific* utility, and its espousal of intrinsically worthwhile ends, provides the maximum and most general utility by its valuation of the knowing and understanding underlying all specific activities and choices that can be engaged in or made.

4.4 The transcendental or presupposition justification

The type of justificatory argument to be now described is used by

Professor Hirst to justify a liberal education where this is construed as the development of the rational mind: 'It is an education concerned directly with the development of the mind in rational knowledge, whatever form that freely takes.[5] Since I am embodying the idea of the development of the rational mind in my description of a liberal education I want to consider Hirst's justificatory argument which, if it applies at all, will apply here. I shall be discussing the views of Hirst again in connection with the content and substance of a liberal education in Chapter 7. It is perhaps necessary to explain here that Hirst believes rational knowledge to be differentiated into a number of 'forms', each one discriminably different from others by virtue of its centrally characterizing concepts and its distinctive tests for truth. To develop the rational mind, therefore, is to involve a pupil in each and every one of the forms of knowledge. This, although brief, is probably sufficient an account for our present purposes. The following somewhat lengthy quotation is necessary for our discussion and should now be meaningful. Hirst writes:

> If the achievement of knowledge is necessarily the development of mind in its most basic sense, then it can be readily seen that to ask for a justification for the pursuit of knowledge is not at all the same as to ask for the justification for, say teaching all children a foreign language or making them orderly and punctual in their behaviour. It is in fact a peculiar question asking for justification for any development of the rational mind at all. To ask for the justification of any form of activity is significant only if one is in fact committed already to seeking rational knowledge. To ask for a justification of the pursuit of rational knowledge itself therefore presupposes some form of commitment to what one is seeking to justify. Justification is posssible only if what is being justified is both intelligible under publicly rooted concepts and is assessable according to accepted criteria. It assumes a commitment to these two principles. But these very principles are in fact fundamental to the pursuit of knowledge in all its forms, be it, for instance, empirical knowledge or understanding in the arts. The forms of knowledge are in a sense simply the working out of these general principles in particular ways. To give justification of any kind of knowledge therefore involves using the principles in one specific form to assess their use in another. Any particular activity can be examined for its rational character, for its adherence to these principles, and thus justified on the assumption of them. Indeed in so far as activities are rational this will be possible. It is commitment to them that characterises any rational activity as such. But the principles themselves have no such assessable status, for justification outside the use of the principles

is not logically possible. This does not mean that rational pursuits in the end lack justification, for they could equally well be said to have their justification written into them. Nor is any form of viciously circular justification involved by assuming in the procedure what is being looked for. The situation is that we have here reached the ultimate point where the question of justification ceases to be significantly applicable. The apparent circularity is the result of the inter-relation between the concepts of rational justification and the pursuit of knowledge.

Perhaps the finality of these principles can be brought out further by noting a negative form of the same argument. From this point of view, to question the pursuit of any kind of rational knowledge is in the end self-defeating, for the questioning itself depends on accepting the very principles whose use is finally being called in question.

It is because it is based on these ultimate principles that characterise knowledge itself and not merely on lower level forms of justification that a liberal education is in a very real sense the ultimate form of education.[6]

One thing that it is important to be clear about in trying to decide whether this justification works or not is exactly what it is we are trying to justify. If the question posed is 'Why be rational?', then the argument clearly works. The question has no point if the value of rationality is not presupposed, and is indeed seen to be an odd question as soon as one reflects about it. Hirst, however, tries to make the argument do much more work than this. He proposes two fundamental principles of justification, i.e. that what is being justified is intelligible under publicly rooted concepts and also assessable according to accepted criteria. I take this to mean that once we undertake justification there are certain rules of reason, of language and logic, that *must* be accepted because that is what justification *is*. This too one can readily accept and if the question asked is something like 'Why bother with the rules of reason when we seek justification?' or 'Why must justification be *rational* justification?' the answer is clearly that the rules of reason must be presupposed to give intelligibility to such questions. So far, so good.

But Hirst pushes the argument still further, for he says that 'to question the pursuit of *any kind* of rational knowledge is in the end self-defeating, for the questioning itself depends on accepting the very principles whose use is finally being called in question.' There is a move from the general to the particular here that rouses our suspicions, for we move from the general idea of rationality itself and its fundamental principles to the particularity of *any kind* of rational knowledge. If this merely means that questioning whether any kind of knowledge should be pursued rationally rather than irrationally is self-defeating then again the argument is clearly sound. But this is not quite what is said. If it means that the pursuit of any kind of rational knowledge is justifiable because of the necessary presupposition of reason in questioning it, then surely this is false. For example, the pursuit of knowledge about ways of inflicting pain on people, however rationally engaged in, can surely be questioned without the question being self-defeating or contradictory. Or, again, we might question the advisability of pursuing further our undoubtedly rational knowledge of how to make nuclear weapons without being hoist by the petard of our own presuppositions. This is not an appeal to something other than reason, or beyond reason, but only a reminder that presupposition or transcendental arguments only work at the level of highly generalizable principles. We cannot logically question the value of rationality, or the principles of justification, but we can, without contradiction, question the advisability of pursuing specific kinds of rational knowledge. All we have to do is show good reasons why not; to show better reasons, that is, than any that can be produced for pursuing the particular knowledge, or engaging in the particular activity.

What exactly does Hirst's argument justify in respect of a liberal education? There is little doubt that if I am talking about *self*-education then the transcendental argument applies. This can be put at three levels: if I ask myself justificatory questions (What ought I to do? How ought I live? How should I develop myself?) then I am committed by the very asking to the adoption of rational principles in answering. This could be pushed further to embrace my commitment to the *development* of my rational mind if I ask justificatory questions. The most general extension of this kind of argument would be to say that I am committed to developing my mind in such forms of knowledge and understanding as I believe to be fundamentally constitutive of a rational mind if I ask justificatory questions or if I claim in any way, even if only to myself, to value rationality. In other words, if I ask justificatory questions I am committed to rationality, if I am committed to rationality I am committed to being as rational as possible, and this means developing my rational mind as well as I can.

The justification we are seeking, however, is the justification that bears upon whoever decides what a national system of education is to be like. At the present stage of the argument it is an unanswered question who that should be. In the United Kingdom at the time of writing the decision lies uneasily and in a not very determinate way with the central government, local government and the actual head teachers and assistant teachers in the schools. Can the transcendental form of argument be used to justify the beliefs and actions of people responsible for the education of others rather than themselves?

It would seem that it can to some extent, but the problem might again be one of how far it can be pushed. A person responsible for the education of others (let us ignore how or why for the moment) is bound to ask what kind of education should be provided and such questioning is only of point if it supposes there to be reasons for providing one kind of education rather than another. This, in turn, presupposes a valuation of reason. So far we are following the Hirstian style of argument: the education-provider, asking himself what he should provide, is committed to proceeding rationally. But, even if he does proceed rationally, will his reason, *must* his reason, necessarily tell him to provide a liberal education of the kind Hirst describes or I have described. Might he not say, in an underdeveloped country for example, 'I know what a liberal education based on reason is, but in the present circumstances of my country the rational policy is to concentrate our education firstly on basic literacy and secondly on the vocational preparation of technicians and administrators'? Clearly there could be countervailing reasons against providing a liberal education such that the provider would not be in breach of his own valuation of reason in heeding them. This is not made clear in Hirst's account but it has important consequences for anyone seeking to justify the provision of a liberal education for all. It would have to be shown, for example, that possible countervailing arguments do not apply in the case under discussion.

The basic reason why Hirst's use of the transcendental argument fails is because in the form he gives it the argument is always self-referenced. What I mean by that is illustrated by my earlier remarks about the argument working if I use it to apply to my own education or development: if I respect reason I ought to develop my own rational mind in all its forms. But what if I am seeking to justify what I should do to others, or get others to do to others? Of course, if *they* already value reason I can demonstrate by using the transcendental or presupposition argument that they are already committed and must welcome my proposals for a liberal education; but if they are not committed already to the valuation of reason then they are not committed to a liberal education and have no reason to accept the proposals that I or Professor Hirst might make. Of particular relevance to this point, of course, is that pupils or potential pupils can hardly be thought of as already committed to the valuation of reason.

What I have to do, therefore, as one asking the question 'What education should I try to provide for others?' and where the described form of a liberal general education is one of the possibilities, is certainly to answer the question as rationally as possible. Doing this, however, will always involve a consideration of possible countervailing arguments with the honest supposition that in some circumstances they might prevail, and should always involve more positive arguments of an ethical nature about why I should seek to influence the beliefs and actions of others one way rather than another.

Although this is clearly to say that the justification of a liberal education cannot rest on the transcendental or presupposition argument alone, at least in the strong sense of 'justification' used here, it is not to say that this form of justificatory argument is unimportant or has no place at all in a theory of liberal education. It is of considerable importance to note, as Hirst does, the inevitable connection between the ideas of justification on the one hand and rational knowledge on the other. To enter into rational knowledge *is* to enter into the business of justifying assertions; to enter into justification *is* to enter into the business of rational knowledge; there is therefore an oddity about seeking a justification for engaging in rational knowledge. About all of this Hirst is, I believe, quite right. Since, as I shall try to show later, part of the methodology of a liberal education is to get pupils to see and accept the bindingness of such necessary connections, and since, as I have said, the argument does work for those who accept the valuation of reason, then liberal educators will in a sense be trying to get their pupils to accept this kind of valuation and this kind of justification. They must, however, engage in the exercise before this comes about, and they must accept that for some, perhaps many, this ideally and intrinsically motivating understanding will never be reached. They therefore need positive accompaniments to the transcendental argument, partly of the kind already urged in Section 4.3, and partly of the ethical kind to follow in the next section.

4.5 The ethical justification

It is rather surprising that ethical arguments for certain kinds of education are not advanced more often than they are. That they are not arises, I think, from a failure to make a distinction discussed in the previous section, namely the difference between justifying a self-referenced action and justifying an other-referenced action. The kind of education I justify providing for myself might have a bearing on the education I justify providing for others, but it is not subject to exactly the same kind of considerations. If, for example, I argue that what I deem worthy for myself I ought to deem worthy for others I am clearly starting to engage in an ethical argument. Arguments like those considered in the previous section, that might convince me of the value of something like a liberal education for myself, do not in themselves justify me imposing it upon others. All they justify regarding others is that I should try to convince the others of the force of the arguments, and that is not enough for our purpose. What we want are grounds for believing it our duty to provide a (possibly compulsory) liberal education for all the youngsters in the state. Such a duty will be a moral duty.

The first point to make in this argument is the desirability of arguing from the idea of adult duties rather than from the idea of children's rights. I am doubtful about the coherences of theories of rights and even more doubtful about their application, their motivating force. The doubt about coherence is too big a matter to be a diversion here, but the doubt about application warrants a mention. The doubt concerns what I suppose is a psychological matter, i.e. what feelings and motivations are likely to be held by possessors of rights as compared with possessors of duties? If a person believes himself to possess a right he has grounds, he believes, for making demands upon other persons which may or may not be responded to, however strongly the right is felt by its 'owner'. The necessary action has to come, not from the right-holder, but from some other who recognizes the right. One who feels that he has a duty, on the other hand, feels that *he ought* to do something. The duty bears upon him, not upon someone else. Another way of marking the distinction is to say that rights arouse demands and expectations which, if not met and satisfied, generate frustration and anger; whereas duties, if realized, move persons directly to action or to feelings of guilt. The point of an argument justifying liberal education must be to convince some people that they have a duty to arrange and provide a liberal education for others. *Who*, exactly, has the duty thus becomes an important issue in this kind of justificatory argument.

This difficulty about rights and duties is worthy of note because much justificatory discussion about education is mounted in a context of claims for human rights to education. A good example is to be found in Brian Crittenden's very interesting book, *Education and Social Ideals*, in his chapter on Education as a Human Right. Crittenden starts his discussion, as his chapter heading indicates, by seeking ways in which the *right* to education can be maintained, but the talk soon changes to an account of *moral obligation*. The following extract shows this happening:

> Thus, given that liberal education, as an initiation into the basic public forms of human understanding, so fundamentally affects the development of significant and distinctive modes of human action, I think the right to education may justifiably be stated somewhat more precisely this way: Everyone has the right to participate in liberal education at the stage of general initiation and to be provided with whatever conditions will enable him to do so to the full extent of his capacities and interests. The claim that this right makes on

political authority is not, of course, one that can be exhaustively satisfied. . . . As a human right, however, it is not simply suggesting what would be desirable, but asserting that political authorities principally have a basic moral obligation to promote the ideal as fully as they can.[7]

What really matters, then, is that some people, political authorities or others, are alleged to have a *moral* obligation, a *moral* duty, to provide and facilitate the liberal education of young members of the national community. It is the source of this moral obligation that needs explicating, and it is precisely this that Hirst's presupposition argument, at least in the form in which it is presented, fails to do. So, of course, does the general utility form of argument in 4.3, since even if it is accepted that a liberal education of the type briefly described does have a profoundly general utility it can still be asked why all the children of a country should be provided with such a generally useful education. A moral argument is required to transfer the presupposition argument from self-reference to other-reference and to under-pin the general utility argument.

Such a moral argument might run as follows:

A commitment to the rational life does not only imply a disposition to justification in terms of knowledge and understanding but also, and importantly, a disposition to value creatures who are the founts or originators of reason, namely persons. Any creature capable of meaningfully asking the question 'What ought I to do?' or 'How ought I behave?' or 'What should govern my conduct?' must also be a creature who should recognize the existence of other rational and potentially rational creatures of the same kind as himself. Not to recognize the existence of such fellow creatures would be to ignore features of the human condition obviously relevant to the rational answering of the questions posed. Not to take the existence of other rational creatures into account in these considerations about conduct would be analogous to a studied indifference to the existence of physical objects in deciding how I should move about the physical world. The recognition of persons is of course not the recognition of them merely as physical objects, rather it is a recognition of them as sources of reason, centres of consciousness, possessors of interests and purposes; and this recognition carries with it the recognition of an appropriateness of treatment of, conduct towards, such creatures. Such an awareness of appropriateness of conduct towards other persons is what is embodied in the idea of respect for persons as described in 2.3. The central point of such respect is basically a respect for reason in the form of individualized consciousness, the only living form that reason can take. Respect for persons is a special kind of respect because it is essentially a respect for embodied and living reason: the kind of conduct owed by all creatures trying to be rational to all creatures capable of rationality. Kant caught the spirit of this idea in various forms of his categorical imperative. For example, 'Act only on that maxim through which you can at the same time will that it should become a universal law' picks out the idea of an appeal to the universality of reason, whereas 'So act as to use humanity, both in your own person and in the person of every other, always at the same time as an end, never simply as a means' picks out the complementary idea of respect for persons as founts of reason, centres of consciousness and possessors of interests and purposes.[8] The formal appeal to rationality and the respect for all creatures capable of rationality are but two aspects of the same framework of morality.

To apply this kind of moral commitment to myself and other adults has two consequences. The first, already noted, is that in regard to myself there is an obligation to improve my own rational mind in so far as I am able. I have expressed this in terms of the duty an individual has to continue his own liberal education. Kant expresses it thus:

> It is the duty of man to himself to cultivate his natural powers (of the spirit, of the mind and of the body) as a means to all kinds of possible ends. Man owes it to himself (as an intelligence) not to let his natural predispositions and capacities (which his reason can use some day) remain unused, and not to leave them, as it were, to rust.[9]

Secondly, however, this moral commitment cannot extend in any sense to my imposition of this requirement upon other persons if they are adult. That part of my respect for them which notes their capacity to act as free agents would forbid this. I might morally urge, facilitate and certainly not hinder the rational development of my fellow human creatures, but I should not try to compel it. There is a large and interesting area of discussion possible here concerning the desirability of state governments taking positive steps both to encourage the rational development of its adult citizens and to act against such forces as might hinder that rational development. Recognizing persons as free agents does not necessarily mean that a government should be entirely passive on such an issue, especially if what might be described as anti-rational forces can be shown to be over-influential for whatever reason.

This brings us to the consideration closest to our present purpose. What is the implication of the framework of moral obligation sketched above for the moral obligation adults might have towards children and young persons in the national community?

Some aspects of the moral duties adults owe to children are no different from those owed to other adults. I should not take the life of children nor inflict unnecessary pain upon them; I should not use them merely as means to my ends; I should aid them in avoiding suffering wherever possible. The difficulty comes, however, in the more sophisticated forms of conduct towards others warranted by the conception I have of them as rational and autonomous agents. This children clearly are not, and to act towards them as though they were would be a perverse kind of cruelty, particularly perverse if done in the name of reason. What they equally clearly *are*, however, is *potentially* rational and autonomous; they can, with help, become rational and autonomous at least to a greater rather than a lesser degree. The 'with help' here is of great importance to the idea of our moral duty towards children and young people. Personal autonomy is not a characteristic which has had its child-rearing antecedents widely investigated and we could do with a great deal more empirical research in this area. It seems highly likely, however, that personal autonomy does not come automatically by some unfolding process of maturation, nor does it come by any old process of interaction with adults or peers, but it is rather a product of certain kinds of adult help and encouragement, without which it is unlikely to develop at all. Furthermore, there are certain others kinds of adult interaction with children and young persons that can be shown to be directly opposed to the kind of development I am favouring here. Children do not 'flower' if they are left alone, though they may well 'vegetate', and they can all too easily be conditioned and indoctrinated into beliefs and conduct that will act against their own best interests as creatures potentially capable of a future of reason and autonomy.

If all this is so then the moral duty of adults towards children is reasonably clear and has two parts. The positive part is a duty to help children, in all ways possible, to become increasingly rational and autonomous up to the point where the moral duty to do this for themselves might reasonably be expected to take over. The negative form of this duty is an obligation not to allow or encourage the social environment to foreclose on the possibilities and life-styles open to a child's future as a rational and autonomous being. It is my contention that the main way of exercising both of these responsibilities is to provide for the child a programme of general and liberal education of the kind outlined, and to defend the priority of such a liberal education from encroachment or replacement by other claims.

Now this really completes the moral justification for the provision of a liberal general education in broad terms, but it leaves a number of questions unanswered. I have not yet said exactly *who* might be expected to provide such an education. Clearly the responsibility cannot be left to float diffusely among the adult population as a whole. A long and honourable tradition has held that this responsibility falls clearly upon parents who may delegate but may never entirely abdicate the obligation to educate their own young or to see to it that they are educated. There are, of course, a number of difficulties in the way of parents educating their own children and thus exercising their responsibility directly. It is worth listing some of them:

(i) Division of labour and the extensive employment of both men and women outside their own homes leaves little time for effective, prolonged and continuous teaching.

(ii) Direct parental instruction, as a major part of the child's education, would isolate the child from social experiences forming in themselves a part of a liberal education.

(iii) Increased expectation of the breadth and depth of a liberal education makes it unlikely that more than a few parents would be capable of providing it.

(iv) Although it might be argued that parents have a particular responsibility for their children's education, the persons influenced and affected by the state of education of a country's young people constitute a much greater number.

(v) Differential provision by the varied exercise of parental responsibilities is particularly unjust given the significance of education for a child's future and present life.

Reasons such as these have led to varied forms of the delegation of parental responsibility to tutors, governesses and grand or small independent schools, often of a boarding kind where much more than the directly educational functions of parents were taken over for long periods. These practices of the wealthy and relatively wealthy became extended to the less wealthy by means of charities, endowments and religious beneficence until eventually central and local government also became involved and included the provision, if not always the direction, of education under its expected mandate. There has been a feel about the patchy history of educational provision of ever larger and more bureaucratic agencies taking on the erstwhile duties of parents. It would not be correct, however, to see these larger and more powerful agents of educational provision as simply taking over the responsibilities of parents. Such agents, especially central and local governments, would claim to represent a much wider constituency of educational interest and concern than that of parents alone. At one level this is only to say that agencies like governments will take notice of special groups like, for example, employers and manufacturers. Such groups come to expect that both their workers and the buyers of their products will have received a reasonable level of education. More profoundly and importantly than this, governmental provision of education might be seen, indeed has been seen, as defending and liberating children by compelling their involvement in an education well beyond that which parents alone could have provided, or, in many cases, would have wished to provide.

On this argument there is a prima facie case for government provision of education by one means or another; but if a government accepts this responsibility it has the grave moral responsibility of ensuring that the education provided *is* liberating and not further restricting. The great temptation lying in wait for governments is to see education as merely instrumental to any particular end seen as important at that time by the particular government, like manpower provision, wealth-creating, or the unity of the nation.

I must return to these matters, but at this point it is enough to note that I am claiming that the moral duty for the adult community to liberally educate its young is best taken up on behalf of all by a democratically elected government as one of its duties of provision. This must not, of course, be taken to mean that the members or officers of a government are the best persons to determine the content or methodology of a liberal education. On these matters, too, there is much more to say before our theory is complete.

Content and Method

part II

5 Some preliminary ideas

5.1 Introduction

The main intent of this and the following two chapters is to sketch
an account of what should actually be taught, and hopefully learned,
as an adequate body of a liberal education. It is necessary to prepare
the ground for this. One of the major faults of many of the proposals
for an appropriate curriculum for universal and compulsory schooling
is that lists of subjects are laid out without any real attempt at explanation or justification of why one should favour the particular list
being offered. What is necessary is to show at some length why the
particular recommendations are made.

We have already gone some way along this road in our discussions
of the nature and justification of a liberal education. Claims for a
particular content must clearly flow from and be compatible with
these earlier characterizations and justifications; and what these earlier
arguments point to is some characterization of what is to be taught
and learned in terms of intrinsic worthwhileness, fundamentality,
rationality and capacity to liberate pupils from the contingencies of
the present and the particular. This in itself provides at least some
broad criteria to weigh proposals against.

Perhaps the first important introductory point to make is that the
content and substance of a liberal education is not the same as the
content and substance of a *total* curriculum for schools of universal
and compulsory education. It would be most extreme to maintain
that the *only* activities to go on in such schools should be those activities essentially constituting a liberal general education. I shall want to
argue for the highest priority for the liberal education elements in the
schools and to point to the unjustifiable emphasis often given to other
and less important considerations; but even this is not to argue that
nothing other than liberal education should take place. What else might
take place in schools, of course, will need different and additional
justifications to those considered here for a liberal education. The
content and structure to be argued for here, then, is peculiarly that of
whatever part of a total curriculum is to be considered a general and
liberal education.

Some consideration must be given to the proposals of other writers on this subject. This does, however, present difficulties since most other proposals are not solely concerned with liberal education, neither do they clearly demarcate within their proposals which are intended to be there for purposes of liberal education. This is not a trivial point nor an unimportant difficulty in trying to think straight about a school curriculum. Those elements of a curriculum there for liberal education purposes are to be justified differently from those elements included for long- or short-term instrumental (usually vocational) purposes, as I have argued earlier, so to conflate them in common proposals can be confusing.

Many writers on the curriculum do seem to take it for granted that vocational claims will loom large. For example, Anthony O'Hear, in pursuing the point that the deprivation of the liberty of the child in school is to be justified by the extent to which his schooling 'promotes his own individual liberty and the respect he has for the liberties of others', goes on to specify:

> The academic core of the curriculum, some (unspecified) vocational training, and moral education are justified to that extent, the academic core because it forms the basis necessary for personal decisions in life, moral education because it leads to an understanding of the rights of others and vocational training because it will provide the basis of self-sufficiency.[1]

Similarly, Robin Barrow believes that vocational studies should be introduced to pupils among other elements at about the age of 13-15, but what he describes seems to be what others call 'careers education', involving little more than an introduction to the kinds of job likely to be available to school-leavers and the skills necessary for them. Barrow's arguments are utilitarian, as they are throughout:

> It is worthwhile that the school should do what it can in terms of preparing the individual child to take on a job to which he is suited, because such preparation can only lead to an increase in personal pleasure for the individual. Greater personal satisfaction for individuals can only lead to greater harmony in society as a whole.[2]

Yet again, the important directive, *The School Curriculum*, issued by the Secretary of State for Education and Science in England and the Secretary of State for Wales in March 1981, and which is likely strongly to influence the curricula of schools in England and Wales for some time to come, states as one of its three propositions about secondary education: 'School education needs to equip young people fully for adult and working life in a world which is changing very fast indeed.'[3] Like the proposals of Barrow, this seems to involve mainly careers education and contacts with industry; *unlike* Barrow, the problem of justification is largely ignored. One is tempted to observe that it is precisely because the rate of technological change in the world is so great that it is *not* possible to prepare pupils in school *fully* for it, but we must leave these arguments for the moment. One last example will suffice for the point being made. Tim Devlin and Mary Warnock in their book, *What Must We Teach?*, include aspects of careers education and other instrumental preparations for life in their 'outer circle' which covers those activities which are to be compulsory but not examined, though the justification here appears to be connected with the desirability of focusing pupils' critical faculties upon the near, the immediate and the particular, rather than always upon the distant and the generalized.[4]

The point of this somewhat arbitrary selection of writers who make reference to vocational or quasi-vocational studies in their proposals for the curriculum is only to indicate the mixture that one finds. Instrumental justifications are simply not sufficiently distinguished from the more fundamental requirements of a liberal education. I shall leave any further consideration of non-liberal or utility claims on curriculum time to a later chapter, and deal here with the considerations that bear directly on the content and substance of a liberal education. In order to do this it will be necessary to look with some care at the work of three writers who have made detailed proposals that *do* claim to have the fundamentality I am concerned with and *do* rest on some substantial attempt at justification. Before doing this, however, and then attempting my own positive account, I want to consider briefly some concepts central to this discussion. They are: fundamentality, information, knowledge, truth and understanding.

5.2 Fundamentality

This notion was introduced and briefly characterized in 3.3.2 where it was claimed that the knowledge and understanding to be gained in a liberal education must be as fundamental as possible in order to have the generality of application that is more rather than less liberating. The origins of the word 'fundamental' are connected with the idea of a foundation or basis upon which other things might stand or be built. Historically the idea has developed from its purely physical connotation to the modern reference to less immediately material things like knowledge, so that the 'OED' can now give the following meanings that convey the idea intended here. 'Fundamental' is held to mean:

of or pertaining to the foundation or groundwork, going to the root of the matter;

51

serving as the base upon which to build. Chiefly and now exclusively in immaterial applications. Hence forming an essential or indispensable part of a system;

primary, original; from which others are derived.

It is a possible temptation here to be carried away into some absolute reification of the idea of a substantive 'fundamental' or a number of such 'fundamentals'. This temptation must be resisted: there are, of course, no studies that are absolute and permanent foundations of everything else we might wish to do. Nevertheless, there are activities that are more fundamental than others and as the fundamentality increases so does the generality of the application: fundamentality is opposed to superficiality as generality is opposed to specificity. Although it is not a logical connection it does also seem to be the case that what is fundamentally known changes rather more slowly than the multitudinous ideas of more superficial information that we have at any given time. For example, the items of railway and bus timetable information that I need to have vary from time to time, as do the various ways in which such information might be presented. Ways of measuring and recording time, however, change more slowly, and an understanding of them is fundamental to understanding any time-tables whatsoever.

The idea of what knowledge and understanding is fundamental is somewhat like, though not identical with, the philosophical idea of what has necessarily to be supposed in order to make sense of something else. Morality, for example, only makes sense on the necessary presupposition of the existence of free agents. To put this another way, it is more important in moral education that a child should come to understand what it is to be a free agent than simply to conform to a particular rule like not stealing, since the point of the latter can only be understood in the context of the former. Hence the notion of free agency is fundamental.

It is not only *within* certain kinds of knowledge that some concepts and propositions are more fundamental than others. For it is also the case that some whole frameworks of knowledge and understanding can be considered more fundamental than others. It is in this sense that animal biology is more fundamental than animal training, and human nutrition more fundamental than cookery.

What is fundamental is not to be confused with what is *elementary* or what is *rudimentary*. Both of these notions are related to the idea of simplicity, but in different senses. Elements are simple, that is irreducible, parts of a whole: the parts we would need to put together in order to understand the whole. Rudiments are beginnings, not in the sense of foundations, but in the sense of easy or imperfect starting points. We might say, for example, that the *elements* of science likely to be first taught will be but *rudimentary* and cannot yet display the ideas *fundamental* to science. This is an important distinction in education, since the idea of teaching something because it is fundamental does not immediately reveal the order in which that something should be taught.

5.3 Information and knowledge

5.3.1 *Information*

Claiming that a liberal education liberates people from the contingencies of the present and the particular by involving them in fundamental knowledge and understanding calls for some explanation of what kind of knowledge I am talking about. I am not talking about information, at least not in the modern sense of that term. The earlier sense of 'inform' and 'information' would have made this distinction less necessary. The notion of information was once a richer package than it now is, and carried the idea of the 'formation or moulding of the mind or character, training, instruction, teaching' ('OED'); so that to inform would be 'To form, mould or train (the mind, character, etc.) esp. by imparting learning or instruction; hence, To impart instruction to (a person), to instruct, teach (in general sense)' ('OED'). The 'OED' is quite clear, however, that this sense is obsolete or rare and that the prevailing sense is much narrower, and common observation confirms this. The modern sense of 'information' is 'communication of the knowledge or news of some fact or occurrence; the action of telling or the fact of being told something'; and the modern sense of 'inform' is 'To impart knowledge of some particular fact or occurrence to (a person); to tell (one) of or acquaint (one) with something' ('OED').

There are two significant points about this contemporary usage of the word 'information'. Firstly, there is the emphasis on relatively isolated facts, events or occurrences that one is informed about and the relatively non-evidential nature of the presentation. To be informed that plants grow towards the light, for example, is simply to be given that information, that fact. I need be given no reasons, demonstrations, explanations for this to be a piece of information. Of course I would need to have some grasp of what a plant is, and what light is, but this kind of understanding need only be minimal. Secondly, there is the emphasis on straightforward *telling*. Information, typically, involves facts being passed on from one person to another or others by word of mouth, print, or something similar. There is nothing in this conception of one individual helping another to come to see *why* he should believe something to be the case, only the transfer or the sharing of the information that it is.

There are many occasions where information, even on this narrowly restricted conception, is all one needs. This may be because the understanding of the context in which the particular piece of information is to fit can safely be assumed, or because the recipient needs the particular piece of information for practical purposes of an immediate kind where evidence and understanding in any extensive sense are not necessary. In all cases, however, the recipient must trust the giver of the information, or have reason to believe that the giver is knowledgeable and unlikely to deceive or misinform. Much information, though not all, is transitory as to its truth and value: knowing the present price of timber is fine if I want to buy timber *now,* but that information will be useless to buyers next year, though it might continue to be of value to economic historians. It is the transitoriness of information, its isolation from frameworks of understanding and evidence, and its dependence upon the trusted information-giver that separates information from more fundamental knowledge and understanding. Information will have a place in schooling, inevitably, but the content and substance of a liberal education can never consist simply of a body of information, however extensive and diversified that collection might be.

5.3.2 *Knowledge improperly so called*

Teachers sometimes give knowledge a low rating among all the things they see as important in education. The arguments against knowledge take various forms, all, I want to argue, involving a wrong conception of what it is to know. A typical account of what I am calling a wrong conception of what it is to know is that knowing is simply being able to give back or repeat a given piece of information. The following are all examples of this:

(i) A teacher tells a class that the area of a parallelogram is to be found by multiplying the base by the perpendicular height. The pupils are subsequently asked how to find the area of a parallelogram and reply that this is done by multiplying the base by the perpendicular height.

(ii) After reading in the textbook that gaps are sometimes left in railway lines to allow for expansion, pupils are asked why gaps are sometimes left in railway lines. They reply that this is to allow for expansion.

(iii) Pupils are told that to divide fractions by fractions you turn the divisor upside down and proceed as if multiplying. The pupils then proceed in this manner whenever doing division of fractions.

(iv)   A pupil is told that Nelson was killed at the Battle of Trafalgar in 1805. He then responds correctly to the following questions: In what year was the Battle of Trafalgar? What famous English admiral was killed at the Battle of Trafalgar?

It is not necessary to claim that many, or even any, teachers engage in bringing about learning in quite such a starkly verbalistic manner as this, though some undoubtedly come dangerously near this extreme. What is interesting to note is that it is this kind of model that some teachers have in mind when they claim to be concerned with more than knowledge. They want pupils to be able to relate propositions together, to apply them to other situations, above all to understand them. Knowing, as exemplified here, does not involve any of this. Each piece of information is a separate piece, not necessarily related to anything else. Information is simply given back, regurgitated, with no understanding necessarily indicated. In extreme cases of such learning it does not even appear necessary to understand the meaning of the words. This is why such learning is characterized as parrot-like and earns the generally derogatory (at least nowadays) title of rote-learning. Teachers are right, therefore, to deplore such learning and to seek for better things.

They are wrong, however, to characterize such learning as *knowledge*. What is involved here is not knowledge at all. In the examples given it should be plain that there *is* something wrong or odd about calling whatever the pupils have acquired 'knowledge'. If we consider (i), (ii) and (iv), how could we really be sure that a given pupil *knows* what he claims to know? He might, after all, just have guessed the right answer and surely what is guessed cannot be knowledge. Even if the pupil had not guessed but had correctly remembered there are still doubts. Of course the pupil can claim, and correctly claim, to know *what the teacher or textbook* said; but is knowing that the teacher said that Nelson was killed at the Battle of Trafalgar the same as knowing *that* Nelson was killed at the Battle of Trafalgar? Try it with less usual examples: Is knowing that the teacher said that all Conservatives are foolish the same as knowing *that* all Conservatives are foolish? Is knowing that the teacher said that trade unions are too powerful the same as knowing *that* trade unions are too powerful? If knowing 'that X' is the same as knowing that the teacher or any other authority said that X, how will a pupil ever be able to know when and if a teacher or authority is wrong? More importantly, what will count as knowledge for the pupil when no teacher is around to tell him?

Example (iii) is not quite the same and appears to avoid these strictures. This is only, however, because the pupil almost inevitably introduces his own additional reasons for the correctness of the procedure by seeing that it works. This might be at the crude level of seeing that he gets ticks instead of crosses; but it might be something like seeing, say, that there are four halves in two and using this direct awareness to check the method: i.e. $2 \div \frac{1}{2} = 2/1 \times 2/1 = 4/1 = 4$ which is what the pupil would have expected. If the pupil does something like this he begins to acquire something much more like knowledge properly speaking. He moves away from a reliance upon the teacher's 'say-so' as the only grounds for belief. The teacher could, of course, have helped the pupil to this piece of realization, but that is to jump ahead in the argument a bit. The point to make at this stage is that it is this derogatory model of *mere* knowledge, non-evidential knowledge, knowledge without understanding that has made many teachers claim that their professional task is not so much with knowledge as with other more demanding and meaningful aspirations. This model, however, has never really deserved the title 'knowledge' at all. It is a caricature of knowledge, a parody, bearing very little resemblance to knowledge as understood by those who have genuinely to use knowledge — scientists and technologists, for example — or by those who examine the nature of knowledge in that branch of philosophy known as epistemology or theory of knowledge. It is to this richer conception of knowledge that I now turn.

5.3.3 *Knowledge properly so called*

Most cases of knowing that we are concerned with in school fall under one or other of two heads: knowing how to do something and knowing that something is the case. A convenient shorthand often used is 'knowing how' and 'knowing that'. 'Knowing that' is sometimes alternatively referred to as propositional knowledge, because knowing that something is the case can always be expressed in terms of knowing a given proposition.

'Knowing how' seems to require proof in performance. Examples of such knowing could be:

knowing how to ride a bike
knowing how to adjust a bunsen burner
knowing how to mend a puncture
knowing how to cut a screw thread on a lathe.

To show that you know how to ride a bike you must get on and ride one. We would be suspicious of a person claiming to know how to mend a puncture if the task was always avoided when circumstances required the demonstration and materials were available. Knowing how to adjust a bunsen burner seems the same as correctly adjusting one in appropriate circumstances. But is it really the same? We must be careful not to conclude that because we normally ask for proof by performance there is no difference between the knowing and the performing. We might at least raise some questions. For example: suppose someone who normally rides a cycle to have an accident so that he can no longer ride. Does he now not know how to ride a cycle? In some sense surely he does (very likely) *still* know how to ride a cycle even though he cannot now give proof by performance. We say this partly because he gave his proof so recently, but not only because of this, but also because *knowing* how to do something suggests *more* than simply being able to do it. What this *more* is does not seem very obvious. That we suspect the existence of something more is revealed in what we say confidently and what strikes us as odd. That a computer is able to compute is plain enough, whereas claiming that a computer *knows* how to compute strikes me at least as odd. Similarly, an automatic pilot flies an aeroplane, that is without doubt; but it sounds odd to speak of the automatic pilot *knowing* how to fly an aeroplane.

We might be in a better position to pursue this question when we have had a look at the other kind of knowing — 'knowing that' or propositional knowledge. Examples of propositional knowledge could be:

John knows that metals expand when heated
Mary knows that Washington is the capital of the USA
Jean knows that water expands as it turns to ice
Rodney knows that Wellington led the British army in the Peninsular
    War
Jack knows that symbolism is used in 'The Great Gatsby'.

What is known here in each case is a proposition which comes after the word 'that': 'metals expand when heated', etc. It is always the case with propositions that something is asserted about something else, and that this assertion can be true or false. There seems little doubt that much of what teachers do in schools is concerned with getting children to know in this propositional sense. As we shall see, however, knowing where the object of knowledge is a true proposition is not 'mere knowledge' as described and criticized in the previous section. A little analysis will help to demonstrate this.

To know that, for example, water expands as it turns to ice cannot mean simply that a pupil can repeat the words 'water expands as it turns to ice' in response to an appropriate written or spoken question. There are three reasons for doubting such a simple conception. I have mentioned already that such a pupil might admit to guessing the right answer. Now the peculiar thing about guessing is that we only guess what we *do not know*. Guessing is incompatible with knowing. If I know I do not need to guess, and if I guessed that is to admit that I did not really know. There is nothing particularly deep or philosophical about this, it is just that this is how we normally use the words 'guess' and 'know'. We must note, however, that guessing *is* compatible with simply uttering the proposition 'water expands as it turns to ice', or whatever, correctly.

In the second place the pupil might utter the words correctly yet himself believe the proposition to be false. Such cynical responses to teachers' questions are far from unusual in situations where pupils try to guess what teachers want. Knowing that something is the case seems to require that the knower *believes* it to be the case. Uttering words correctly *might* indicate the holding of a belief in the truth of the proposition, but clearly it does not necessarily do so.

In the third place, and not so obviously, there is the question of *why* the utterance was made. Even if the pupil *does* believe in the truth of the proposition, on what is that belief based? One of the reasons why guessing does not count as knowing is that even if someone chooses to *believe* something on the basis of a guess this hardly seems sufficient warrant for the belief. To substantiate a claim to know that something is the case we normally expect that there is a belief and, further, that the belief is justified in some way: there must be some evidence, grounds or warrant for the belief. Only with all these conditions satisfied are we really talking about knowledge properly so called.

Now if this is right it begins to look very different from the earlier idea of mere knowledge. We have two important ideas that will need considerable further exploration. Firstly, the idea that the pupil must in some sense come to believe for himself if he is to really know, and, secondly, the difficult and far-reaching idea of evidence or grounds that must be grasped, understood, by the pupil if he is to really know. These will be highly important considerations for the content and substance of a liberal education, but also for our later attention to the appropriate methods of liberal education. We might sum up the account of knowledge properly so called in this way: I can claim to know that something is the case when I have a belief that appropriately conclusive evidence entitles me to be reasonably sure about.[5]

Notice that nothing is said here about ideas like 'absolute certainty', which some people, going from one extreme to another, wish to attach to the idea of knowing. The emphasis is upon 'appropriately conclusive evidence'. What can count as appropriate evidence under differing circumstances we have yet to discuss. The point to make at the moment is that without such evidence beliefs cannot count as knowledge, with it they can. Again, there is nothing more mysterious or stipulative about this than an explication of the way in which the word is normally used. 'How do you know that?' we say, in response to somebody's claim to know; and when we do that we are asking for the evidence without which we do not accept the claim as knowledge at all.

Let me now return briefly to 'knowing how'. I raised doubts, a few paragraphs back, about saying that knowing how to do something was no more than being able to perform the appropriate action. We are now in a position to have a closer look at this. What I am getting at here is simply that it is more useful and less ambiguous to say something like 'is able to' or 'can' when *all* we are speaking about is the performance, i.e.

He can ride a bike
He is able to make boxes
She can make silk screen prints.

'Know how' can then be kept for all those cases where we *are* suggesting rather more than mere performance. The 'more' might be something like:

(i)   having some conception, presented to myself in some form, of what I am doing and how it is differentiated from other things that I might be doing;
(ii) having some understanding of what I am doing in the sense of knowing why I do certain things to achieve other things; and perhaps
(iii) providing evidence of (i) and (ii) in an account given to another person.

Another way of putting all this is to say that we talk about *knowing* how to do something when the performance is, as it were, an intelligent performance executed with a background of evidential beliefs about it. We might thus define it: I *know* how to do something when I perform the action correctly (or have recently done so more than once) and have a background of at least some beliefs about the action that appropriately conclusive evidence entitles me to be sure about. Of course, I am going to say that the objects of liberal education, in so far as they concern pupil performances, must be to get pupils to *know* how to do things and not merely to be able to do them. The full implications of this significant distinction, like much else I am sketching here, must await further elaboration.

5.4 Truth: what we ought to believe

Many philosophers, in giving an analysis of what it is to know, build in an additional condition to those given for propositional knowledge in my definition. They want to say that knowledge is justifiable *true* belief. This sounds very much the same but it is different in one very important particular. What is being insisted upon is that my belief that something is the case, to be knowledge, must not only be supported by appropriately conclusive evidence, but it must actually in some sense *be* true. I do not think this is right. Indeed I think it is a very confused and difficult position to maintain.

The main objection is that the truth condition can never really be satisfied meaningfully in the additional way that seems to be expected. If I believe something to be the case, on good grounds or evidence, what can I produce additionally to show that my belief *is* true? Of course, there are cases where such claims are shown to be wrong, but this is only when the false claim had ignored, or been unaware of, some additional *evidence* that someone else can demonstrate. This is simply that one belief is shown to be less justifiable than another, and in such a case only the *more* justifiable belief can count as knowledge. Science, for example, progresses by the constant replacement of beliefs justifiable in their time by beliefs that are *more* justifiable. To talk of false beliefs being replaced by true beliefs hardly seems to fit the case when we know that there is a considerable likelihood that many of our 'true' beliefs will themselves have to be replaced. The point, then, is that there cannot be any sense of 'true' which is more than the most justifiable belief we can get. We have probably been led astray by the apparent certainty obtainable in the truths of logic and mathematics to imagine that such certainty lurks elusively to be sought for in other areas of knowledge. But the certainty of logic is a special case, depending on the internal form and relationships of formal systems. This certainty is just not to be found anywhere else.

To insist on the truth condition makes the grounds of knowledge and belief sound all of a piece, whatever kind of belief we are thinking about. To ask only that beliefs be justifiable, warranted, grounded in *some* way, is more flexible and allows for variations in what is to count as appropriate evidence. This supports our intuitive awareness that scientific propositions, moral propositions, mathematical propositions and religious propositions, for example, *do* seem to require different kinds of justification.

A dogmatic attachment to the idea that there are truths and falsities and that education is concerned only with truths can lead to rather odd educational practices. A pupil can be told, for instance, that he ought to believe something *because* it is true. This presents a blank wall to the pupil. He can do nothing about it. He is faced with a mystery and a cult where some have access to truths which are transmitted, as seen fit, to recipients in schools. Because the teacher knows certain things to be true his sole concern comes to be that pupils should believe them, not necessarily that pupils should be helped to see why these things are believable. John Stuart Mill labelled truths communicated in this way 'dead dogmas' as compared with 'living truths' and it is worth noting at some length what he says:

> There is a class of persons (happily not quite so numerous as former-ly) who think it enough if a person assents undoubtingly to what they think true, though he has no knowledge whatever of the grounds of the opinion, and could not make a tenable defence of it against the most superficial objections. Such persons, if they can once get their creed taught from authority, naturally think that no good, and some harm, comes of it being allowed to be questioned. Where their influence prevails, they make it nearly impossible for the received opinion to be rejected wisely and considerately, though it may still be rejected rashly and ignorantly; for to shut out discus-sion entirely is seldom possible, and when it once gets in, beliefs not grounded on conviction are apt to give way before the slightest semblance of an argument. Waiving, however, this possibility — assuming that the true opinion abides in the mind, but abides as a prejudice, a belief independent of, and proof against, argument — this is not the way in which truth ought to be held by a rational being. This is not knowing the truth. Truth, thus held, is but one superstition the more, accidentally clinging to the words which enunciate a truth.[6]

Mill does not deny that it is useful to mankind to increase the number of truths — i.e. beliefs that are no longer contested — but he fears that the very acceptance of these truths presents problems about the way they are to be passed on to other generations who have not shared in the excitement of their initial battle for acceptance:

> The loss of so important an aid to the intelligent and living appre-hension of a truth, as is afforded by the necessity of explaining it to, or defending it against, opponents, though not sufficient to outweigh, is no trifling drawback from, the benefit of its universal recognition. Where this advantage can no longer be had, I confess I should like to see the teachers of mankind endeavouring to provide a substitute for it; some contrivance for making the difficulties of the question as present to the learner's consciousness, as if they were pressed upon him by a dissentient champion, eager for his conver-sion.[7]

What I am suggesting is that if we take the view that it is justifiable beliefs that we are concerned about, rather than some reified 'truths' we are more likely to do something like Mill wishes 'the teachers of mankind' to do, but there need be no contrivance about it. To involve pupils in knowledge *is* to involve them in the evidence, the reasons for believing, and this can only be done if the atmosphere is one of questioning, discussion and critical examination of the kind that initially accompanied the discovery of the 'truth' in question.

Now, of course, people *do* commonly attach much importance to the idea of truth and are likely to be properly suspicious of what looks like an attempt to dispense with it. What I am doing, however, is only concerned with dispensing with the dogmatic reifications of 'truth' that I have described. I certainly do want to say that 'Statement p is true' can always be translated without loss of meaning into 'Statement p ought to be believed because there are good reasons for believing it.' The only test for such a definition is that it might be more useful and lead to less difficulties and pseudo puzzles than others. It has the added advantage of drawing our attention to the need for involving pupils in the evidence and justification for the beliefs we want them to hold.

What is *not* relinquished here is what we might call the moral concern for truth. 'Teachers should be concerned about truth' becomes 'Teachers should be concerned that beliefs are justifiable,' and this expresses one side of our moral concern about truth, namely, that statements should not be made flippantly or carelessly, but should be uttered, as it were, seriously — with care about their justification. Indeed, the concern is that the truths stay living, even when transmitted in education, by virtue of not being dissociated from the evidence and justification that gave them life: hence the emphasis on justifiable belief rather than 'truth' which gets cut off from its justificatory base and becomes dead dogma.

The other side of the moral concern for truth that these arguments need not diminish is the concern for honesty. In other words we still, of course, want people to say what they believe to be the case and not pretend that something is the case when there are reasons, known to the speaker, to believe otherwise. In particular we should want teachers to involve children with beliefs that the teachers can honestly justify, in an atmosphere in which the pupils can openly and honestly accept and reject beliefs on evidence available to them. Honesty and sincerity are not abrogated by anything said here. These matters must be examined more closely in considering the methods of liberal education.

5.5 Understanding

Unlike the characterization of knowledge by some teachers in the derogatory sense described earlier, understanding is nearly always given the stamp of approval by contemporary teachers. What exactly it is to understand may not always be very clear but that it is to be valued few, if any, appear to doubt. Indeed, discussions all too often focus on reasons for pupils not understanding or misunderstanding without any adequate positive conception of understanding to hold these shortcomings against. Since I am arguing that the content of a liberal education must rest on sound conceptions of knowledge and understanding I must give some account of understanding here.

A first important point to make is that understanding occurs in individual minds. Even if some might claim (though controversially) that stocks of *knowledge* can exist in libraries, and on films and tapes, independent of individual minds, the idea that *understanding* could so exist strikes us immediately as ridiculous. If machine intelligence is raised as a challenge to this general point there might be more to be said; but it is probably sufficient here to say that in so far as constructions capable of artificial intelligence can be said to understand, they are acting in the significant respects *like* individual minds. Their existence does not destroy the point being made, but it might widen our conception of what counts as individual minds. (See Margaret Boden: *Artificial Intelligence and Natural Man*[8].) In education, at least, it should be fairly obvious that the understanding we bring about, or seek to bring about, must be fashioned in the minds of individual pupils, since there is nowhere else that such understanding can occur. I make this point, not because it is seriously challenged elsewhere — I cannot believe that anyone seriously doubts it — but rather because it is rarely given the emphasis that it deserves and many classroom practices appear to be ignoring its truth. Bringing about understanding in individual minds, and ascertaining whether such understanding has been achieved, are two of the main tasks of liberal educators.

This does not say much about what understanding is, though it points to some things that it is not. To move rather closer we can note that 'understand' is sometimes used to mean 'know', as in: 'I understand that metals expand when heated' or 'I understand how to solve simultaneous equations'. If this was all the word 'understand' meant it would clearly be a redundant term. There is another reason for not supposing 'understanding' to be synonymous with 'knowing', which is to do with the idea of correctness associated with knowing and not necessarily with understanding. The logical and conceptual structure of ideas picked out by 'understanding' is in some ways more complex than that picked out by 'knowing'. The difference is mainly that to know something I must have a belief that is, in some sense at least, correct. To understand something always leaves open the further questions of (a) whether it is appropriate to talk of this example of understanding as correct or not, and (b) if so, whether it *is* correct or not. Another way of putting this is to say that 'understand' can have two different but connected meanings which generate different opposites.

1	Understand	=	make sense of something in a way meaningful to me.
	Not understand	=	fail to make any sense of the something meaningful to me.
2	Understand	=	make sense of something in a way meaningful to me and correct in some publicly demonstrable way.
	Misunderstand	=	make sense of something in a way meaningful to me which can be shown to be incorrect in some publicly demonstrable way.

In the second sense of the word we often speak of having *an* understanding, where this can mean various things. It might mean that although a person has *an* understanding of something he has put it together incorrectly − e.g. he understands a whale as a fish. On the other hand it might mean, when we say that he has *an* understanding, that his understanding is one among many equally possible ones, or that his understanding is one among a number of controversial understandings, where not all can be correct but the issue is not yet decided. For example, there might be various 'understandings' of a picture − one person might see Breughel's picture of the harvesters under the tree as an essay in yellow and gold, another sees it as a masterpiece of perspective, yet another sees it as a statement about man's innate gluttony and sloth. Each 'understanding' is possible and no one excludes the others. On the other hand one person might understand violence as something to be morally condemned in all circumstances, whilst another person believes violence to be sometimes justifiable. Here both cannot be right, yet it is difficult to see how one clearly demonstrates the mistake, the misunderstanding, of the other. These areas of inquiry which appear to allow, quite properly, for kinds of understandings not reducible, or not easily or readily reducible, to one correct kind, are of the greatest importance for the curriculum and for teaching methods.

What is common, however, to all these usages of the word 'understand' is the idea of making sense of something in a way meaningful to me. Clearly and strictly, if the sense is not meaningful to *me* there is no sense made. Nevertheless, it is important, I think, to stress the 'meaningful to me' part to reinforce the point already made about understanding going on in individual minds, and to remind ourselves, as teachers, that for something to be clear and meaningful for us is only part of the exercise of getting it to be clear and meaningful to someone else.

What is it, then, for something to make sense in a way meaningful to me? The main answer to this, I believe, lies in three key ideas:

(i)   relationships or linkages,
(ii) non-arbitrariness, and
(iii) coherence.

If I am struggling to make sense of something that at the moment puzzles me I am normally trying to make relationships or linkages of some kind: What is this like? What is it not like? How could it be used? Is it a kind of 'X'? Is it long enough, heavy enough, light enough, tough enough for an 'X'? These kinds of questions refer, of course, to attempts to understand some physical object, but similar questions arise about ideas, words, sentences, theories or any 'thing' capable of being understood. The object of the exercise is always to fit the 'thing' to be understood into some framework of relationships which, of course, must already partly exist in some form in my own mind. In order to make this fit I may have to alter the framework of meanings I already have in my mind. Piaget's account of adaptation by assimilation and accommodation is an elaboration of this idea.[9] All understanding is making, enlarging, sophisticating, modifying systems of relationships or linkages.

Individual understanding is greatly facilitated if the individual is assisted, by say a teacher, to enter into those great assemblages of relationships already shared by the minds of many others and variously described as disciplines, forms of knowledge, realms of meaning, and so on. To grasp the way in which an idea, a theory, a word, an object, a tool already fits in a framework of ideas known to others (and increasingly to the person trying to understand) as physics, or geography, or history is far easier than to fit every isolated object of cognition or perception into frameworks of purely individual construction. It is this necessary interplay between the personal mental constructions that *must* be made if understanding is to occur, and the already established, shared and public bodies of knowledge and understanding, that constitute the challenge and difficulty of education. As the shared and public knowledge increases in volume and complexity, the temptation is to shortcut or ignore the necessity for real individual understanding, and the result can be disastrous.

The idea that the linkages and relationships have to be *non-arbitrary* is a simple but necessary counter to the madder forms of idiosyncrasy. It is not to say that the pattern of relationships constituting a person's understanding must be just like everyone else's pattern, for to say this would deny the possibility of any kind of discovery, creativity or innovation; but it is to say that the relationships must embody *some* system, *some* rule, *some* process of ordering, either already existing or newly capable of demonstration. Indeed, a relationship that does not invoke these characteristics raises difficulties about how it can be conceived of *as* a relationship.

The idea of *coherence* is the idea of 'things' sticking together but the adhesive idea has clearly become metaphorical. What is normally held to supply the adhesion when we are talking of the coherence of a network of related ideas are the twin notions of consistency and connectedness.[10] Most writers admit that perfect coherence is an ideal rather than a realizable experience. In a perfectly coherent system of propositions not only would no proposition contradict any other, directly or by implication (consistency), but every proposition would entail all the others 'if only for the reason that its meaning could never be fully understood without apprehension of the system in its entirety'.[11] It is the last idea, that of the interdependence of each idea, concept or proposition on each and every other idea, concept or proposition, that constitutes the 'connectedness' part of coherence. The supposition that in its complete form coherence is an unrealizable ideal should not be taken to detract from its importance as a criterion of understanding. The important idea to grasp is that there is *no* way in which ideas, concepts, words, propositions, etc., can be grasped, made meaningful, in isolation. Meaning can only come by the grasping of the interdependent body of relationships in which the idea, etc., has its being. This is not merely an important idea in education. It is no exaggeration to say that it is the central and most characterizing idea of a proper liberal education. Pupils must be initiated into the most fundamental networks of ideas and activities mankind has evolved, in a way which gives them each an individual knowledge and understanding of these great systems to whatever extent is individually possible. No other procedure can properly liberate each individual pupil from the particular dependencies of time and place, nor properly fulfil the moral duty that one generation owes to the next.

5.6 Summary

It is perhaps useful at this point to attempt a summary of these preliminaries.

Building on the characterization of a liberal education set out earlier, I am now arguing that the criterion of fundamentality cannot be satisfied by seeing liberal education as a purveying of information, even where such information might be considered immediately useful. Schools will always have to supply *some* information, of course, both in its own right for immediate or short-term usefulness, and as instrumental to the more profound purposes of liberal education; but it is the deeper purposes of knowledge and understanding in their full senses that must provide the mainsprings of a liberal education. The understanding criterion involves the initiation and engagement of pupils in those frameworks of interrelated ideas and activities that have stood the test of time in terms of fundamentality, non-arbitrariness and coherence, and the knowledge criterion involves the initiation and engagement of pupils in frameworks of interrelated, evidentially held beliefs where ideas of justifiable correctness are significant. In both cases the suggestion of 'initiation and engagement' distinguishes an attitude to knowledge and understanding as profoundly different from that appropriate to the purveyance of information, the handling of 'mere knowledge', or the transmission of 'truths' in the 'dead dogma' sense castigated by Mill. The methodological implications of 'initiation and engagement' will be considered more fully in a later chapter.

6

Three accounts considered

There is a large literature of suggestions for the curriculum of schools of universal education. As indicated earlier, however, much of this literature is of little use in an endeavour to find proposals based on fundamental principles, and much of it is almost hopelessly entangled with considerations other than those appropriate to the justification of a curriculum for a liberal education. Before enlarging the general suggestions so far made into a more specific account of the content and method of a liberal education I intend to consider the views of three writers, all philosophers of education, who have attempted to base recommendations on principles which, though different, are considered to be fundamental. The three are:

(i) P.H. Hirst: based on an epistemological analysis of the nature of knowledge.
(ii) P. Phenix: claims to be based on the idea that 'knowledge in the disciplines has patterns or structures and that an understanding of these typical forms is essential for the guidance of teaching and learning', but is probably best seen as based on a phenomenological account of the differentiated areas of 'meaning' evolved by humankind.
(iii) J. White: based on the educational implications of a subjective theory of values.

6.1 P.H. Hirst and the forms of knowledge

Although the work of Philip Phenix mainly concerned with curriculum content appeared in the year before that of the appearance of Hirst's earliest curriculum paper it is convenient to consider the work of Hirst first, partly because of its very considerable influence in the philosophy of education over the last decade and a half, and partly the better to understand the base from which Hirst mounts his most trenchant criticism of Phenix. It is also the case, I believe, that the thesis propounded by Hirst is the most serious attempt so far to get at what might be a fundamental basis for the curriculum of a liberal education.

Hirst first discussed his ideas about liberal education in his paper, Liberal Education and the Nature of Knowledge, which appeared in 1965. This paper contained the essentials of the thesis which have remained relatively unchanged in their most important parts in more recent writings, though a number of significant modifications of detail have emerged in later papers and in lectures to students taking the Education Tripos at Cambridge. Fortunately, nearly all the relevant material has been published in the collection 'Knowledge and the Curriculum' and most of my references are to that volume.

Earlier I noted that Hirst justified a liberal education by a pre-supposition argument, namely that an education concerned with the development of the rational mind was itself presupposed in all justificatory questioning. Liberal education, then, for Hirst, is essentially the development of the rational mind in the individuals being educated: 'It is an education concerned directly with the development of the mind in rational knowledge, whatever form that freely takes.'[1] The connection between 'knowledge' and 'mind' is seen by Hirst as a conceptual one, not to be confused with attempts to shape or mould the mind to some external reality, since this would be to presuppose a philosophy of metaphysical realism, and Hirst does not want to tie his thesis necessarily to such a philosophy. Neither does Hirst see mind as having some inbuilt structure or process of operation of the brain which itself develops into certain differentiated kinds of knowledge or ways of knowing. He is thus concerned to free his thesis from any kind of 'realist' determination from, as it were, the outside or the inside. The context is rather one of human interaction, an initiation into conceptual schemata developed in the social and public interactions of the past:

> to have a mind basically involves coming to have experiences
> articulated by means of various conceptual schemata. It is only
> because man has over millennia objectified and progressively
> developed these that he has achieved the forms of human
> knowledge, and the possibility of the development of mind as we
> know it is open to us today.[2]

The link between mind and knowledge is, then, for Hirst, a logical relationship:

> from which it follows that the achievement of knowledge is
> necessarily the development of mind — that is, the self-conscious
> rational mind of man — in its most fundamental aspect.[3]

Before we take the next expository step, which is to look at what Hirst goes on to say about the nature of knowledge, now seen to be indissolubly linked with the nature of mind, it is important to note

69

another link of a logical and conceptual kind that Hirst makes. This is the link between the idea of knowledge and the idea of meaning. Some indication of this was given in Hirst's early paper, where he says, for example:

> To acquire knowledge is to become aware of experience as structured, organised and made meaningful in some quite specific way.[4]

and where he is at pains to point out that it is not only knowledge in its minimal sense that consists of publicly statable conceptual structures, but that:

> The various manifestations of consciousness, in, for instance, different sense perceptions, different emotions, or different elements of intellectual understanding, are intelligible only by virtue of the conceptual apparatus by which they are articulated.[5]

and that without the human development of cognitive frameworks embodying public criteria:

> all other forms of consciousness, including, for example, emotional experiences, or mental attitudes and beliefs, would seem to be unintelligible.[6]

Thus, on Hirst's account, to find meaning, intelligibility or understanding in any aspect of conscious life is only possible under the diverse cognitive structures that constitute different forms of knowledge. To classify knowledge, if that is possible, is to classify meaning. There is no wider class of meaning of which knowledge is only a subclass.

What is not quite so patent in the earlier paper is the extent to which this linkage between meaning and knowledge rests on a form of the verificationist theory of meaning: the idea that a proposition or statement is only meaningful if we know, at least in some sense, how the statement might be tested for truth or falsity. That he attaches importance to this idea is made clear by Hirst in his much later paper directed against Phenix:

> all aspects of meaning necessitate the use of concepts and it is only by virtue of conceptualisations that there is anything we can call meaning at all. And no concepts can be the basis of shared meaning without criteria for their application. But the criteria for the application of a concept, say 'X', simply are the criteria for the truth of statements that say something is an 'X'. By this chain of relations, that meaning necessitates concepts, that concepts necessitate criteria of application and that criteria of application are

truth criteria for propositions or statements, the notions of meaning and true propositions, and therefore meaning and knowledge, are logically connected.[7]

This tight connection between meaning and true propositions is an essential part of Hirst's structure of ideas. It turns out to be a very restricting and harmful part of his thesis, as we shall see when I turn to criticism. But now I must move on to Hirst's account of the forms of knowledge themselves.

These are to be not merely discriminable conceptual frameworks, but discriminable bodies of true propositions, and are indeed seen to be distinguishable, one from another, by an examination of those aspects which are 'the necessary features of true propositions or statements'. These aspects are:

(i) Certain central concepts that are peculiar in character to the form.
(ii) A network of possible relationships between concepts in which experience can be understood. A distinctive logical structure.
(iii) Distinctive tests against experience in accordance with particular criteria peculiar to the form.
(iv) Particular techniques and skills for exploring experience and testing their distinctive expressions.

In later papers far less attention is given to (iv) and it is fairly clear that the significant and important distinguishing criteria came to be regarded by Hirst as the idea of specific conceptual structures based upon some centrally characterizing (if not categorial) concepts, and the idea of specific and discriminate truth tests. For instance, in the paper against Phenix we have:

These forms, I have argued, can only be distinguished by examining the necessary features of true propositions or statements: the conceptual structures and the truth criteria involved.[8]

and in another place:

the three elements in which the differences are to be found are the concepts and the logical structure propositions employ, and the criteria for truth in terms of which they are assessed.[9]

In trying to enumerate the exact forms of knowledge distinguished by these criteria there appears to have been some confusion, to be noted more fully later, as to whether logically discernible forms are being listed, or empirically discernible *claims* for such status are being listed. In the early paper there seemed little doubt that what Hirst had in mind was a list of what seemed to be revealed by his analysis, when he wrote:

In summary, then, it is suggested that the forms of knowledge as we have them can be classified as follows:

I   Distinct disciplines or forms of knowledge (subdivisible): mathematics, physical sciences, human science, history, religion, literature and fine arts, philosophy.[10]
II Fields of knowledge: theoretical, practical (These may or may not include elements of moral knowledge).

To this list Hirst added another suggested classification based on organizations of knowledge:

formed by building together round specific objects, or phenomena, or practical pursuits, knowledge that is characteristically rooted elsewhere in more than one discipline.[11]

He gives geography as an example of such a 'field of knowledge', being a theoretical study of man in relation to his physical environment drawing on more than one form of knowledge. Engineering is given as an example of a practical field which similarly draws on more than one form for practical, rather than purely theoretical, purposes. Thus Hirst finishes his description:

It is the distinct disciplines that basically constitute the range of unique ways we have of understanding experience if to these is added the category of moral knowledge.[12]

By this point in the argument it is clear that in order to be liberally educated pupils must, according to Hirst, be engaged in some way in each of the distinguishable forms of knowledge, since that is what it is, in our historical time, to develop a rational mind. This does not mean that the content of a liberal education would simply be each of the forms taught separately. *How* pupils are to be best initiated into the forms will depend upon many things of a psychological, practical and organizational kind. Integrated studies, for example, are not automatically ruled out. Nevertheless, Hirst is emphatic that, however it is done, the objective must be that pupils become able to know and to understand in each of the forms of knowledge.

Hirst is also at pains to point out that he does not see a liberal education as synonymous or coterminous with a general education:

Certainly liberal education as it is here being understood is only one part of the education a person ought to have, for it omits quite deliberately for instance specialist education, physical education and character training.[13]

In writing about the forms of knowledge thesis in later papers, and in replying to criticism, Hirst has not seriously altered his general thesis but two modifications are worthy of note before turning from exposition to criticism. The first concerns the characterization of the suggested forms of knowledge. The chapter on The Curriculum in the well-known introductory text, 'The Logic of Education', written jointly by Hirst and Richard Peters in 1970, says:

> Detailed studies suggest that some seven areas can be distinguished, each of which necessarily involves the use of concepts of a particular kind and a distinctive type of test for its objective claims.[14]

and the seven are given as:

   (i) the truths of formal logic and mathematics
  (ii) the truths of physical science
 (iii) awareness and understanding of our own and other people's minds
 (iv) moral judgments
  (v) objective aesthetic experience
 (vi) religion
(vii) philosophical understanding

The most significant difference here is the removal of difficulties associated with the previous suggestions that 'history' and 'human sciences' constituted discriminate forms. Hirst himself notes that he came to believe that the social sciences and history were at least partly empirical studies, not logically distinct from the physical sciences, but that:

> On the other hand, history and some of the social sciences are in large measure not concerned simply with an understanding of observable phenomena in terms of physical causation, but with explanations of human behaviour in terms of intentions, will, hopes, beliefs, etc. The concepts, logical structure and truth criteria of propositions of this latter kind are, I would now argue, different from, and not reducible to, those of the former kind.[15]

A second important difference is to cease talking of literature and the fine arts and to talk instead of 'objective aesthetic experience'. This is to meet the fairly obvious objection that literature and the fine arts includes under its umbrella title a vast range of activities, many of which it would be extremely difficult to consider in terms of the truth or falsity of propositions. Similar objections could be made about religion. In dealing with these objections Hirst says:

> The suggestion that in literature and the fine arts and also in religion we have distinct forms of knowledge has not surprisingly provoked opposition. Let me therefore make it clear that they can to my mind only be regarded as such in so far as they involve expressions that

have the features of true propositions. We certainly do talk of the arts and religion as being cognitive, as providing distinctive types of knowledge. Whether this is justifiable and there is a form of knowledge in the arts, depends on whether or not artistic works themselves have features parallel to those of propositions with related objective tests.[16]

What these modifications of the delineation of the forms adds up to, I believe, is a tightening of the thesis around the idea (which was there from the start) that what is being talked about as forms of knowledge are discriminable bodies of true propositions. Whilst undeniably tightening the logic of what is being said, this does have the effect of making it more difficult to justify within the thesis the inclusion in the curriculum of a liberal education of large bodies of practical and expressive activities thought by many to be important.

As against this tightening of the thesis against criticism there has been a corresponding but less noted weakening which is the second and different modification to be indicated.

In the 'Logic of Education' chapter it was still being said that the seven areas 'can be distinguished', the assumption being that these seven areas were revealed in some way by the logical and conceptual analysis. This impression is strengthened by the words, *'Detailed studies* suggest that some seven areas can be distinguished.'[17] Later in the same passage, however, the word 'claim' starts to appear. Morality, for example, 'must be recognized as having serious claims to independent status. We are also told that there are 'claims for a distinctive mode of objective aesthetic experience' and that 'Religious claims in their traditional forms certainly make use of concepts which, it is now maintained, are irreducible in character.'[18] The idea that we are not now always talking about a number of forms actually logically and conceptually distinguishable by analysis, but rather about *empircally observed claims* to such independent status is put more openly in the brief reference to the forms in Hirst's paper against Phenix: 'On this basis it seems to me that we must at present acknowledge serious claims to some seven distinct categories of meaning and knowledge.'[19]

With the noting of these changes and modifications we must now consider the exposition of Hirst's views reasonably complete and turn to criticism.

There is much to be said in favour of Hirst's approach from the point of view of the necessities of a liberal education sketched earlier in this work. Most importantly, Hirst is trying to get at what is fundamentally necessary for an education to be liberating. If his account is correct nothing could be more fundamental than the forms of knowledge. By definition they would be irreducible, either to one another or to anything else that could be knowledge. This is fundamentality indeed, and if the account is correct then the forms of knowledge would have to be the basis of a liberal education, since they would underlie, characterize, give meaning to, anything that anyone could undertake or choose. Undeniably, also, if correct the thesis satisfies my criteria of rationality since the development of the rational mind is at the very heart of the thesis. Intrinsic worthwhileness is pointed to by the difficulty of imagining how anything else could be valued if the conceptual and cognitive framework necessary for knowing and understanding it were not valued in some prior way and to some extent. The rational man may value any or none of a great number of things, but he must at least value the development of his own rational mind. Hirst does not say this specifically, but it seems implicit in all he does say that he believes the value of the development of the rational mind to be objectively justifiable and not a subjective value which one might take up or lay down as one pleases.

All of this, then, comes admittedly nearer to satisfying the characteristics of a liberal education than anything else I have seen in print, certainly nearer than the other proposals I shall look at more briefly. Yet one must nevertheless say that as the thesis stands it will not do. There are serious and gravely weakening difficulties that must be considered.

The main difficulty arises in any serious attempt to enumerate distinct forms of knowledge possessing, and therefore distinguishable by, the specific and categorial concepts and the distinctive tests of truth required by the thesis. It is first of all necessary to be very clear what kind of an exercise this is. There are three seemingly similar exercises which are in fact quite different:

(a) the classification of knowledge and understanding into discrete forms by a demonstrable analysis of different and distinguishable categorial concepts, conceptual frameworks and tests of truth;

(b) the noting of bodies of alleged knowledge and understanding that proceed *as if* they had demonstrably distinguishable categorial concepts, conceptual frameworks and tests of truth; that is, it could be said of such bodies that they could only be coherent *if* they had such concepts, frameworks and tests, but it is not demonstrable that they have, or it is *controversial* whether they have;

(c) the noting of empirically observable claims by many or few persons that such and such bodies of alleged knowledge and understanding have the independent status that distinctive categorial concepts, conceptual frameworks and truth tests would give them.

Without some success in actually indicating forms that satisfy the distinguishing criteria the thesis of Hirst is reduced to one of prescriptive definition: If an 'X' is to be a Hirstian form of knowledge it must have distinctive categorial concepts, conceptual framework and tests for truth. The class of forms so defined might be a null class! It might have one proper member as scientific reductionists would argue. It might have two, as the logical positivists who shared Hirst's attachment to a verificationist theory of meaning, argued. What Hirst has not done, and to be fair does not claim to have done, is to demonstrate that there actually *are* the seven he suggests. What he increasingly says, as I have noted above, is that some 'X's are the subjects of *claims* to be considered as having a separate status, e.g. religion; whilst other activities can only be considered coherently as forms of knowledge if, or in so far as, they can be shown to have distinctive categorial concepts, conceptual frameworks and tests of truth, or in such part of them as can be so shown. Thus the appeal is indeed sometimes to (a), but it is also sometimes to (b) or (c).

This apparent confusion has a number of implications, all important and harmful to the thesis. We are no longer clear, for example, exactly what it is that justifies a particular knowledge activity in the curriculum of a liberal education. Is it to earn its place by a satisfactory outcome of the (a)-type analysis? Mathematics might satisfy this test, and most people might be prepared to accept that the physical sciences do, too. But beyond these two we enter areas of considerable controversy as to the distinctive concepts, structures and truth tests. Or is a possible knowledge activity to be included in the curriculum by some (b)-type conjecture? If so, this produces odd results. Someone convinced of the importance of literature and the fine arts, for example, notes with satisfaction that they seem to get into the curriculum of a liberal education on Hirst's account. Closer inspection, however, especially of Hirst's debate with Scrimshaw,[20] reveals that what Hirst means by this form of knowledge is nothing like the rich mixture of making, doing, appraising, expressing, criticizing and appreciating that most lovers of the arts have in mind. This whole area only satisfies Hirst's criteria *in so far as* it, or *in such part of it* as, can be conceived of as a body of true propositions. Speaking of both religion, and literature and the arts Hirst says, as we have already noted:

> Let me therefore make it clear that they can to my mind only be regarded as such (i.e. forms of knowledge) in so far as they involve expressions that have the features of true propositions.[21]

The debate here has hinged around whether or not art can be thought of in any sense on the model of making statements of a propositional kind like those normally made in ordinary language or in symbolic

forms that can be translated into ordinary language. It is highly doubtful whether the visual arts, music, dance, drama, or even the more
imaginative aspects of literature can be fitted neatly into this paradigm.
It is virtually certain that they cannot without loss of much that is
considered not only of value, but is essentially characteristic of them.
Thus even if the debate is resolved in Hirst's favour it is only likely to
show, at an improbable best, that some part of, some types of, art
might be thought of as propositional. This would not meet the main
objection, which is the intuitive belief that the richer aspects of art,
music and literature, form of knowledge or not, propositional or not,
have a claim to be included in the content and substance of a liberal
education; nor will it abate the consequent suspicion that there must
be something wrong with a theory that seeks out a highly speculative
cognitive core in the arts as being what is most fundamental to them,
and by so doing relegates beyond the pale of a liberal education precisely those aspects of art most valued by those who practise and
appreciate it.

The difficulty about religion is not quite the same. There is little
doubt that for many people there is a body of true propositions constituting religion in general or, more likely, a particular religion. The
difficulty here is that it is precisely the suggestion that this body
consists of *true* propositions that is challenged by other, equally intelligent, people. This is an obvious enough social phenomenon, yet it
presents itself as an oddity on Hirst's account in two ways. Firstly,
religion could only be included in the curriculum of a liberal education
on some kind of (c)-type argument − i.e. it would be there because at
least *some* people claim it to be a form of knowledge. But what of
those who claim it is not? And what proportion of people would have
to be in each camp to settle the issue one way or another? For note the
second aspect of the oddity: where there is dispute as to whether some
community of discourse is actually a form of knowledge or not there is
no truth test apparently available to decide the matter, for while truth
tests are, on Hirst's account, unique to each form of knowledge, there is
no overriding truth test that can be applied. If it is claimed that it is
philosophy, itself a form of knowledge, that is to fill this honorific
role by virtue of its second-order nature, surely this in itself would be
controversial? Are we really to suppose that theologians will see judgments about the nature of the subject of their enquiries as purely
philosophical? Will artists, musicians and poets readily accept the adju-
dication of philosophers as to the nature of their activities?

What all this reveals, I believe, is that, whereas the forms-of-
knowledge thesis looks as if areas of knowledge are to earn their place
in the curriculum of a liberal eduation by emerging as distinctive and
irreducible after appropriate logical and conceptual analysis, in fact

some at least of those suggested are listed because they are observed to be communities of discourse of largish numbers of intelligent people. These are, of course, no more than empirically observed claims to the status that the logical and conceptual analysis would give if it could.

What is also revealed by these considerations is that the content and substance of a liberal education, on Hirst's account, would not be so rich as appears at first sight. In fact, when all the qualifications are noted the basis would be very narrow indeed and this narrowness has led to significant criticism. Jane Roland Martin attacks quite vigorously:

> The received theory's liberally educated person will be taught to see the world through the lenses of the seven forms of knowledge, if seven there be, but not to act in the world. Nor will that person be encouraged to acquire feelings and emotions. The theory's liberally educated person will be provided with knowledge about others, but will not be taught to care about their welfare, let alone act kindly towards them. That person will be given some understanding of society, but will not be taught to feel its injustices or even to be concerned over its fate. The received theory conceives of a liberally educated person as an ivory tower person: one who can reason, but has no desire to solve problems in the real world; one who understands science, but does not worry about the uses to which it is put; one who grasps the concepts of biology, but is not disposed to exercise or eat wisely; one who can reach flawless moral conclusions, but has neither the sensitivity nor the skill to carry them out effectively.[22]

This is somewhat heated polemic but most of it is justifiable criticism. I have already exampled literature and the fine arts as areas where only an attenuated form of both would really earn their place. Martin's reference to moral education is certainly fair comment. Here Hirst makes a distinction between moral understanding, which is properly part of a liberal education, and the development of moral character and commitment which extends beyond a liberal education. Hirst is obviously concerned about these kinds of limitations, perhaps far more so than Martin gives him credit for, but he is prepared to pay the price because of the fundamentality achieved by his analysis. This also has the effect of making Hirst distinguish, as already noted, between a liberal education consisting of involvement in the discriminable forms of knowledge and a wider *general* education still to be separable from specialist training:

> To equate such an education (i.e. a liberal education) with 'general education' is also unacceptable if that is taken to be everything a total education should cover other than 'specialist' elements. The

lack of concern for moral commitment, as distinct from moral understanding, that it seems to imply, is a particularly significant limitation to this concept's usefulness. Nevertheless, it emphasizes, by drawing them together, precisely those elements in a total education that are logically basic, and the exclusion of all logically secondary considerations gives it importance at a time when the ends of education are often looked at purely pragmatically.[23]

That I sympathize with this attempt to find what is basic or fundamental has been made abundantly plain; but where is the division between what is logically basic and what is purely pragmatic and instrumental to be drawn? Hirst's account leaves off in a peculiarly unsatisfactory way. There is to be a class of general education which all should have and which will have things like physical education and moral education in its full sense within it. There is to be a smaller class of liberal education, a part of general education in the sense that all should have it, but more limited in that it should contain only the forms of knowledge as strictly characterized. Then there might be all kinds of instrumental activities, variously justified and presumably not compulsory for all, beyond both the former.

I have already noted the difficulty of thinking that the strict characterization of the forms of knowledge, and the way this justifies a place for an area of 'knowledge', is at all straightforward; but there are two other difficulties to note. Martin draws attention to the fact that the term 'liberal education' is not neutral but value-laden. To say that something should be a part of liberal education is to attribute a special kind of value to it. It follows from the justification of a liberal education that I have discussed in previous chapters that I would agree with this. Thus it is not a matter of indifference to relegate certain parts of some activities to sit somewhere in general education but not in liberal education. To do so is inevitably either to devalue them or to suggest that somehow the importance of the elements to be included in liberal education is perhaps not so great as was at first claimed. The other, and connected, difficulty is that in supposing that, as well as liberal education, there is to be a wider general education containing elements that all should have, a justificatory gap arises. For the liberal education components Hirst provides, as we have noted, a justification in terms of a presupposition argument. For the general education area, though we are told that all pupils should have the elements within it, like physical education and the development of moral character, we are nowhere told why. If there *is* a justification that appeals to common humanness in some way, and not merely to particular instrumental needs, then surely these are parts of a liberal education too? I find it very difficult to see what would justify the inclusion of any activity or any inquiry in a *general* education for all, separable from any kind of instrumental education, that is not at the same time being justified as part of a liberal education. This is why, up to this chapter, I have written of a 'liberal general education' or, sometimes, of a 'general liberal education', where 'general' does *not* only mean 'to be taken by all' but means also 'of general rather than specific application'.

In particular, I find it difficult to see why it is only to be those parts of literature, art and morality, and other aspects of human action which can be construed as bodies of true propositions which are to be within liberal education, whilst those parts of these areas of human 'goings-on' which are the actions, makings, doings, dispositions, expressions and interactions which give meaning, point and significance to these propositions are to be excluded.

These difficulties are generated to a very large extent by the way in which Hirst uses the concept of meaning. 'Meaning', for Hirst, is always used in the context of the meaning of statements. He can thus always make the connection between 'meaning' and 'knowledge' mentioned earlier. For a statement to be meaningful, so the argument runs, we must at least in some way be able to indicate what would make the statement true or false. To analyse meaning, then, becomes an analysis of knowledge truth tests. As we shall see, Hirst uses this conception of meaning in a sharp attack upon Philip Phenix who claimed to be examining different kinds of meaning. Verificationist theories of meaning have run into a good deal of criticism, often because of their empiricist or positivist connections.[24] Hirst is not open to most of these criticisms largely because he does not say what kind of truth tests would apply, only that there must be some. When the logical positivists, for example, suggested a verificationist theory of meaning to depend upon truth tests they also suggested that there were only two kinds of truth test and explained what these were, namely those of empirical observation and experiment and those of analytic logic. Hirst suggests that there are seven but makes no serious attempt to show what these would be.

Now, of course, the meaning of statements is one important way in which we can talk about meaning, and when we do so the relationship between meaning and the way in which statements are to be tested for truth and falsity does seem significant. Even so one would need to be careful about characterizing knowledge as bodies of *true* propositions in the light of Karl Popper's claim that science advances by continuous falsifying of propositions and that verification in the sense of establishing truths is not what goes on at all. Even if we took a slightly modified view of the relationship between the meaning of statements and tests of truth and falsity, to take account of Popper's views, it would still surely be wrong to suppose that meaning *only* attaches to statements.

Hirst more than once refers approvingly to Wittgenstein's ideas of meaning, language games and forms of life as reinforcing his own ideas, but I am not convinced that Wittgenstein actually provides such reinforcement. For Wittgenstein the meaning of words and sentences was to be seen in their actual use in more or less self-contained language games themselves set in forms of life. In his 'Philosophical Investigations' he gives examples of the multiplicity of such language games:

Giving orders and obeying them
Describing the appearance of an object, or giving its measurements
Constructing an object from a description (a drawing)
Reporting an event
Speculating about an event
Forming and testing an hypothesis
Presenting the results of an experiment in tables and diagrams
Making up a story; reading it
Play-acting
Singing catches
Guessing riddles
Making a joke; telling it
Solving a problem in practical arithmetic
Translating from one language into another
Asking, thanking, cursing, greeting, praying

and he goes on to say

> It is interesting to compare the multiplicity of the tools in language and of the ways they are used, the multiplicity of kinds of words and sentences, with what logicians have said about the structure of language.[25]

The point here is that much of this is not to do with statements, yet is nevertheless meaningful on Wittgenstein's account. Whatever Hirst may be doing, Wittgenstein was not reducing meaning to seven sets of characterizations!

Perhaps more importantly, 'meaning' has a different kind of sense which is connected with notions like significance and importance. It is in this sense that people can talk of religion or art being significant in their lives or giving meaning to their lives. This sense is *not* metaphorical or parasitical on the 'meaning of statements' usage, but is rooted in the language in its own right. The import, signification and denotation of *words*, and consequently of sentences embodying propositions, is a widespread, but certainly not paradigmatic sense of 'meaning' as any study of the appropriate 'OED' articles will show. People *mean* to do things, in the sense of intention; they have *meanings* in the sense of purposes; and they find *meaning* in the sense of finding importance or significance in something or some activity. Heidegger, in his subtle considerations of the relation of language to the being of man, criticizes the tendency to limit considerations of signification to the study of statements and assertions, and suggests that a proper philosophical investigation would need to take much more into account:

> we must inquire into the basic forms in which it is possible to articulate anything understandable, and to do so in accordance with significations; and this articulation must not be confined to entities within-the-world which we cognize by considering them theoretically, and which we express in sentences.[26]

'[T]he basic forms in which it is possible to articulate anything understandable' sound remarkably like Hirst's forms of knowledge, but the difference is immediately signalled by what Heidegger goes on to say; for Hirst limits the analysis of the forms to precisely those theoretical sentence expressions that Heidegger warns us against. Heidegger, like Wittgenstein, accepts a richness of articulatable understandings that Hirst appears to deny. Thus, when someone claims that art constitutes a discriminable way of finding meaning in his experience he is not necessarily committed to reducing the significant part of art to a body of true propositions or their equivalents. He is not required to do this even if, in some sense, he relates art to truth, as indeed Heidegger does, for 'truth' too can have meanings other than the correctness to be found in testable statements, as Heidegger argues in his lecture, The Origin of the Work of Art.[27] Our art-lover (not necessarily a Heideggerian!) might be talking, and quite properly, about the significance and importance for him of certain kinds of makings, doings, expressions, appreciations and dispositions. Similarly, 'Nature means much to me,' is not a nonsensical utterance, neither is its significance to be fully rendered by a succession of subsumed true propositions.

There is thus a richer, and perfectly proper, sense of 'meaning' which might allow us to reunite those important areas of human thought and action which Hirst's account appears to dismember, and if this is so we might yet gather into the content and substance of a liberal education those creative and expressive activities which many people intuitively believe have a rightful place.

Regretfully, then, I must for the time being say of Hirst's account, seminal though it is in its determination to seek out fundamentality, and illuminating as it is in its attempt to characterize the forms of knowledge, it is handicapped by its particularly strict characterization of meaning and thus of the forms of knowledge, and this leads to an unduly impoverished basis for a liberal education, especially in the areas of the arts and the humanities. I must now look, rather more briefly, at two other attempts to delineate such a content.

6.2 Philip Phenix and the realms of meaning

Philip Phenix produced his main theory of the curriculum for a general
education in 1964 in his book 'Realms of Meaning', though there
was some indication of his line of thought in an earlier work, 'Philosophy
of Education', in 1958. One view of the work of Phenix is to say that
he has tried to do the same job as Hirst but that his logical analysis
is faulty and collapses plainly under the criticism of Hirst. There is
certainly justification for this view, as I shall try to show; but it is
possible, I believe, to take another view of what Phenix has done which
is much more favourable to the account. After some brief exposition
I shall say something about each of these views.

Phenix starts his account by a consideration of human nature and
he is obviously attracted by the classical philosophical description of
man as a rational animal where 'This power of thought distinguishes
man from everything else in the creation. In human nature reason is
of the essence.'[28] But Phenix also, and importantly, has reservations
about this description:

> This philosophical answer suffers from the limitation that such
> ideas as rationality, reason and mind tend to be narrowly construed
> as referring to the processes of logical thinking. The life of feeling,
> conscience, imagination, and other processes that are not rational in
> the strict sense are excluded by such a construction, and the idea
> of man as a rational animal in the strict sense is accordingly rejected
> for being too one-sided.[29]

The concept that Phenix proposes instead of rationality is *meaning*, a
concept of some importance which we have already found necessary to
examine at some length in talking about Hirst. In one sense Phenix
obviously sees 'meaning' as a convenient word embodying a richer conception of reason and mind than the strictly ratiocinative idea that he
has rejected; but he also has a notion of a very wide range of different
meanings which are probably not trapped at all within normal, not
necessarily strict, conceptions of reason:

> This term is intended to express the full range of connotations
> of reason or mind. Thus, there are different meanings contained in
> activities of organic adjustment, in perception, in logical thinking,
> in social organization, in speech, in artistic creation, in self-
> awareness, in purposive decision, in moral judgment, in the
> consciousness of time, and in the activity of worship. All these
> distinctive human functions are varieties of meaning, and all of them
> together — along with others that might be described — comprise
> the life of meaning, which is the essence of the life of man.[30]

It appears obvious to Phenix, though clearly not so to non-naturalists, that:

> If the essence of human nature is in the life of meaning, then the
> proper aim of education is to promote the growth of meaning.
> To fulfill this aim, the educator needs to understand the kinds of
> meaning that have proven effective in the development of civilization
> and to construct the curriculum of studies on the basis of these
> meanings.[31]

In order to make this broad conception of meaning, however, into a sensible and workable basis for a curriculum, Phenix now has a problem of selection, the more so as he believes that: 'Theoretically there is no limit to the varieties of meaning. Different principles of meaning formation can be devised ad infinitum.'[32] He rejects the idea of an a priori analysis of classes of meaning in favour of an attempt to determine 'the forms of meaning that have actually demonstrated their fecundity'.[33] These he finds in the actually established bodies of scholarly and intellectual activity bound together in communities of discourse:

> comprised of persons bound together by common responsibility
> for a particular kind of meaning. Each such community has its
> characteristic discipline or rule by which the common responsibility
> is discharged. The discipline expresses the particular logic of the
> meaning in question.[34]

It now looks as if the problem of selection is to be solved anthropologically. We are to look around and observe the great and significant communities of discourse, transcending barriers of class, nation and time. Using criteria of growth and fruitfulness – Phenix cannot escape the debt all American philosophers of education owe to Dewey! – we select those most important shared cultural enterprises into which the younger generation of the world should be initiated. Thus expressed the idea is attractive. It avoids some of the difficulties of Hirst's account, since we do not fall into problems about truth tests. Religion, for example, is clearly a manifestation of human being, quite apart from the truth of its propositions. Phenix seems to point to this when he says:

> Whether or not the claim of the religious believer is affirmed, the
> type of meaning intended by the faithful should be clear. Regardless
> of the results of the search, religious inquiry is directed toward
> ultimacy, in the sense of the most comprehensive, most profound,
> most unified meanings obtainable. At the very least, faith refers
> to an ideal and a hope for maximum completeness, depth and

integrity of vision. On these minimal terms, in which no transcendent realities are posited, everyone should be able to acknowledge some religious meanings.[35]

Unfortunately, Phenix does not go on consistently to work out the implications of such an anthropological or phenomenological approach. He is lured back into logical analysis. We might have anticipated this since in enumerating the custodians of meaning to be discerned within human culture there is a patent attachment to those who manipulate propositions, rather than meanings in other forms. For example: artist-critics are mentioned, not just artists; theologians, not just religious believers; moralists, rather than moral people; and scientists, rather than technologists. Perhaps the areas of meaning are not being selected quite so empirically, after all; at least there is ambiguity. The ambiguity extends into the classification that Phenix proposes. On the one hand it is to be no more than a matter of convenience, not really logically fundamental in some Hirstian manner:

> There is no single basis of categorization that any body of material forces on the investigator. Classifications are to some extent arbitrary, depending on the uses for which they are intended. Since the purpose of classifying meanings in education is to facilitate learning, it is desirable to organize the disciplines along lines of general similarity of logical structure. In this manner certain basic ways of knowing can be described, and these may be used to allocate studies for general education, that is, for the education of persons in their essential humanness.[36]

On the other hand, the logical classification actually proposed has all the suggestion of a fundamental, a priori classification of cognitive meaning. It just does not seem like a relatively arbitrary device of selection. For what is proposed rests on the claim that *all* cognitive meaning has two logical aspects, those of quantity and quality. Quantity can be expressed as singular, general or comprehensive; and quality can be expressed as fact, form or norm. One would have thought that a full permutation of these would give nine different kinds of meaning, but Phenix combines them into six, as shown in Table 6.1.

Phenix is quite clear that a proper curriculum for general education will enable a pupil to be involved at some depth in each and every one of the six realms of meaning, and it is worth concluding this brief exposition by quoting him fairly fully on this:

> A program for the curriculum of general education in schools may then be conceived as providing for instruction in all six of the fundamental types of meaning — in language, science, art, personal

Table 6.1 Logical classification of meanings[37]

Generic classes		Realms of meaning	Disciplines
Quantity	Quality		
General	Form	Symbolics	Ordinary language, mathematics, non-discursive symbolic forms
General	Fact	Empirics	Physical sciences, life sciences, psychology, social sciences
Singular	Form	Esthetics	Music, visual art, art of movement, literature
Singular	Fact	Synnoetics	Philosophy, psychology, literature, religion, in their existential aspects
Singular	Norm }	Ethics	The varied special areas of moral and ethical concern
General	Norm }		
Comprehensive	Fact }	Synoptics	History
Comprehensive	Norm }		Religion
Comprehensive	Form }		Philosophy

knowledge, ethics and synoptics — over a period, say, of fourteen years, with some opportunity for concurrent specialization where individual capabilities and interests and social needs indicate its desirability. To achieve a well balanced program it may further be recommended that the program be divided approximately equally among the six realms . . . .

For example, during fourteen years of general education a student could study not only his own everyday language, but also mathematics and one or two foreign languages. He could study several of the sciences — physical, biological, psychological and social — and, among the arts, at least . . . music, the visual arts, the arts of movement (in physical education), and literature. He could have regular opportunities for gaining personal insight, through a program of social activities and of work with skilled guidance counsellors. He could have instruction and practice in making moral decisions, through the study of moral problems and the methods of ethical enquiry consummated by responsible participation in decision making where the common good is at stake. Finally, he could be given a thorough grounding in history and a basic understanding of religious commitment and philosophic interpretation.[38]

This is undeniably a rich and attractive package; so much so that few people would deny that recipients of such an education, conducted in the spirit Phenix clearly intends, would have received a liberal education. The tragedy is that the attempts by Phenix to set all this in an explanatory and justificatory framework, to say clearly, that is, *why* pupils should have such a package, have been partly misguided and partly ambiguous, and have thus provided a focus for quite destructive criticism. One of the main critics, as might have been expected, is Hirst in the paper already noticed. Here Hirst leaves few of Phenix's logical weaknesses unprobed. His most damaging criticism is that the classification of Phenix rests on a confusion, namely that there is no consistent treatment of the logical objects of knowledge enabling them to be compared in different kinds of meaning. There is, claims Hirst, 'ambiguity about the objects of knowledge and appropriate classification criteria for them'.[39] Hirst is maintaining, of course, that the account he himself gives, whereby the logical objects of knowledge are true propositions classifiable on the basis of their necessary features of central concepts, conceptual structures and truth tests, is the only coherent and consistent way of achieving the classification of meaning that Phenix attempts. As compared with this, the objects of knowledge, or meaning, for Phenix are sometimes logical but sometimes what Hirst calls 'everyday' objects. Hirst points to the way in which this confuses the issue in the examples of Phenix's realms of 'symbolics' and 'synnoetics'. In the case of symbolics Hirst says:

> Only if the objects of knowledge are taken to be 'objects' in the everyday, non-philosophical sense, does it seem to me to be possible to assert that the domain of symbolics is that of a distinct type of knowledge . . . . Symbols as such designate no logically distinct domain of knowledge any more than any other particular 'object', in the non-philosophical sense, does. A knowledge of chairs, say, may be of many different fundamental kinds, scientific, esthetic, even moral or religious. No 'objects' in this sense pick out logically distinct types of knowledge.[40]

A similar point is made about synnoetics: 'Again a category of "objects" in the non-philosophical sense is the focus of a type of knowledge, existential experience of these being a second distinctive factor.'[41] It is clear from Phenix's own account of synnoetics that the type of understanding he has in mind here is 'relational insight' or 'direct awareness', and that: 'This personal or relational knowledge is concrete, direct, and existential. It may apply to other persons, to oneself, or even to things.'[42] Since it is direct and not concrete, what this form of knowledge or understanding does *not* apply to is propositions, for this would be indirect and abstract. It is not propositions *about* people that are known in this way, but *people*; not propositions *about* oneself, but *oneself*. Hirst is therefore right to point out the varied types of objects of knowledge that Phenix is dealing with, and to compare this with his own more rigorous consistency. I do not see, however, that Hirst is right in all cases to claim that the objects dealt with by Phenix are 'everyday' rather than 'philosophical'. True propositions are not the only logical objects of knowledge generally recognized by philosophers, as Hirst himself admits. Knowledge with a direct object is accepted as a kind of knowledge by many philosophers, especially when discussing interpersonal understanding. It is therefore somewhat arbitrary of Hirst to rule this out of classificationary respectability simply because it does not fit the logical tidiness of basing the whole thing on true propositions.

Hirst is also critical of the way in which Phenix rests his account on distinctions of fact, form and norm. One difficulty here seems to be that, on the one hand, form and norm are to be distinguished *from* facts, yet on the other they are to be classified as certain *kinds* of facts. Another is that norm is limited to ethics when it seems fairly obviously to have something to do with aesthetics, which Phenix limits to form. Further difficulties arise from Phenix's handling of quantity. Why, asks Hirst, are historical facts alleged to be comprehensive when clearly many of them are singular? Is symbolics always to be general, even in relation to mathematics and non-discursive symbolic forms?

Lest it be argued that Phenix was doing a *different* job, more connected to the idea of meaning than to knowledge, Hirst is at some pains to claim that this is not so. First Hirst claims that this is 'quite contrary to Phenix's own account of what he has sought to do'.[43] I am not convinced that this is quite so obvious as Hirst says, as I shall try to show below. Hirst is concerned to show, as I have already mentioned, that 'the categorization of meaning is in the end a matter of categorizing knowledge or at least knowledge claims' and he claims that Phenix himself, 'implicitly at least', accepted this. Hirst does appear to make some concessions to the idea that meaning is a wider concept than knowledge:

It is quite true that the domain of what is meaningful extends vastly beyond the domain of what is known. For every true proposition that can be the object of knowledge there is an infinite number of false propositions which are meaningful but not the objects of knowledge. Even among utterances meaning extends beyond stating propositions to a myriad of other uses of language in commands, questions, curses, etc. Actions too and events can be said to have meanings. What is more, appreciating the meaning of something may well at times have the kind of dimensions that Phenix outlines.[44]

This seems like an important acceptance of Phenix's position. But Hirst then goes on to use the argument we have already encountered in the previous section; namely, that meaning is impossible without concepts, concepts have to have criteria of application and these involve truth tests for statements that something is an 'X'. Thus 'the notions of meaning and true propositions, and therefore meaning and knowledge, are logically connected.' So meaning *does* reduce to knowledge and true propositions, after all! One might question, however, whether what Hirst has to say about the necessary connection of conceptualization with meaning really does rebut the argument that not all that is meaningful is made up of true propositions. For example, to utter the imperative 'Open that door' is to utter something that is meaningful and yet is not a proposition, as Hirst acknowledges. Now, of course, the concepts of 'open' and 'door' could only be operated with by one who was in at least some sense aware of appropriate criteria for distinguishing such concepts from others, and thus aware of the truth tests of propositions expressing such distinguishing criteria, as Hirst also points out. Neither of these two claims appears to be controversial; it is the way they are connected by Hirst that causes the trouble. Hirst wants to say that because of all he has said about concepts, even though 'Open that door' is not a proposition, its meaning rests on the grasping of certain true propositions asserting what 'open' is and 'door' is. Surely what this shows is only that there is a *necessary* connection between meaning and conceptualization, and thus between meaning and true propositions, but not that there is thereby a *total* or *sufficient* connection. When we note that imperatives are meaningful, though not propositions, we are still asserting something significant; and we are certainly demonstrating that an utterance does not have to *be* a proposition, true or otherwise, in order to be meaningful. Thus we *are* demonstrating that the objects of meaning are not *identical* with objects of knowledge, as Hirst seems to want us to suppose, though they may have, as Hamlyn carefully puts it, 'certain conceptual connections'.

In so far as Hirst does battle with Phenix on terms of his (Hirst's) own choosing, there is little doubt that he wins. Phenix's analysis and classification *is* open to charges of ambiguity and confusion and inconsistency. Most of the points vigorously made by Hirst are well made *if* we assume that Phenix was attempting a classification of fundamental knowledge in something like the same way as Hirst. Yet one emerges from the rather one-sided debate with a strong suspicion that the victory is not somehow as complete as Hirst sees it to be, and this is mainly because Phenix's treatment of meaning is *not* exactly as Hirst sees it in his desire to equate it with his own conception of knowledge. If one takes a more flexible approach, deliberately seeking in Phenix's work for a different interpretation of a more cultural and phenomenological kind, I believe it is there to be found, often partly buried by the misguided attempt at analysis. Let me now try to quarry this alternative view.

It is necessary for this purpose to recall what was said about meaning in the previous section. There I claimed that the 'meaning of statements' sense of 'meaning' was certainly not the only sense that could be given to the word, and that there was another range of senses connected with the ideas of significance, purpose, importance and value. It is in reference to this kind of usage that one can see an alternative interpretation of what Phenix was doing. When Phenix says, for example: 'This thesis grows out of a concept of human nature as rooted in meaning and of human life as directed towards the fulfillment of meaning,'[45] this has more of a ring of concern for meaning in all that people do in their actions and makings, rather than a concern solely for the meaning of written or spoken statements. He further affirms that one temptation of a revival of interest in knowledge:

> is to construe knowledge too narrowly in purely intellectualistic terms. The present analysis shows that meanings are of many kinds and that the full development of human beings requires education in a variety of realms of meaning.[46]

A connection, even an identification, of meaning with a wiser conception including values and purposes seems clearly enough intended, especially where Phenix is expressing his fears of meaningfulness:

> The human situation is such that mankind is always threatened by forces that destroy meaning. Values, purposes, and understandings are fragile achievements and give way all too readily to attitudes of futility, frustration and doubt.[47]

In particular Phenix appears to claim meanings in the areas of synnoetics and ethics that are not limited to the propositional. Phenix uses the term 'synnoetics' to pick out the specially direct and experiential knowledge and understanding that people claim to have of themselves, one another and of things; and he says of such knowledge:

> Thus synnoetics signifies 'relational insight' or 'direct awareness'. It is analogous in the sphere of knowing to sympathy in the sphere of

feeling. This personal or relational knowledge is concrete, direct, and existential.[48]

Similarly:

> ethics includes moral meanings that express obligation rather than fact, perceptual form, or awareness of relation. In contrast to the sciences, which are concerned with abstract cognitive understanding, to the arts, which express idealized esthetic perceptions, and to personal knowledge, which reflects intersubjective understanding, morality has to do with personal conduct that is based on free, responsible, deliberate decision.[49]

Here we seem to have at least the following counted as meanings, as well as statements embodying propositions, which would of course also be counted:

   (i) relational insight;
  (ii) direct awareness or apprehension;
 (iii) expression of obligations, presumably in actions or dispositions;
 (iv) idealized perceptions of an aesthetic kind;
  (v) intersubjective understanding.

Now, of course, it is possible to argue, as Hirst does, and as indeed I have myself in another place, that some of these claims to meaning are not very coherent claims. But, as I have argued above, some of the claims to the status of a Hirstian form of knowledge are not very coherent either! If the judgment of importance and value is to be at least partly empirical and phenomenological, like Hirst's *claims* to forms of knowledge status, then it must be acknowledged that claims are extensively made for understandings and meanings of the kind Phenix indicates. In other words, whilst Phenix's logical analysis may be faulty, his perception of what people actually *do* in their attempts to find meaning and understanding, his grasp of the *phenomenon* of the human search for meaning, seems sharper than Hirst's.

Phenix actually gives summaries of his position in the later part of his work in which the logical analysis is virtually abandoned in favour of an account of the phenomenologically observable proclivities of human beings:

> human nature itself supplies the clue to the minimal scope of the curriculum. Human beings are characterized by a few basic types of functioning. They use symbols, they abstract and generalize, they create and perceive interesting objects, they relate to each other personally, they make judgments of good and evil, they re-enact the past, they seek the ultimate, and they comprehensively analyse, evaluate and synthesize. These are the universal, pervasive,

and perennial forms of distinctively human behaviour. They are
the foundation for all civilized existence. All of them are deeply
woven into the texture of life whenever it transcends the level
of biological and social survival.

. . . the curriculum should at least provide for learning in all
six of the realms of meaning: symbolics, empirics, esthetics,
synnoetics, ethics and synoptics. If any one of the six is missing,
the person lacks a basic ingredient in experience . . . . Each makes
possible a particular mode of functioning without which the
person cannot live according to his own nature.[50]

This is not only interesting and persuasive, but it owes nothing to all
the earlier analysis of meaning into the singular, the general and the
comprehensive, or fact, form and norm, which Hirst properly criticizes.
In that this thesis is separable from the unacceptable logical analysis
it is also separable from most, if not all, of the criticism Hirst has
mounted against it. What we are discerning, then, in this alternative
interpretation, is a quasi-anthropological, or at least phenomenological,
investigation into the fundamental meaning-cultures of mankind. One
can criticize Phenix, of course, for muddling this up with something
pretending to a sharper philosophical focus, but we would be wrong,
I think, to join Hirst in rejecting the whole account because of this.
There are two reasons for this caution.

Firstly, I have already indicated that Hirst's own account rests
much more than appears at first sight on straightforwardly observed
empirical claims to certain kinds of knowledge status. There is no
need to repeat all that has already been said on this; but, by way of
example, it is interesting to compare Hirst and Phenix on religion.
Hirst is unable to maintain that religion *is* a form of knowledge, with
distinctive central concepts, a conceptual framework and truth tests,
since large numbers of intelligent people deny this. So the argument
is that religion should appear in the curriculum of a liberal education
because many people *claim* to see religion as a distinctive form of
knowledge. This is empirical or phenomenological observation. Phenix
sees religion as concerned with meanings to do with the ultimate. He,
too, cannot claim that all people perceive such meanings or accept
that religion is thus meaningful. Religion would therefore be dealt
with in the curriculum because a sufficiently large number of people
give to religion the meaning and significance attributed to it by Phenix.
This is empirical or phenomenological observation. The two views
are not all that different when it comes down to it. *Both* writers try
to stretch their logical analysis beyond what it will bear, and fall back
on empirical claims for what they actually want in the curriculum.
What is wrong with both of them is the failure to acknowledge this.

The second reason for not completely rejecting Phenix's account is that there is a richness about Phenix's awareness of phenomenological nuances in meaning that we shall need to keep in mind in delineating our own account.

As with Hirst, then, I am bound to say that the account of Phenix, interesting and sensitive though it is, will not do as it stands. The justification and analysis *are* ambiguous and unclear, and much of Hirst's criticism is justified. However, if looked at in the less philosophical and more phenomenological way that I have described, there are insights here to be made use of in trying to fashion a more coherent account of the content and substance of a liberal education.

6.3 John White and subjective values

In this section I shall consider the views put forward by John White in his book, 'Towards a Compulsory Curriculum', which appeared in 1973.[51] White has recently, however, produced another book, 'The Aims of Education Restated', 1982,[52] which presents a rather different point of view. Since there appears to me to be distinctively different emphases in the two works, and since the influence of the former work has been considerable, I shall retain the intention to treat mainly of the argument in the earlier work, reserving some remarks for the more recent work until the critical part of the section.

The main interest of the earlier work lies in its explicit espousal of a subjective theory of value, and it is worth pausing a moment to be clear as to what this means. To say that values are subjective is to say that there is no sense in talking of values unless what we are talking about, the object of value, is actually valued by at least one individual. On this account, what is valuable is what is valued: things are seen to be valuable *because* people value them, and for no other reason. In the extreme form of the view there would even be no point in providing reasons why a person *ought* to value something, since once there are reasons of this kind attached to values they become objective rather than subjective. This distinction is an important one for educational decisions in this way: If it is possible to point to something as being *objectively* valuable, then it is possible to move from that to a claim that it, or something about it, should be taught to pupils as part of a liberal education. The only issue would be one of *how* objectively valuable the thing was, and whether there might not be other things of even more objective value. Hirst's theory is essentially like this in the sense that the forms of knowledge are to be seen as objectively valuable; there are good reasons, spelled out in a transcendental or presupposition argument, for valuing them; and therefore they should collectively constitute a liberal education in which pupils are not only

brought to be able to operate in these ways of knowing and understanding, but are brought to permanently care about and value them.

I am not concerned now with whether Hirst is right about all this.
The present point is that he does offer an argument to support the
claimed objectivity of the values in which he wants to involve pupils.

Now suppose that a writer on the curriculum believes values to be
subjective. That is, he believes that there are *no* reasons for believing
that any one thing is more valuable than anything else, but that things
are only to be valued as individuals happen to value them or as instruments to such individually valued ends. Such a writer now has a
problem if he or she wishes to make curriculum proposals, for it seems
that the only proposals consistent with a subjective theory of value
would be those of an extremely child-centred kind, whereby children
would choose, more or less at all times, what they wished to do. Some
writers, P.S. Wilson for example,[53] appear to have said more or less this.
It is the special significance of what White has done that he has tried to
combine this belief in the subjectivity of values with suggestions for
compulsory and common elements in the curriculum. Few would guess
from the title of his book that it is driven throughout by a passionate
concern for individual liberty, an affirmation of individuals' right to
determine their own values, and a strong belief that it is the duty of
anyone who would coerce or compel pupils to produce satisfactory
justificatory arguments for such compulsions.

White is quite clear that what is wanted for its own sake can only
be determined by an individual actually doing this wanting on his own
behalf, and that it cannot be determined for a person by someone else.
He presents what he calls an ideal case, which is quite important to the
subsequent argument:

> In the ideal case what is wanted for its own sake on reflection is
> what a man would want for its own sake, given at least (a) that
> he knows of all the other things which he might have preferred at
> that time and (b) that he has carefully considered priorities among
> the different choices, bearing in mind not only his present situation
> but also whether he is likely to alter his priorities in the future.
> ((b) effectively rules out any preference adopted in a state of
> depression, euphoria, etc.: a depressed person is shut off by his
> depression from considering certain options which would otherwise
> be open to him.)[54]

Any person, considering what might be intrinsically worthwhile for
him, can be in something like this ideal position:

> Knowing nothing of my wants, someone else has no grounds at
> all for saying that any particular thing that I may want to do is

intrinsically valuable. But I am in a different position. Let us
say that I have as broad as practicably possible an acquaintance
with the various things I might want and have reflected on priorities
among these over a considerable period and come to a settled
opinion about them. I have some grounds for saying that the ends
I now prefer are the most intrinsically worthwhile since I am in
something like the ideal situation – en route, even if I can never
hope to arrive there.[55]

White draws our attention to three important features of the intrinsically valuable as he has described it:

First, it is something formal not substantive. We cannot identify
it with any particular pursuit or way of life, the reflective life,
for example . . . . *Second*, it must be subjective in the sense that
it can only be given substantive content once one knows what a
particular individual wants in the ideal situation – and this may
vary from person to person. On the other hand, taken at the formal
level, it is the same for all men, and is in this sense objective. *Third*,
. . . it is something ideal, not in any value sense of this term, but in
the sense that, strictly speaking, it may well be unrealizable because
of the conditions (a) and (b).[56]

Such a view of what is intrinsically worthwhile enables White to dismiss
the extreme child-centred view of not trying to teach the child anything
he does not at present want to know as being irrational. What we have
to do is to get the pupil as near as possible to the ideal situation.
Leaving the child free to choose *now* would not be the best way of
doing that:

The least harmful course we can follow is to equip him, as far as
possible, for the ideal situation . . . . To do this, we must ensure
(a) that he knows about as many activities or ways of life as
possible which he may want to choose for their own sake, and
(b) that he is able to reflect on priorities among them from the
point of view not only of the present moment but as far as possible
of his life as a whole. We are justified, therefore, in restricting his
liberty as far as is necessary to ensure (a) and (b): we are right to
make him unfree now so as to give him as much autonomy as
possible later on.[57]

Before looking at the next move White makes, which takes us
closer to curriculum content, it is worth noting how White anticipates
objections. We might argue, for example, that knowledge, reflection
and autonomy are all being objectively valued and that the position
is not quite so totally subjective after all. White recognizes this and has

answers to such objections. I do not find these answers convincing and I shall return to them in criticism later.

Reflection, says White, might appear to be valued since it is necessary to work out, in the ideal situation, what is intrinsically worthwhile for oneself:

> But this is not so. Just because the man has reflected on what he most wants for its own sake, it does not follow that the answer he comes up with must be some form of reflective pursuit. It might be: he might decide on philosophy or writing tragedies. But, equally, it might not be, since he might choose ten-pin bowling or swimming.[58]

On autonomy White is similarly clear that although it must be pursued as an educational aim this is only to allow the pupil eventually to choose what to value. At that stage he might choose to abandon his autonomy:

> I am not advocating any necessary commitment to an autonomous way of life. The child 'must' become autonomous, to be sure, on the completion of his education: this follows from the preceding argument. But whether the pupil then chooses to stay autonomous is up to him: if he becomes a slave or a 'true believer', that is none of the teacher's business, at least on the argument so far . . . .
> Autonomy, we might say, is a 'must' if we are looking at what is educationally worthwhile; what is worthwhile in itself as an ideal of life is quite another question.[59]

White himself appears to have worries about this strange position, since he returns to it in the last two pages of the book, but his view, at this point, seems clear enough.

Like autonomy and reflection, knowledge is only to be valued (eventually) if the person wants to value it. Knowledge must be acquired in some sense, however, even if only temporarily, in order to be as near as possible to satisfying condition (a) of the ideal situation. Condition (a) is only satisfied if the person 'knows of all the other things which he might have preferred at that time', i.e. at the time of making a choice of what he will value. How can a pupil, in his limited period of education, be brought into knowledgeable contact with *all* the activities from which he might eventually choose? If, indeed, it was necessary to introduce pupils to all possible activities the task would be impossible. White, however, supposes this not to be necessary because of a convenient twofold categorization that he believes to characterize all activities. His first indication takes all activities that need to be learned and claims that:

These can be divided, exhaustively, into two classes, in which:
(1) no understanding of what it is to want X is logically possible without engaging in X
(2) some understanding of what it is to want X is logically possible without engaging in X.[60]

A page later the two categories have changed slightly in that 'understanding of what it is to want X' becomes 'understanding of X' as follows:

Category I: No understanding of X is logically possible without engaging in X . . . .
Category II: Some understanding of X is logically possible without engaging in X.[61]

Criteria for what is to count as 'some understanding of X' are offered, namely, 'either a correct verbal account, sufficient to distinguish X from other things, or correct identification of cases of X'. The paradigm case of an activity in Category I is given as linguistic communication; and of Category II, climbing mountains. The logical point is then easily made since with no engagement at all in linguistic communication how could anyone entertain any idea about it at all, let alone judge whether one wanted to value it? Climbing mountains is clearly different, in that I could gain *some* idea about such an activity without actually engaging in it.

White maintains that communication in general, mathematics, physical science, appreciating works of art and philosophizing are important Category I activities, though not an exhaustive list; whereas speaking a foreign language, playing organized games like cricket, cookery and woodwork, creative activities in art and music, vocational and leisure pursuits of innumerable kinds are all examples of Category II activities. The curriculum implications up to this point are plain: there are good grounds for compelling pupils to engage in Category I activities like those listed above, but there are no grounds of this kind for *compelling* pupils to engage in Category II activities, at least if no other arguments can be adduced. White notes, pertinently, that children in English schools nevertheless *are* compelled to engage in Category II activities, games for example, whilst *not* always being compelled to engage in all Category I activities. He deals, incisively and cogently, I think, with a number of popular but bad arguments attempting to justify the compulsory involvement of pupils in foreign languages and organized games.[62] The issue of justification is important throughout for White, it being just as wrong not to compel where there is justification as it is to compel where there is not. It is perhaps necessary to point out again that the justification here is all in the service of the ultimate liberty of the pupil.

One comes back to the principle of liberty and the justified
overridings of it. If children were left free not to speak, study
mathematics, physics, philosophy or contemplate works of art, then
this might well harm them, since they might never come to know of
whole areas of possible wants, both those connected with the
pursuit of these activities for their own sake and those dependent
on an understanding of these activities for their intelligibility. It
might not only harm the child to be cut off from all these possible
options: it might also . . . harm men in general if others were
incapable of grasping what they wanted to do. The principle of
liberty may be overridden, therefore, to prevent harm both to
the pupils themselves and to men in general.[63]

The account of the curriculum so far, it could be argued, is rather
limited, though it contains that part of White's proposals most frequently referred to, and also, on my view, that part of his account
which is most closely argued. The remainder of the book is much looser
in style and rather more tentative. There are, however, three important
elements still to be included in White's curriculum: studies aimed at
giving the pupil a view of diverse ways of life; studies aimed at practical
decision-making; and studies helping the development of a moral and
personally integrated life-style.

It follows from White's subjective views about values that he sees
life-styles or ways of life as open to individual choice. So that children
may come to have a free choice as to their life-styles two things are
necessary: firstly, they must be introduced to as wide a range of life-
styles as possible and, secondly, school teachers must not foreclose with
their power and influence on the possibilities opened to their pupils.
The main subject agencies for effecting the introduction are history
including biography, literature including foreign literature in translation, the study of religion and philosophy, especially ethics.

White does not only want the pupil to know about different ways
of life in some general and detached manner, but to see this as an
issue significant for himself. The pupil has to shape a coherent life-style
for himself. White sees this as a blend of two ideas. The first is that all
individual things learned have to be seen in what R.S. Peters has called
a cognitive perspective, that is, with some relationship to one another
and in the light of one another, rather than in isolation and having
nothing to do with each other. The second is that all learning must
relate to a 'coherent pattern of life' for the individual. White is at
pains to point out that the integration he is looking for here is not just
a linking of everything together in the way sometimes favoured in the
sillier versions of integrated studies, but something on the one hand
more personal and on the other more social, moral and political. The

pupil, he is saying, has to come to have some coherent and integrated conception of his own life stance, but he also has to include in his coherent view the idea that there are others to be considered too — his coherent style, ideally, is to become universalistic.

White, like many other writers on the curriculum, believes that pupils should be involved in practical matters, but he does not mean by this the sometimes isolated skills in woodwork, metalwork and the like that are often meant. Rather he means skills:

> which help one to understand means to ends, obstacles and ways round them. They will not necessarily require physical skill: some understanding of economic affairs, for instance, would seem an obvious candidate for this part of the curriculum.[64]

He also believes that in some way these practical studies must be integrated with the understanding of ends hopefully produced by the studies mentioned already.

White is tantalizingly sketchy as to the curriculum implications of all this. The sketch seems to indicate a kind of relatively sophisticated introduction to social, political and economic affairs:

> At any rate there is clearly a need at this point to work out the contours of a basic minimum in this curriculum area other than the ones already described. It will perhaps be drawn partly from sociology, economics, economic geography and political science; and also partly from moral and social philosophy.[65]

It is emphasized that the approach to all of this should be a critical one, not leaving students with the impression that all can only be done, ends only achieved, within the given system. Like many other writers on curriculum matters White appears to take it for granted that all pupils should have some kind of careers education, and he asserts that this should be part of the basic minimum — 'an integrated part of the school's educational activity'.

Lastly, White notes that the ends a pupil might go on to choose are not only affected by social, political and economic factors, but by psychological factors as well. The main concern here seems to be to acquaint pupils in some way, not necessarily by a course in psychology, with the various kinds of psychological impediment hindering people's rational decision-making and determination of ends.

It is now necessary to comment critically on these ideas. In doing so I shall make some reference to White's later (1982) work where this seems relevant to the points of criticism I want to raise.

There are many aspects of White's work with which I find it easy to sympathize. The emphasis upon the need for justification echoes my own concerns. What is to be compulsory needs justifying, repeatedly affirms White, and where there is no justifiable basis for compulsion then the activity must be voluntary for pupils in a strong sense. That is, pupils must be free to not do it at all. There is a weak sense of 'voluntary' where a number of 'voluntary' subjects are offered and pupils *must* select one. There is little justification for this unless the alternatives are all types or variations of some general activity held to be justifiably compulsory. Where the alternatives are simply diverse voluntary activities, then in the strong sense of 'voluntary' pupils must be free to do nothing at all if they so wish. White's emphasis of the logic of this important difference between what is justifiably compulsory and what is not must surely be endorsed. It will appear radical to most schools where little is really voluntary in quite this sense.

White's fine sense of the place of the individual in the physical, political, social and economic world, though not the most systematically worked out part of his account, is also worthy of support. There is a richness of perception here compared with which some other accounts, and many actual practices look distinctly crude. Similarly, White's continual emphasis on what is necessary for rational autonomy should be noted. Pupils are to be helped to develop a coherent system of ends for themselves and to come to realize all that is involved, not only in the individual competence to achieve the ends, but the problems and responsibilities of achieving them within a moral and democratic system of other similarly autonomous choosers. All this is difficult to explain and systematize, and White's book is too short to give all this the argued basis that he gives only to the first part of his case. Much of it seems sketchy if sensitively illuminating.

I place last as an area of agreement that which in most discussions of White comes first. This is his claim that if we can justify a basic minimum curriculum it ought to be compulsory in the sense that all schools should be required to provide such a minimum and oblige all their pupils to take it. How this is to be done is not the subject of a chapter of content and substance, but the logic of the claim is surely not to be denied.

Despite these points of sympathy and agreement I cannot, however, say that White's account can stand as a coherent philosophy of content for a general liberal education. There are too many difficulties by far, and these must now be considered.

The major objection is to the attachment of White's view to a subjective theory of value. In the first place White himself is not consistent. There is little doubt that White does attach objective value to rationality and autonomy, otherwise why should he bother to *argue* his case and why should he attach importance to justification? White, like the present writer, clearly believes and affirms that teachers and administrators *ought* to justify their actions and particularly the making

of studies compulsory. To say that people ought to value something
– i.e. justification – is to say that there are good reasons for valuing
that something. And to say that there are good reasons for valuing it is
to say that the valuing is objective and not subjective. Whether a given
individual actually comes to value justification is, of course, a contingent matter; that one *ought* to value what there are good reasons for
valuing is, however, an objective matter when the reasons are demonstrable. Similarly White clearly believes that people ought to value
autonomy. His strange idea that, once we have helped pupils become
autonomous, it is then up to them whether they remain so, as though
abandoning autonomy is to be considered merely one exercise of
autonomy, clearly will not do. White himself appears to admit the
oddity of this when, in his later book, he changes his mind. The teacher
he now says:

> has good reasons to care that the person he has brought up to be
> autonomous stays that way, unless he finds the burden of autonomy
> too great, reasons to do, as before, with the conflict-ridden nature of
> human life, the need for some kind of resolution and the
> misguidedness of trying to find ethical experts on whom to rely.[66]

This is, of course, sound argument; but it supports the idea of the
objective valuing of autonomy and therefore undermines the whole
basis of White's earlier construction.

Similar remarks can be made about White's views on reflection and
knowledge. Not only are *particular* kinds of reflection and knowledge
conceived of in subjective value terms – i.e. mathematics is only
valuable for Johnny *if* he comes to value it – but reflection and knowledge, generally speaking, are also only to be considered subjectively
valuable. In other words, it does not particularly matter if a person
comes not to value reflection and knowledge, providing that educationally we had given him the opportunity. This seems to me to be
wrong generally and contradictory, particularly even within White's
own framework of argument. Why should we value (and be told we
ought to value) the acquisition of certain kinds of knowledge and
reflection necessary for autonomous choice *only* during the period of
education? Why should we not go on valuing them for similar reasons
– i.e. as continuing to be necessary for the exercise of autonomous
judgment? The idea that education provides the opportunity for choice,
that the choice is then exercised and henceforth only the knowledge
chosen as valuable at that point is needed, seems to me a monstrously
odd idea. Surely the truth is that if I take my autonomy seriously there
are certain kinds of knowledge and reflection, broadly constituent of
a rational understanding of the human situation, that I must continue
to exercise and expand whilst I continue to value my autonomy. It is

precisely the interrelated nature of the ideas of autonomy, rationality, morality and knowledge that provides the objectively valuable aspect of them. It simply is not the case that one can, without inconsistency, take or leave these essential characteristics of personhood one at a time. If I am to make *choices* rather than mere reactions, I must value *reasons* for choices. I must value, therefore, at least some amount of reasons and reflection and the knowledge and understanding connected with such thought. The strong point of Hirst's arguments, whatever else we might have criticized, is his recognition of these necessities.

White, again, appears to make a rather grudging acknowledgment of the necessity of knowledge in his 1982 book. Here he admits the necessity of knowledge for moral autonomy, but only in a kind of subsidiary way.[67] That is to say, it is moral autonomy that is really valuable but knowledge happens to be a necessity for it and has no value in its own right. Similarly, White places knowledge in this neces- sary but subsidiary relationship with certain dispositions and virtues that loom large in importance in the 1982 work. In Chapter 6 of this work, in which the Educated Man is characterized, White argues for the centrality of certain dispositions and virtues as educational aims. 'Knowledge is necessary to virtue,' he affirms, 'but knowledgeableness is not a self-justifying state on its own.'[68] The virtues and dispositions include:

caring about one's own well-being
being morally virtuous
being prudent, courageous, temperate, benevolent, just, truthful, tolerant and reliable, lucid, wise, autonomous, detached, imaginative
being independent-minded oneself and sympathetic to independent- mindedness in others
being humorous, vital
having a chosen life plan.

In order, as it were, to service and support these desirable (and presum- ably justifiable) dispositions, the educated man must have knowledge of:

the variety of ends in themselves
something of the means for obtaining and adopting them, and such knowledge is only to be valued because of such service to the disposi- tions and virtues.

The major fault here, and it is to my mind a great one, is to suppose for one moment that there can be this kind of separation between the virtues and dispositions on the one hand and knowledge and under- standing on the other. The virtues and dispositions favoured by White are not just dependent upon knowledge in some trivial way, they are totally inconceivable without knowledge and understanding. No non-knowing creature could possibly be characterized as prudent, courageous or tolerant, since all these virtues positively embody both a knowledge of what one is doing and why one is doing it. Non-human animals cannot be humorous for precisely the same reason – only knowers can be humorous. Independent-mindedness not only needs knowledge and understanding for what one is being independently minded about, but the very act of *being* independent is an affirmation of a certain kind of known conception of oneself: one acts out of this conception of oneself as autonomous. It is not just that autonomy is the name of a certain class of performance or behaviour, it is rather, as Julius Kovesi has pointed out about moral concepts,[69] that autonomous action is only made possible by the possession of the concept. In other words I have to *know* I am autonomous in order to be so. To say simply that certain kinds of knowledge are necessary to dispositions and virtues is to understate the case in a profound way. In truth virtues and dispositions, in the typical human case, are as much compounded of knowledge and understanding as they are of consistencies of behaviour: indeed, we would not know whether particular behaviours constituted virtuous behaviour unless we knew something of the knowledge and understanding in which the behaviour was set.

Of course, the knowledge and understanding is not the whole of a virtue or a disposition, any more than the peel or the flesh taken alone is the whole of the orange; but if that is all White means he has unloaded a truism. Of course, also, we want people to exercise the virtues and not just to know about them. If that is what White means, I agree with him; but there is no need to demean knowledge and understanding in the process. Indeed, the greater danger is that teachers will take short cuts to establish certain kinds of behaviour seen by them to be prudent, virtuous, etc., without rooting the behaviour in the framework of knowledge and understanding necessary for the behaviour to be really autonomous. In brief, but most profoundly, the child must come to *know* what he is doing and to *know* why he is doing it. All else is manipulation and a deep lack of respect for the child. White, I am sure, would not want this, but his denigration of the place of knowledge and understanding in his scheme of things is more than likely to lead in that direction.

As with Hirst and Phenix, then, one is left praising certain insights and illuminations but unsatisfied with the total structure. In the case of White the confusion starts, I believe, with his apparent rejection of objective values, but is compounded by the difficulty of giving any coherence to parts of the thesis unless certain objective values *are* presupposed; in particular, rationality, autonomy, respect for persons and knowledge and understanding. The constant attempt by White to reject these as essentially valuable, whilst frequently dragging them back in as necessary instruments destroys any fundamental coherence in his theories.

Any satisfying account of a necessary content for a liberal and general education must affirm these values as objective and build upon them. The next chapter attempts to do this.

7 The content of a liberal education

Introduction

In discussing the characteristics of a general liberal education, in attempting to justify such an education, in outlining some preliminary ideas about content, and in criticizing the ideas of Hirst, Phenix and White a number of guiding principles for the content and methods appropriate to liberal education have been argued for. I list them here as a convenient summary, together with indications of where the detailed discussions have arisen.

The contents and methods of a liberal general education must be such as to be:

1 liberating from the restrictions of the present and the particular; (3.3.1)
2 concerned with knowledge and understanding that is fundamental and general; (3.3.2) (5)
3 concerned with intrinsically valued ends; (3.3.3)
4 concerned with the development of reason; (3.3.4)
5 of the most general (rather than specific) utility; (4.3)
6 concerned with justifiable belief and action; (4.4)
7 respectful of the pupil as person or potential person; (4.5)
8 concerned with the actions, makings, doings, dispositions, expressions and interactions which give meaning, point and significance to propositions, and not only with the truth and falsity of propositions; (6.1)
9 concerned with a 'rich' sense of 'meaning' rather than a solely propositional sense; (6.1) (6.2)
10 concerned with what is objectively valuable, that is, what is justifiably to be valued. (6.3)

It is not, of course, claimed that these conditions are logically exclusive. In fact they overlap and interlink considerably. Neither is it claimed that every item of content and every suggested piece of method must satisfy each and every one of these conditions. The point of guiding principles is much more flexible than that, and the relationship between principles and subsumed items much looser. Nevertheless the principles *are* principles and have been argued for. If the theory being expounded here is to be at all coherent then the principles listed here should not only be individually justifiable but should not, at least, contradict one another. Similarly, an item of content or method might not necessarily have to do with *all* the conditions but it must not contradict any one of them. There must be a coherent structure in at least this sense. If the structure coheres more closely and tightly, in terms of mutually supporting and mutually implying or presupposing ideas, as I believe it does, then so much the better.

What kind of content structure can be built on these principles and these terms?

7.1 Underlying ideas and assumptions

I believe, like Hirst, that we must look for logical distinctions in human forms of inquiry; but unlike Hirst I believe the number of logically distinct forms to be quite small and nothing like in number the seven or eight that Hirst suggests. Since this chapter is to be a positive account I shall not go over again the difficulties that Hirst runs into in claiming to discern the number of forms he picks out.

Distinctions in the curriculum are not only to be made on logical grounds, though we should start from there. It is perfectly proper to make judgments about content on the purely empirical or pragmatic claim of something having been considered important, significant, to large numbers of intelligent human beings. We might thus have a hierarchy of distinctions to be made, where the most fundamental distinctions are logically distinct forms of inquiry, confused only at the cost of the gravest category mistakes and consequent misunderstanding, and where subsequent sub-divisions are less purely logical and more to do with discerned foci of human import. There might also be a case for yet further sub-divisions based on individual interest once we are reasonably sure that the major divisions are being attended to. It will also be necessary to inject into this framework what I shall call 'the serving competencies', by which title I mean to name those skills, understandings, practices, facilities and dispositions without which no desire to understand, to inquire, can be kindled, maintained, developed and serviced.

The whole of this framework, yet to be fleshed out, must serve an integrative idea — namely that of a developing person, born into a world of persons inhabiting a physical world understood to some extent and manipulated to some extent by persons, and seeking to understand and operate in such a personal, social and physical world.

I must now try to construct this framework of content for a liberal and general education by discussing in turn:

7.2 The integrative idea

All educational ideals reflect a world view and fail to satisfy if the world view they reflect is too idiosyncratic or held by too few people. The world view reflected here is basically humanistic in the broadest sense of that word. The vision is that all human beings are born into — as it were — a kind of double world: a world of persons and a world of physical material and structures. To suggest such a duality is not to prejudge arguments about the material or otherwise nature of persons. The duality rests upon the apparent fact that only some 'parts' of the universe are capable of trying to understand their situation, and these 'parts' are persons. Persons have to come to know enough about the physical world they find themselves in to be able to operate in it — that is, to shape purposes for themselves and to seek to satisfy those purposes. This is no easy task, but it is further complicated by being born into a world that is also, very significantly, a world of other persons who have collectively inherited, and continue to gain and share knowledge and understanding of their world. The child, as part of grasping what he is meshed in with, has to come to see what it is to be a person with other persons. He or she has not only to understand the world, but also to understand what it is to be one who tries to understand the world among others similarly engaged and frustrated.[1] Education, in its liberating sense, is appropriate for persons because only persons act out of their *own understandings* of situations they find themselves in. They do not simply react or live out built-in instincts or behaviour patterns. Persons enter into a world already perceived through the understandings, meanings and practices shaped and modified by countless generations of persons before them, and these understandings have themselves to be understood by young persons, not merely received as passed on to them. This is the vision, and to manage this with integrity is the task of liberal education.

To be subject, through education, to this integrative idea, and indeed to come to see the world ultimately and personally with this integrative idea in mind, the pupil does not necessarily have to have been subject to what are sometimes called integrated studies. The integrative idea here is nothing to do with joining subjects together for whatever likely or unlikely reason, but it is much to do with the idea of coherence, both in a programme of education and in a person's own conception

107

and understanding of his or her situation. One can, without inconsistency, maintain clear conceptual distinctions between forms of
inquiry, subjects or parts of subjects, whilst still carrying all these
distinctions in one's mind in some kind of coherent framework. Indeed,
how could one have coherence *without* making and maintaining justifiable distinctions of a logical and conceptual kind? Attempts to erect
structures or frameworks without attending to necessary distinctions,
or even distinctions of convenience result only in confusing muddles.

7.3 The fundamental logical division

Whatever sub-divisions it might subsequently be necessary or desirable
to make there are only *two* basic kinds of inquiry, two basic kinds of
'goings on' that we can try to understand in making sense of our
situation. Michael Oakeshott puts it this way:

> There are two categories of identities to be reckoned with,
> predicating categorially different 'orders' of inquiry. To the first
> belong 'goings-on' the identification of which includes the
> recognition that they are themselves exhibitions of intelligence:
> for example, a 'going-on' identified as itself an engagement to
> understand (a biologist at work, . . . an audience at a play, a boy
> learning Latin), a 'going on' identified as a human action (that is,
> an agent responding to an understood situation meaning to achieve
> an imagined and wished-for outcome), a subscription to a 'practice'
> which requires to be understood in order to be participated in, a
> work of art, an artefact, an argument, a barrister addressing a court
> of law, an expression of moral sentiment, a statement of belief
> or of policy, etc. . . .
>
> To the second category belong 'goings-on' recognized, in virtue
> of their characteristics, *not* themselves to be exhibitions of
> intelligence: for example, a rock formation, a wave breaking on the
> shore, metal fatigue, a thunderstorm, a butterfly on the wing, the
> facial resemblances of children and parents, a chameleon changing
> colour, melting ice, etc.[2]

Within each of these categorially distinct orders of inquiry
Oakeshott also posits sub-divisions which he considers idiomatically
but not categorially different. For example, marks on a piece of paper
might be recognized categorially as manifestations of intelligence but
remain ambiguous until we can decide whether the marks constitute
art, symbol (a trademark or emblem), or a sign. Each particular idiom
in both orders of inquiry will have methods and theories constituting its
particularity. For example we have ethics, jurisprudence and aesthetics,
all being inquiries into manifestations of human intelligence. Similarly

physics, chemistry, biology and psychology are distinguishable idioms, all being inquiries into 'goings-on' not themselves exhibitions of intelligence. These idioms are not exclusively separable because the distinctions are not categorial. For example, chemistry might be reducible to physics and psychology to biology; nevertheless there are well established differences in terms of conceptual usage, theories and methodologies.

One more Oakeshottian idea helps us to link the fundamental logical division of two categorially different orders of inquiry to the more idiomatic and pragmatic or convenient distinctions actually to be found in human life – this is the idea of a practice. The idea of a practice, as used by Oakeshott, is an extraordinarily rich and illuminating idea, especially significant in our context since education can be viewed both as itself a practice and also the means of initiating pupils into the practices of interrelating human agents:

> what joins agents in conduct is to be recognized as a 'practice'; that is, a procedure proper or useful to be observed and therefore capable of being neglected or violated and capable, also, of being observed only in the chosen subscription of agents.

> A practice may be identified as a set of considerations, manners, uses, observances, customs, standards, canons, maxims, principles, rules and offices specifying useful procedures or denoting obligations or duties which relate to human actions and utterances. It is a prudential or an authoritative adverbial qualification of choices and performances, more or less complicated, in which conduct is understood in terms of a procedure.[3]

A practice may be relatively simple or relatively complicated. Three great human practices specifically mentioned by Oakeshott are language, morality and education:

> like every other transaction inter homines, this engagement to educate is itself utterances, actions and responses governed by a practice in which a relationship, distinguished from all others, is articulated: the relationship of teachers and learners.[4]

Typically, human agents are rarely involved in mere performances, their actions rather being governed by an understanding of an appropriate practice which can only be gained by learning. The kind of task often referred to as 'practical', says Oakeshott, is not a mere performance but rather 'conduct in respect of its acknowledgement of a practice'. What persons engage in within such practices are not to be seen as processes, since this is the appropriate term for 'goings-on' *not* manifestations of intelligence, but rather as subscription to *procedures* evolved by previous generations and subject to change and fluctuation in method and perceived utility.

Indeed, agents as historic persons composed of acquired beliefs, understandings, sentiments, imaginings, aptitudes, arts, skills, etc., and capable of self-disclosure in actions, themselves emerge in a transaction between the generations called education, in which newcomers to a local human scene are initiated into its 'mysteries'; that is, into practices which human beings have invented for themselves.[5]

Here, then, is a rich conceptual view of the human situation against which to plot the content of a liberal education; far richer than the propositional distinctions of the Hirstian view criticized earlier. We start with a truly logical and categorial distinction of fundamental importance whereby the two great orders of inquiry are distinguished. These two great and fundamental orders of inquiry can then be subdivided, but on a different basis, into particular idioms of inquiry which are themselves the practices of human agents. These particular idioms of inquiry, these practices, can be judged objectively but pragmatically in terms of the importance and significance they have had for generations of human beings, and for the significance of the meanings and understandings handed on to fresh generations to re-assess and modify. Other practices, rooted in the results of various attempts to understand, are not themselves purely attempts to understand but rather are the makings and creations of human agents individually and collectively. Art and technology, for example, undeniably practices and rooted in understandings, are not themselves attempts to understand but rather attempts to create, to make, and to solve instrumental problems.

The essential starting point, then, in constructing the content of a liberal education, is that some studies will be initiating pupils into inquiries and practices only understandable as manifestations of intelligence, and other studies will be initiating pupils into inquiries whose objects are only understandable as *not* being manifestations of intelligence. To start to perceive this is the first step to intellectual liberation. I shall expand on this, and examine the relationship of this major division to the lesser divisions subsumed under it, when I have introduced the idea of the serving competencies.

7.4 The serving competencies

A liberal education, I have said, is concerned with knowledge, understandings, makings and doings valuable in themselves. Nevertheless, much of what is learned in such an education must of necessity be instrumental, not in the sense of serving specifically prescribed purposes beyond a liberal education, but rather in the sense of making the more substantive objectives of such an education attainable. This is especially the case in the early stages of a liberal education, when young pupils must learn how to learn by acquiring the appropriate means, skills and dispositions. Much of primary education will be taken up with the mastery of these serving competencies which make the rest of a liberal education possible and much else besides.

About most of these serving competencies there is little dispute that I am aware of. The first necessity, of extreme and undeniable importance, is that the child acquires competency in at least one operating language to as high and broad a level as possible. The child must come to be able to talk with ease, fluency and confidence; he must become an attentive and discriminating listener; he must attain considerable skills of reading and abilities in writing language himself. All this can be said in a few words but constitutes, as all teachers of young children know, a very large, complex and challenging educational task. Here we are dealing not only with the important tools of communication but with the very stuff of discursive reasoning itself. It is not necessary to enter the debate about the necessity or otherwise of language to rational and logical thought in order to accept that for most people there is little reasoning that is not supported, facilitated or even made possible by language. Here is the first great practice of human agents into which children must be initiated.

It is also generally argued that alongside literacy must go numeracy. Little further study can progress unless at least some elementary grasp of numbers, order, quantitative comparison, simple measurement, parts and divisions, and so on, is attained. Such elementary competency, of course, as well as being of general service – and thus counting as a serving competency – lays the foundation for entering into mathematics as a study, worthwhile in its own right, of one way of making sense of experience. As a serving competency, however, we are concerned with simple numeracy, relating very much to language (i.e. the special language of cardinal and ordinal numbering, parts, multiples, and so on) on the one hand, and to logical reasoning on the other.

Indeed, logical reasoning itself is another great serving competency which has received nothing like the attention that has been given to literacy and numeracy. In order to enter the substantive areas of inquiry pupils need to come to operate logically: to be able to infer, to avoid contradiction, to hypothesize, to discern what is logically possible and what is not. To progress here is no easier than learning to read, write and compute; but in essence it is no more difficult, at least in its more elementary moves, either. Piaget[6] and his followers have charged some of the developmental paths here and de Bono[7] has indicated some possible ways of developing critical thinking quite deliberately. Bruner and his followers[8] and associates have attached more importance, rightly I believe, to the development of critical thinking by means of interrelated inquiries making use of the established intellectual devices of the existing disciplines. However it is done, little will be done successfully in any area of inquiry unless logical thought is encouraged and developed as a serving competency. One way of developing language, of course, is by developing the logical use of language. When the specific teaching of grammar and other rules of language became unfashionable, largely because of some deplorable and meaninglessly rote methods of teaching such rules, the teaching of the precise and logical use of language often fell by the wayside also. This is a pity, since the use of language with semantic precision and logical accuracy is perhaps the greatest mental liberator of all skills.

To study well pupils must be reasonably fit and healthy. This, of course, cannot be solely the responsibility of schools, but schools must play a part. Physical education enthusiasts have tried to establish much more honorific justifications for the place of physical education in recent years, but as a serving competency physical fitness is a perfectly justifiable objective which needs no embroidery. Neither does it need, necessarily, costly equipment nor all the trappings of competitiveness with which physical education has become associated. These may have another place in the curriculum, but as a serving competency all that is needed is a reasonable balance of physical activity, recreation and outdoor activity, with some planned and systematic exercise.

Some of the serving competencies, as with some of the substantive items of content still to be discussed, are dispositions rather than skills or items of knowledge and understanding. This is not to assume, as White seems to have done, that there is some clear difference between dispositions on the one hand and knowledge, understanding and skills on the other. Each depends upon the others. Nevertheless there is an affective characteristic of dispositions that makes them separately worthy of notice. To be disposed to attend, concentrate or cooperate is certainly to take the view (to believe, to know, to understand) that I ought to attend, concentrate or cooperate in certain circumstances; but it is also more than this because it is to be affectively moved actually *to* attend, concentrate or cooperate, or at least to feel guilt if I do not.

To be disposed to do something clearly differs from being compelled to do something. Although a teacher can compel certain behaviour likely to facilitate the exercise of dispositions, the self-directing nature of dispositions can sometimes be very difficult to get at. Children still fail to cooperate, attend, concentrate and persevere, say, even when the teacher has pressed in the strongest way and threatened the direst sanctions. Yet other children, in the complete absence of such force or threat of force, sometimes exercise all these dispositions quite freely.

There is a kind of double necessity about the dispositions which are to be seen as serving competencies of a liberal education: they must be acquired and developed, and they must be brought to bear in appropriate circumstances. The reason for failure in the second of these is sometimes, though not always, simply a consequence of failure in the first. A young child cannot exercise cooperation, say, in an appropriate circumstance, if he does not know what it *is* to cooperate. A disposition to do something can be withheld even after being acquired, but it clearly cannot be exercised if it has never been acquired in the first place. The acquisition, development and appropriate exercise of dispositions is not the most thoroughly studied branch of educational psychology by any means. I shall need to say more about this in the next chapter. For the present I list some of the main dispositions that will best serve in liberal education:

the disposition to
- (i) attend to something or somebody,
- (ii) concentrate on something,
- (iii) cooperate with others,
- (iv) organize time, materials, thought and actions,
- (v) reason,
- (vi) imagine possibilities, and to
- (vii) inquire — try to understand.

Much of this is to do with the overcoming of whim and impulse in the interest of sustained, rational and purposive action. Such dispositions develop slowly, perhaps, but there is little doubt that once developed and exercised they serve further endeavours in liberal education.

Lastly one must note that as technologies change, especially those of communication and information processing, so some of the important serving competencies will change. Reading and writing stood for centuries as the main agents of communication and information-handling, if under 'writing' we include printing. Radio and television in themselves seemed hardly to threaten this dominance, at least in education, but the rapid development of the micro-electronic industry seems a much more significant change. Computers, micro-processors and electronic word-processors seem likely to mean that certain keyboard skills and probably certain programming and operating skills will increasingly come to be necessary serving competencies. The problem might well be one of ensuring that these skills are kept in a *serving* capacity with reference to liberal education and do not come to dominate it.

The ideas I have discussed so far, in beginning to draft the content of a liberal education, relate together in something like Figure 7.1.

In the early stages of a liberal education the serving competencies will take up most of the time, gradually becoming more involved with

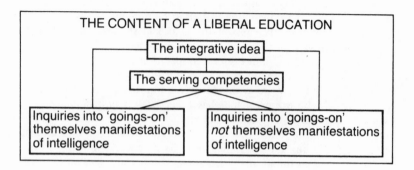

Figure 7.1 First draft of the general ideas shaping the content of a liberal education

substantive inquiries, studies and activities. Another trend proper to a liberal education would be that both kinds of inquiries will increase in the use of school time at first, but in the later stages the inquiries into 'goings-on' themselves manifestations of intelligence will loom larger. Diagrams are speciously precise, but the idea would be something like that shown by Figure 7.2. The increasing proportion of time spent on matters concerned with manifestations of intelligence in the later years is intended to reflect the idea, proper to a liberal education, that the world of persons is to be considered more important than the world of things, however sophisticated the 'things' might be.

To counter a possible objection at this stage it is perhaps necessary to make a reminder that I talk here solely of the content appropriate for a liberal and general education. Nothing is said here of how a country might go about its specialist training. It may be, for example, that liberal education, as here described, should stop at age 16 and other, more specialist and vocationally oriented training and education, take over. This is the proper subject of a later chapter. What we must do now is to put some more substantial flesh on this bare skeleton.

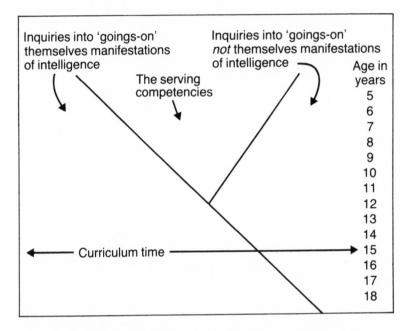

Figure 7.2 Roughly relative proportions of time on major parts of a liberal education

7.5 The convenient and pragmatic divisions

Divisions within each of the two main orders of inquiry are difficult to make on purely logical grounds, as we saw in examining the ideas of Hirst. This does not mean, however, that any divisions made must therefore be arbitrary. Divisions based on interest or convenience need not be arbitrary divisions since they can indicate long-established divisions arising from the diversified activities and practices of humankind, whereby persons notice, attend to and deal with certain abstracted aspects of their experience, rather than others which they might have chosen or might choose at another time. Some of these, like certain facts of the physical world, or certain historically dominant features of social, political and economic life, rather force their attention upon people and assume an importance because of this. Others, like art and literature, perhaps do not impose in quite this kind of way. In valuing such activities, practices and understandings we must have recourse to historical and anthropological judgments on the part they have played in the developing understanding of their situation by human beings. Let me try to make this clear with one example. Religion is undeniably a convenient name for a number of diverse practices of human beings in which rituals, actions, behaviours and beliefs are set within certain kinds of understandings of how things are. The importance of this body of practices for a liberal education does not lie in judgments about the truth and falsity of supposed bodies of propositions constituting these understandings. It lies rather in judgments about the significance of these understandings in human history and development. Since the significance is certainly great then attempts to understand religious understandings should form part of a liberal education. This claim could be supported even by a liberal educator, himself a secular humanist, believing most allegedly true religious propositions to be false.

Let us start, then, with inquiries into 'goings-on' identified as themselves manifestations of intelligence and see what sub-divisions can be made in this rich area which might help us further to indicate the content of a liberal education.

7.5.1 Divisions within inquiries into 'goings-on' identified as themselves manifestations of intelligence

It is convenient to make one major division. On the one hand we have attempts to understand human understanding and action themselves in some very general way, not in the way of either psychological inquiry or philosophical conceptual analysis, but rather in the way of a more general inquiry into the essentially human condition. That is to say, into the condition of being a person who tries to make sense of his situation and to act out of his own understanding of this situation to create and achieve purposes, individually or with others. This is perhaps the integrative idea of the humanities, whether explicitly understood or not, and literary fiction, from the simple stories of early childhood to the great wealth of classical and modern literature, probably provides the major entry into these inquiries. To these must now be added the more recent facilities for imaginative fictions on film, radio and television. What all these creative forms can do is to open minds to the countless imaginary possibilities of human agency set against different visions or understandings of the human situation. A work of fiction, itself imaginary, can widen my awareness of the human condition even when I can only test this knowledge indirectly against my direct experience. Sometimes, of course, such a reading enables me to see my erstwhile experiences differently, recast them, as it were. However it works there is little doubt that modern men and women are shaped in their understandings of how things are by the verbal and visual imaginative creations they engage with as well as by their more immediate, but usually less wide, direct experiences. It is also reasonable to suppose that imagination, sensitivity of inter-personal perception and relationships, and tolerance of variety can all be developed by broad involvement in works of creative imagination and, in turn, move pupils away from the worst forms of ethnocentricity and egocentricity so characteristic of over-concern with the present and the particular.

All pupils in British schools are involved with literature in some way and for some length of time, but one might voice two criticisms. Firstly, at just the age when literature becomes most influential, say from 14 years onwards, our examination system both cuts some pupils off from much study of literature (those who do not choose it as an examination subject) and, secondly, for those who do so choose it the subject becomes more like a specialist study of literature *per se*, and less of a contribution to the general understanding of the human condition.

Other subjects, too, contribute to this basic inquiry. History, rightly, has always been at the heart of the humanities. It holds this place most properly when the study is essentially one of interrelating and decision-making persons changing and developing their vision of how to live together. There are ways, still called 'history', of diverging from this. Certain ways of writing and teaching about economic and technological history *de*personalize the study. This has little to do with the focus of the study but more to do with the mode of treatment. A life of Brunel or Trevithick can have as much 'humanities' content as one of Wordsworth or Milton; whereas over-emphasis on the growth of capital investment in the railways, the growth of the steel industry or the changing constitutions of political parties — anything quantified or abstracted into group movements — is less likely to have such content, though it might serve other purposes.

To these traditional and basic approaches to the understanding of human understanding and action in its most general sense we can add certain aspects of religious education. To gain some sense of man's quest for religious understanding is to gain an understanding of man's attempt to understand himself. To this will be linked another great

117

practice of humankind, that of morality. Any proper moral education that goes beyond mere moral instruction will involve attempts to understand persons in relation to the moral judgments they make.

This great corpus of study, almost infinitely expandable, a lifetime's liberal education in itself, should be the main focus of a liberal education in schools of general education. The aim here is not simply to try to understand a number of human practices, though that must come; it is rather to try to understand human understanding and action itself in the most general way. The generality here is not something that can be abstracted, since it is itself a sum of interrelated particularities. There is no simple 'human nature' to be grasped because there is no such abstractable notion. There is, instead, an imaginable variety of human possibility, some of it already to be discerned in the stored imaginings in books, libraries, films and tapes, and much of it yet to be imagined. There is, instead, a sensitive awareness of the humanly proper and the improper, the decent and the indecent, the good and the bad that have flowered from the judgmental proclivities of human persons.

All this, then, is on one side of a division that can be made in all the inquiries into 'goings-on' identified as themselves manifestations of intelligence. On the other side of this divide are the various practices, of greater or lesser importance, that mankind has evolved. This is the great list of the makings and doings of man from which only a selection can be made for inclusion in a liberal education. To repeat, the selection cannot be made on purely logical grounds. Each and every one of these practices can only properly be understood as a manifestation of intelligence and the understandings and skills to be acquired are to do with procedures and not performances or processes. In this respect they are logically much more alike than different. To understand politics, art, economics and dance is different from understanding the dispersal of seeds, gravitation, genetic inheritance or the expansion of metals. What distinguishes attempts to understand politics, art, economics, and dance is not essentially a logical distinction, it is rather the particular focus of interest and attention of each of these activities and understandings – 'a set of considerations, manners, uses, observances, customs, standards, canons, maxims, principles, rules and offices specifying useful procedures or denoting obligations or duties which relate to human actions and utterances'.[9] It can certainly be said that understanding what it is to be a person at all in a world of persons, all that I have so far indicated as properly forming the humanities, is a necessary accompaniment (though not logically prior) to an understanding of *any* of the practices, and therefore *must* be a part of a liberal education in some way. But the practices themselves do not have this kind of necessity. The *more* practices one comes to understand the better educated one is, no doubt, but in the time available for a general liberal education in a period of compulsory schooling one can only come to have some understanding of those practices judged to be the most important. Some judgment has to be made on grounds of importance and significance. Neither can these practices really be collected, classified, into convenient groups. It is not the case, for example, that the visual arts, music, dance, drama and literature are all somehow similar branches of aesthetic activity, at least not in any way that is useful. Trying to understand or participate in the great human practice of music, for example, has no significant transfer of understanding or skill to other practices like drama or the visual arts. Dance may have a closer connection to music, but it is still a diversified practice in its own right. Since practices are not to be distinguished on logical grounds they can clearly overlap, share concepts, interconnect and have relationships in all sorts of ways. Educationally, however, we should not make too much of these interconnections. To be initiated into a practice will always be to be involved in the particularities of *that* practice and not another. In particular some practices will have evolved organizing categories that come near to being the distinguishing central concepts that Hirst claimed to discern, and pupils will need to grasp these as necessities of understanding the practice.

If the selection is not to be made on logical grounds neither is it proper for a liberal education for it to be made on grounds of *individual* interest or perceived significance, as the more radical child-centred theorists would have us do.[10] This is to go to the other, and unnecessary extreme. The duty we have is to involve all pupils in attempts to understand the most significant makings and doings of man, where 'significant' means something like 'of universal significance' or at least 'significant over long periods of time to large numbers of people'. To fail to attempt the involvement of a pupil in one of these major practices purely on the grounds that he or she manifests no present interest in it is to betray the pupil in the long run. Most teachers have long understood this, though their judgments of importance have not always been clearly justifiable.

There is one other important consideration to note before attempting a list of such important practices that should be part of a liberal education. That is to raise the question of where to draw the line between those practices that should be compulsory studies and those that pupils should be free to choose or not. Again it does not seem to be the case that this decision can be based on simple logical grounds. The judgment of what is to be a compulsory part of the curriculum, in a compulsory system of liberal education, can only be on grounds of perceived human significance of a general kind. Other writers appear to recognize that their purely logical constructions cannot contain this requirement. Hirst, for example, acknowledges that there are some things like physical and moral education which all pupils should have, even though they are not distinguishable as forms of knowledge. Phenix's test of 'meaningfulness', as I have argued earlier, is not a test of logical distinctiveness but one of significance or importance. White's attempt to distinguish logically between Category I and Category II activities has been seen to lose its point when other activities have to be added, even though not satisfying the justifying criterion. In short, even writers trying to decide the compulsory/voluntary issue on logical grounds have to fall back on to judgments of what is generally significant or important.

Such judgments are not arbitrary. They are not judgments of purely personal interest and they are not judgments as to numerical popularity. Rather they are judgments as to the enduring significance of certain activities and inquiries for human beings. There is little doubt, too, that such judgments are at least partly moral judgments. That is to say that something judged as an important human activity, and worthy of compulsory inclusion in a programme of liberal education, is also being judged as in some sense morally commendable. The sense of 'morally commendable' here would be something like —

> is likely to at least respect the pupil as a rationally autonomous
> person, or potentially so, and enhance his or her development as
> such, and at best is likely to enhance his or her developing awareness
> of others as moral agents worthy of treatment as such.

The force of such a moral component in the judgment would be mainly the negative one of ruling out certain activities as unworthy of study in any directly participatory way: i.e. fighting, picking pockets, torturing and swindling — all of which have been significant human activities in the purely statistical sense of 'significant'.

Judging human practices on this basis will produce no absolutely clearcut division between those inquiries that should be compulsory and those that should not. There will be a continuum from the highly desirable to the less desirable. It must be remembered that the areas of the serving competencies and the humanities properly so called, which we have already considered, would be deemed so highly desirable, and so necessary to any further inquiries and understandings, as to be compulsory.

After this lengthy preliminary on the nature of the judgments being made it is now possible to attempt a list of those practices, the makings and doings of humankind, that should be included in a liberal and general education. I shall give the list first, then make brief comments on each area of inquiry. All pupils should have some introduction, including direct involvement in the activity where that is appropriate, to the following activities of humankind or manifestations of human intelligence:

Social and political institutions
Economic, commercial and industrial institutions
Mathematical and logical systems
Religion and morality
Art, craft and design
Literature and drama
Music and dance
Games and physical activities

A few general points may be made about this list. The order *is* intended to reflect, at least roughly, degrees of importance and thus desirability, as judged on the criteria already referred to above. All or most of these inquiries will have a *historical* component, but serving a different purpose to that of history in the humanities properly speaking, namely that of giving a developmental perspective to the study of the particular practice – e.g. art history, political history, economic history, history of craft and technology. Each one should be studied as a general introduction to the practice, *not* as the beginning of professional training *in* the practice. It is impossible to deal with any of these practices without the conveying of some specific factual information, but the danger of the transitory nature of such information has to be realized against the overall intention of generating general understandings of these practices. Active participation, though necessary, also has its dangers. For example, a pupil engaged in art in a school of general and liberal education is studying and practising with a different purpose from that of a student in an art school. In a school of liberal education we are not trying to produce an artist, but a human being who has some understanding of the arts as great and pervasive human practices.

The following brief notes should be read as indicating my view of what seems important in each of these areas. Limited space precludes the fuller treatment that is really necessary – but this would call for a monograph on each.

Social and political institutions Some consideration of how human beings have come to organize their social and political life. Political/ geographical divisions of the world. Different types of government organization and beliefs underlying them. Political parties. Sources of conflict. Central and local government. Electoral and representational methods. Other social institutions: the family and the community. Health and welfare services. Political and social concepts – e.g. justice, freedom, equality, fraternity.

121

Economic, industrial and commercial institutions Some considerations of processes of manufacture, production and exchange of goods in trade. The role of money and a simple introduction to financial institutions. market economies and planned economies and their relation to political beliefs. Technological development – its benefits and hazards. Trade unions, international and multi-national business organization. Tax and rate systems. Government and economics.

Most of the matters under these first two headings are not taught systematically in many schools at the moment, though they may be encountered in courses of modern history and in some aspects of geography. Some students, of course, do study constitutions or economics but these are normally optional courses selected at the expense of others. What is suggested here is that these matters should be part of the curriculum of a liberal education for *all* pupils because they involve human practices of great significance affecting all people in a very pervasive and general way, whatever else they as individuals might choose to do. I do not argue, as some do, that an informed democracy depends upon knowledge and understanding in these areas, though there is some truth in this claim. The larger truth, however, is that these are the major practices of humankind everywhere in some form or another. The adult community therefore has a duty to initiate the young of the community into an understanding of these practices, not just as a simple initiation or indoctrination into the particular or favoured practices of the community, but as a wider initiation into a framework of understood alternatives from which the particular community has presumably chosen.

It might be objected that these matters are all too complex to be understood by young people below the age of, say, 16. This is an odd argument. If these matters are indeed complex then surely they need prolonged consideration, and one could certainly *start* this consideration long before the age of 16. No person ever becomes *suddenly* capable of understanding the complexities of social, political and economic life, at whatever age; but to start some systematic reflection on these matters whilst still in the relatively detached atmosphere of the classroom at least promises a wider enhancement of such understanding.

Another objection is the susceptibility of these matters to indoctrination, where this is taken to mean the teacher influencing pupils to share his or her belief on issues known to be controversial. This danger cannot be denied but is not in itself a reason for excluding such content. Any danger of *teacher* indoctrination must be weighed against the ever-present danger of indoctrination from other sources, especially radio, television, newspapers, parents and friends. Looked at this way the possibility of teachers being *less* partial than these other sources of information and opinion looks more promising, especially if teachers themselves are aware of indoctrinatory dangers, as increasingly they are.[11]

Mathematical and logical systems An introduction to simple mathematics and measurement, it will be remembered, was to be an important part of what I have called the serving competencies, necessary for all pupils. What is now suggested goes much further than this. Humankind has created great symbolic systems of thought which have become ways of thought in themselves as well as having increasingly wide applications. Number systems, orderings within space and time, algebra, probability and statistics are not *discoveries* of non-intelligent realities in the world, they are creations of intelligence proposing ways of ordering our experience and thought. They are, in this sense, as much intelligently created 'goings-on' as art or politics, and can be studied as such. This is their main liberal education purpose and should not be confused with all the vocationally oriented quantitative and logical applications to industrial and commercial training, which give the enterprise a completely different purpose and are not properly part of a liberal education.[12]

Religion and morality I have already said that some study of religion is necessary to understand the attempt by humans to understand themselves, as is some involvement in a consideration of morality. Both religion and morality can also, however, be inquired into as great human practices. Indeed, for most people, without religious and/or moral considerations there would be no overriding framework of consideration from which to approach inquiries into social, political or economic matters. This is further to emphasize the point that the divisions between these practices are not logical but idiomatic, divisions of significant focus of attention. I do not mean to suggest by linking religion and morality together that they are *necessarily* linked. A person can clearly be moral (and immoral) in ways other than religious ways, and according to principles not dictated by religion. That they *can* be so separated, whilst for some people *not* so separated, is one of the things that pupils must come to see. A liberal education does not set out to make pupils religious, but neither does it set out to prevent them so becoming. It does and should set out to bring pupils to some understanding of religion as a great influence in historical and contemporary affairs. With morality the liberal educator is somewhat less neutral since, presumably, we do want pupils to become moral rather than immoral as well as coming to understand the nature of morality. This was the peculiar dichotomy in the Hirstian account, where it was supposed that initiation into a logically distinct understanding of morality was a proper part of liberal education, whilst the development of moral character was not such a proper part yet nevertheless ought to be attempted for all pupils. What is suggested here, in contrast with the Hirstian view, is that it is precisely *through* a proper understanding of morality, its point and principles, that a pupil (ideally) would come to act morally. The development of moral character is a proper task of liberal education provided it is undertaken in certain ways themselves compatible with the principles of liberal education − that is, by methods which are moral, rational and respectful of the personhood of the developing pupil.[13]

Art, craft and design For many men and women the greatest significance in their lives has come from making and creating. The challenge to produce something pleasing, useful, symbolically meaningful − or in various combinations of all three − has led to the making of some of the most treasured possessions of humankind. At a more humble level this challenge has also led to the development of taste in everyday living concerning, for example, domestic architecture, furniture, domestic tools and utensils, gardens and town-planning. All forms of such making involve design and problem-solving in some kind of way, and all involve some combination of practical skill with aesthetic and functional judgment − a sense of what is pleasing and proper. Typical problems are those of the visual artist in creating the illusion of three-dimensional space on a two-dimensional surface, and those of the technologist in turning ideas into the realities of feasible production.

Pupils undergoing a liberal education must be given some introduction to these enterprises but choices within them present some difficulties to the curriculum-planner. The division between what is to be compulsory and what voluntary becomes a matter of importance here. I would suggest the following principles:

(a) All pupils should have some regular involvement with art, craft and design activities from 5 to 16.
(b) All pupils should have some real instruction in the use of drawing as a tool − i.e. simple representative sketching and the production of simple sketch plans.
(c) All pupils should have an extensive introduction to the visual arts on a wider basis, both making and appreciating.
(d) All pupils should have an extensive introduction to domestic design and making. This would involve simple introductions to architecture, furniture design, fabrics and furnishings design, utensil design and garden design. This only sounds over-ambitious if we make the mistake of thinking that nothing of this kind can be studied

unless appropriate practical work accompanies it. There should, of course, be as much practical engagement in making as is reasonably possible, but we should not avoid some study of, say, architecture on the grounds that the pupils cannot build houses! The general aim would be to bring pupils to a closer understanding and appreciation, both aesthetic and technological, of the humanly made objects which surround them in their daily lives and the possibilities of enriching such surroundings.

(e) There should be a wide range of voluntary art and craft activities which can additionally be studied where pupils wish to.[14]

Literature and drama Created fictions, I have already said, form an important part of the humanities properly speaking, that is, those inquiries in which we seek to understand not just particular human practices but human understanding and agency itself. This is to *use* literature, and a very important task of liberal education this is. But literature and drama are, of course, great human practices which pupils ought to come to know about and be involved in *as* practices. There are three main aspects to these studies: pupils need to study in a systematic way selected works of literature and drama as exemplars of what is held to be good in the practices; they need to be involved in readings and performances of dramatic works and to see and discuss performances of such works; and they need to have some experience in creating fictions themselves in various forms. To pick up a point well made by John White there is every reason for selecting from works of foreign literature in translation as well as from English literature. It is also important to develop the idea that the creation of poetry and prose works is an *ongoing* human activity and not something to be studied solely historically. At least some contemporary writers should be studied and discussed. Again the aim should be the general one of bringing pupils to some understanding of the nature of literature and drama as human practices, not the production of writers or poets. It would be the hope of liberal educators that all pupils *would* become readers, not of course in the merely mechanical sense of being able to read but in the wider sense of wanting to use reading as the main means of sharing in human understandings and imaginings, and continuing to do this long after leaving behind the requirements of school.

Music Though there seems little doubt that a liberal education should include some introduction to music on the criterion of its significance in human life, there is considerable difficulty in determining exactly what to do when one moves on from the general assertion. Here there is a greater tangle than usual of different emphases and different considerations of what is more and less desirable. There are three main ways in which a person can be involved with music:

(a) by coming to know about and understand music by hearing it (recorded and live) in a context of explanations and information of a more or less historical and technical kind;
(b) by performing music in some way, either by singing or by performing on an instrument of a traditional or electronic kind, either by oneself or with others;
(c) by composing (making) music, either in the traditional sense of writing for performance in some agreed convention or by creating music in some more extempore or less formal way.

It is not the job of a general liberal education to produce executant musicians or composers, however desirable these may be, for this is the task of specialist training. The main task of a liberal education in respect of music is therefore that indicated by (a). This, however, is not all that simple since some involvement in (b) and (c) is greatly facilitative of achieving the understanding in (a). The guiding rule should be that involvement in (b) and (c), as compulsory activities at least, should only be taken as far as is necessary to serve the purposes and objectives of (a). The aim is the widest general understanding of music for all pupils. It is not, essentially, the creating of specific performances or the fostering of specific individual talent. This is not to suggest anything wrong with either of these activities, only that they should be desirable voluntary extras and not the main contribution of music to a liberal education.

Dance, games and physical activities other than those mentioned under the serving competencies are good examples of what would count as borderline activities for me. They are undeniable human practices of some significance. There should certainly be opportunities for them in the facilities provided for schools. They fall, however, on the voluntary side of the line for me! I cannot believe that a pupil should be *compelled* to play football or hockey, or to engage in physical activities like gymnastics or dance if he or she does not want to. In the case of competitive games, particularly, I have argued elsewhere that there are other reasons why these should not be compulsory for any given pupil.[15]

There are, of course, in addition to all those now mentioned, a vast range of human activities which are undeniably practices and undeniably of some significance. To start to consider these, however, would be to move on to those activities only involving *some* people, whereas those considered above, it is claimed, are practices in some sense affecting all people. There is clearly room for a good deal of variety between schools as to the voluntary activities that might be offered, based on the skills and interests of the staff and parents. *All* pupils, however, in *all* schools, should be introduced to the major practices of humankind outlined above.

7.5.2 Divisions within inquiries into 'goings-on' identified as not themselves manifestations of intelligence

The *activities* of scientists are, of course, themselves manifestations of human intelligence. If an inquiry was into the activities of scientists this would be but one more practice to be studied additionally to those discussed in 7.5.1. The *objects* of scientific inquiry, however, are not themselves practices with procedures, customs and actions to be investigated. It is convenient to recall the examples given by Oakeshott: 'A rock formation, a wave breaking on the shore, metal fatigue, a thunderstorm, a butterfly on the wing, the facial resemblances of children and parents, a chameleon changing colour, melting ice, etc.'[16]

There is sometimes confusion in education as to whether we are helping children to understand what scientists do, or helping them to understand the 'goings-on' that scientists try to understand. My contention is that for the purposes of a general liberal education it is more properly the latter that should concern us. What we are at is to help pupils to come to some understanding of the physical world they find themselves in: to understand, that is, the properties and processes of this physical world that obtain quite independently of the intervention of thought or intelligence. In order to do this pupils must be encouraged to approach inquiry into the physical world in somewhat the manner of scientists, and not simply to hear or see what scientists have done or proposed. Nevertheless the pupils are not, in a liberal education, being trained *as* scientists. They are being helped to understand the physical world which is inevitably the arena and framework of limiting conditions in which they must seek to realize their individual and collective purposes.

Another preliminary point is that such understandings of the physical world inevitably become involved in understandings of the human practices already considered. For example, understandings of the properties of certain materials affect our understandings of the practices of art, craft and design; understandings of human anatomy and physiological functioning affect our understanding of possibilities in dance and certain aspects of music; understandings of certain causal processes and physical properties affect our understanding of industrial and commercial undertakings, and so on. This does not alter the point of the logical division between the two great orders of inquiry; indeed, it emphasizes the need to be clear about what can be altered by fluctuations in human interest, and what cannot because it is in no way dependent upon that interest. Certain kinds of dance or drama or literary forms might fade from fashion, but metals will expand, water will freeze and radiation be emitted under certain conditions whether or not the interests of human beings change over time.

There are several problems in deciding what, out of the vast and growing assemblage of scientific knowledge, should form part of a general liberal education. Perhaps the first point to remind ourselves of is that the education to be given does not cease to be general and liberal now that we are talking of the sciences rather than the humanities and the arts. Science presents a greater temptation to specific training and preparation than do the humanities and the arts. Science courses in schools seem particularly influenced by science courses in universities, and these in turn appear to assume that students are being trained to be scientists — scientific researchers, in fact. Schools of liberal education, or those teaching in them and managing them, must resist being dragged into a training programme of a scientific and technological nature. The pressures for schools to become so engaged will be great and increase as the rate of technological change (and governments' powerlessness to control and manage such change) increases. This is undoubtedly happening in England at the time of writing and will be further considered in Part III.

Even if these pressures and temptations are discounted for the moment, other problems remain. The field of scientific knowledge is so vast and grows so rapidly that the problem of selection is considerable. Some proposals for a science common core curriculum, whilst worthy in urging that there should be such a common science experience for pupils, contain so much material content that one cannot imagine any pupil other than one proceeding to scientific specialism possibly attaining understanding of it all. (See for example that proposed in Appendix 5.1 of Ingle and Jennings, 1981, note 17 below.) This overloading danger is compounded by the history of the training of science teachers and its roots in the separate disciplines of physics, chemistry and biology. Syllabus constructors inheriting these traditions cannot resist laying the foundations for a 'proper' introduction to physics, chemistry and biology in an additive way, even when the intention is to produce a common core science curriculum for general education. Neither a sufficient appreciation of significant scientific understandings nor a real appreciation of scientific skills and methods can be gained when the list of topics is excessively long and multivarious. As is so often the case we need guiding principles that will help with *exclusion* as well as with inclusion.

To some extent our guiding principles might match the earlier approach to the humanities and the arts. There I suggested that what a person had to come to understand was being a person in a world of persons and their practices. What is needed for the order of inquiry now under consideration is a focus on what it is to understand oneself as a physical living organism among other similar and different living creatures sharing a physical universe. There are some understandings more central to these concerns than others among all the scientific understandings that one *could* come to have. I once asked a Cambridge professor of physics (Brian Pippard) what he thought was the most important aspect of science to be studied as part of a general education, thinking that he would say 'physics', often considered the school science subject of highest status. His actual reply was 'human biology', the topic later placed first on the list of suggestions for a common science element by HMIs in their 11 to 16 curriculum proposals (1977). On my suggested principle of selection what could be more sensible? Second only to my concern to understand myself as a person must be my concern to understand how I work as a physical organism. There is much to be known about my own body that can start with relatively simple understandings, though, of course, there is hardly any limit to the depth of knowledge and understanding that can be developed. Knowledge of our bodies relates clearly to considerations of health and medicine and particularly to food and nutrition. Food, nutrition, health and medicine have clear relationships with ethical and social issues to be studied under earlier headings. They also happen to be areas of understanding in which all persons have to make decisions about their life-styles and consumption habits. This whole area of study is of clear and central importance to all human beings and has nothing to do, at least initially, with whether the pupil intends to be a scientist or not. Neither is this study purely a biological study, though much of the understanding comes from biologists. The human body is as subject to physical and chemical laws as it is to biological ones; and the human body interacts physically with the physical world both unconsciously and through the more simple technologies. These simple technologies are important to understand, not of course as things to be trained for, nor out of nostalgia, but in order to grasp certain natural aspects of the relationship between human beings and their natural environment: a relationship which modern and more sophisticated technologies both weaken and make more difficult to understand and to appreciate.[17]

To know something of our own bodies is to start to know something about our place in a living world of plants and animals. Here again there is much that can be known at a relatively simple level but also a vast area of more sophisticated inquiry to draw us on. What seems to be of the greatest significance here is knowledge of animal behaviour and ecology, rather than details of animal anatomy and physiology, though some such detail should not necessarily be excluded. It is the grasp of some idea of an interrelated, evolved, living whole of which we are part that needs struggling for, rather than the piling up of arbitrarily selected facts having no apparent relationship with one another or with the life of the pupil.

It is also proper for human beings to have some introduction to, and description of, the developed understandings of the non-living material universe in which they find themselves. These understandings, quickly listed but including a great deal of study, concern the science of the world in its place — astronomy and cosmology; the science of the world as an object — physical geography and meteorology; the science of the world's resources of energy and usable materials; and the science of ecology and conservation.

In respect of these scientific understandings it is important for pupils to come to share certain bodies of information together with some insight into this kind of evidence that makes belief in such information warrantable, at least for the time being. The fact that scientific information is continually in a state of change is no argument against trying to equip pupils with a broad basis of understanding of the physical world, provided always that the idea of a scientific knowledge as changing knowledge is part of the very framework of the knowledge to be understood. A growing understanding of the objects of scientific inquiry must go hand in hand with a growing awareness of science as a great human practice. As previously pointed out, these understandings also relate to other human practices like politics, industry and commerce which cannot properly be understood save in their context within an understood physical world. These relationships, however, must not drive educators into thinking that there are no distinctions to be made. Whether the distinction is the main logical distinction between inquiries into 'goings-on' *not* themselves manifestations of intelligence and 'goings-on' that *are* such manifestations, or the more pragmatic and convenient distinctions between one human practice and another or one focus of scientific inquiry and another, such distinctions are important. Before pupils can understand relationships and interconnections they must understand *what* is to be related to and connected with *what*.

An education in certain aspects of scientific understanding is not to be confused with a technical education or an education in technology, even less with specific technical or technological training. Liberal education is concerned essentially with understanding the world, technology (with apologies to Marx!) is concerned with changing the world in some practically useful way. Established technologies, as human practices, are among the things to be understood in a liberal education, but liberal education is not in the business of training people to operate specific technologies. This is not to be taken as any general derogation of technical training. All societies need to engage in technical training for all sorts of specific purposes, and in a time of rapid technical change training might need to be followed by re-training at more or less frequent intervals. The point being made here, to be further developed later when considering politics and education, is that the training of scientists and technicians or technologists is neither most desirably nor most efficiently located in schools of general and liberal education which have their own demanding objectives largely in terms of understanding.

The major divisions of study to form part of a liberal education, then, within that categorial division of inquiries into 'goings-on' not themselves manifestations of human intelligence, might conveniently be listed as follows:

(i) The workings of the human body.
(ii) Health and medicine.
(iii) Food and nutrition.
(iv) Animals and plants — behaviour and ecology.
(v) Simple technologies.
(vi) Astronomy and cosmology.
(vii) Physical geography and meteorology.
(viii) Resources of energy and usable materials.
(ix) Ecology and conservation.

These are, of course, very broad headings, but they are specific enough to indicate what is to be considered important in relation to the governing principles of understanding ourselves as physical organisms in a physical universe. Each heading subsumes considerable detail. For example, heading (viii), Resources of energy and usable materials, in so far as it points to some consideration of the properties of energy and material resources, would include much that at present is to be found in physics and chemistry courses; but since the focus would be on significance to humans there would also be exclusion of some of the items to be found in long lists like that of Ingle and Jennings.

7.6 The place of interest

The guiding principles with which this chapter opened, themselves a summary of earlier arguments, attached importance to the idea of respecting the freedom and autonomy of the pupil. The whole conception of a liberal education being liberating rests on the assumption that the child is to be helped to become autonomous, self-governing, a free chooser of what to believe and to do.

Some educators have given exclusive importance to the idea of freedom, seeing it not only as an object of education but as a defining characteristic of any education truly so called. One writer, P.S. Wilson,[18] has argued that no learning-teaching transaction can count as education

Table 7.1 The content of a liberal general education — outline draft
For explanations of distinctions, the integrative idea and
explanations of the headings, see text of Chapter 7.

Forms of inquiry into 'goings-on' essentially manifestations of intelligence	Serving competencies	Forms of inquiry into 'goings-on' essentially not manifestations of intelligence

The humanities proper	Language
	Numeracy
	Logical reasoning
	Appropriate
	  dispositions
	Physical fitness
	Keyboard skills
		The workings of the
		  human body

Literature		Health and medicine
History		Food and nutrition

Morality		Animals and plants —
		  behaviour and
		  ecology

Religion		
		Simple technologies
The makings and practices of persons		Astronomy and cosmology
Social and political institutions		Physical geography and meteorology
Economic, industrial and commercial institutions		Resources of energy and usable materials
Mathematical and logical systems		Ecology and conservation
Religion and morality		
Art, craft and design		
Literature and drama		
Music and dance		
Games and physical activities		

unless the pupil is freely choosing to develop an interest he or she already has, a value already present. Another writer, M. Bonnett,[19] whilst not wanting to monopolize the concept of education in quite this kind of way, nevertheless attaches the greatest importance to the opportunity for a child to operate with authenticity out of the genuine concerns of the constitutive core self, and rates this as of greater importance than the acquisition of knowledge in the development of autonomy. Indeed, generally pervading the very influential, if not always clearly articulated, ideas of child-centred education is the claim that children must somehow *be* free in education, and not simply be in a state of tutelage or preparation for freedom in the future.

Looked at from one point of view this cluster of ideas could make the delineation of content appropriate for a liberal education a redundant exercise. For, it could be argued, the choice of content should be the pupil's own, otherwise freedom is denied and the development of autonomy frustrated. I want to argue that this is a false characterization of the child-centred position before going on to indicate some of the important truths that are to be found in that position.

The falsity of the claim about choice of content lies in the assumption, often implicit rather than explicit, of a subjective theory of values – i.e., the idea that there is nothing to be called valuable other than that actually valued by an individual. The whole point of the account of an appropriate content for a liberal education outlined in this chapter is the justificatory argument that has accompanied it in terms of what is involved in understanding one's place in a world of persons and simultaneously a physical being in a physical world. If this justificatory account is sound then the *objective* value of the described content is claimed. This is just another way of saying that if one does not value the understandings listed then one *ought* to. One ought to value an understanding of persons; one ought to value an understanding of significant human practices; one ought to value an understanding of the physical world, and so on. The 'ought' here is a kind of moral 'ought', concerned in the case of adults with duties to oneself. In the case of children, however, the duty attaches to responsible adults on behalf of children, and the choice of content, in broad terms at least, is not the responsibility of the child.

The truth in the child-centred claim lies in its correct characterization of real understanding and real knowledge. Understandings are inevitably individual and knowledge is only genuine where the individual grasps the warrant or reasons for holding beliefs to be true beliefs. For a teacher to assume that understandings and knowledge can somehow just be imposed on the pupil whatever the state of mind of the pupil is a misconception that has bedevilled education since teaching began. If understandings and knowledge are to be achieved then the way particular developments of understanding and knowledge come about is significant. It is for this reason that the present interests and concerns of the pupil are important, for it is on to these present interests and concerns, and onto the conceptual frameworks in which such interests have their being, that any fresh knowledge or understanding has to be grafted in some way. It is not true, I am claiming, that completely fresh interests and concerns cannot be developed. If this were true then no education would be possible. It *is* true, however, that any fresh interest or concern, any new development of knowledge and understanding, can only come about by some kind of relationship with the conceptual frameworks, the mental structures, already possessed by the pupil. This idea is no mere truism and will need extensive development in the chapter to follow.

A further truth of the child-centred position is a point about motivation. The claim is that a pupil will work harder, concentrate more, be more generally inclined to apply him or herself to the task in hand, if the task is one of interest to the pupil. This has all the appearance of some empirically confirmed discovery but is in fact largely conceptual or definitional. What I mean by this is that what it *means* to be interested in something is to want to pursue it, to spend time on it, to find out more about it, and so on. Thus to say that I am more inclined to spend time on things that interest me is no more than to say that I am more inclined to spend time on things I am inclined to spend time on! The real truth lurking behind all this is the importance for educators of engendering in pupils the kind of appropriate dispositions discussed in 7.4. It is an educational task to engender concern, care and interest for justifiably worthwhile endeavours.

Yet a further extension of this line of thought is the claim that pupils will be more motivated to engage fully in activities and content that are self-chosen than in those chosen by others. This is a different point from the claim that pupils need to exercise choice in order to develop their autonomy, and it is certainly not merely a conceptual or definitional point. Observation, however, does not lead me to believe that the truth of this claim is at all obvious. For one thing children often choose one activity only to pass quickly on to another, so self-selection in itself appears to provide at least no immediate guarantee of sustained interest and attention. Another consideration is that the very phrase 'self-selected' is deceptive. How do ideas and activities which I might conceivably develop come to me for consideration in the first place? The answer, presumably, is that such presentations come in a multitude of ways: some by pure chance or accidental contiguity, but many by more deliberate encounter through books, magazines, radio, television, friends and, of course, teachers. There is also a complex story to be told of why some of these hold my attention and grow into more developed concerns and others do not. Of course part of this story is to do with my constitutive core self, compounded of my present concerns and interests. I have, as it were, no other self from which to encounter new experiences; no other self from which to conceptualize, understand and know. But this core self is not static. It has developed and will continue to develop, and is therefore alterable. Novelty itself is attractive and motivates many activities and changes of activity. People strive deliberately to develop new activities and to this end often welcome the presentation of new ideas and proposals from others.

All this is but a sketch of the confusions attaching to the place of interest in education. What emerges, I believe, is that there is no need for immediate pupil control of the determination of the broad content of a liberal education; indeed, there is strength in the opposed view, namely, that all pupils should be involved in all the areas deemed to be important by convincing justificatory argument. There should, to be blunt, be an extensive compulsory core curriculum. Beyond this there is no reason why schools should not have facilities for offering all kinds of activities and studies to be chosen on the basis of personal interest. The charge at the moment, regarding English schools, is that the compulsory and common core is neither broad enough nor lasts long enough to be a satisfactory general and liberal education, and that the choice area comes too early and is too large a part of a young person's curriculum.

What emerges also is that problems of motivation are not essentially problems of choice of content, but methodological and strategical problems of pedagogy concerned with how to engage pupils in what is demonstrably worthwhile. This is a main concern of the next chapter.

8 The methods of a liberal education

8.1 Introduction

Although the idea of a liberal education is appropriately attached to certain kinds of curriculum content rather than to others, it is equally importantly attached to certain teaching styles, strategies, methods and intentions rather than to others. Even if an item of curriculum content was carefully selected from the body of such content already discussed it could fail to constitute a part of liberal education by the manner in which it was taught. The reason for this concern for teacher style, strategy, method and intention is connected with our initial characterization of, and justification for, liberal education. Liberal education has been characterized in this work as that education which is liberating from the ties of the present and the particular, concerned with knowledge and understanding which is fundamental, general and intrinsically worthwhile, and concerned with the life of reason. Methodological considerations also arise from the ethical nature of the main justification of liberal education that has been given. In dealing with this justification I said:

> the moral duty of adults to children is reasonably clear and has two parts. The positive part is a duty to help children, in all ways possible, to become increasingly rational and autonomous up to the point where the moral duty to do this for themselves might reasonably be expected to take over. The negative form of this duty is an obligation not to allow or encourage the social environment to foreclose on the possibilities and life-styles open to a child's future as a rational and autonomous being.[1]

We thus have a number of considerations which point to treating people in certain ways rather than in others while they are being liberally educated; or, to put it more strongly, in order to be sure that they *are* being liberally educated. We must teach in such a way as to liberate people and not bind them or restrict them; so as to bring about in them genuine knowledge and understanding rather than the possession of some rote repertoire; so as to bring about real concern for what is

justifiably worthwhile; so as to bring about concern for and competence in the life of reason; and so as to ensure that pupils are respected,
and come to respect themselves and others, as rational and autonomous
persons. We must try to avoid teaching them in ways that act against
these intentions.

It is tempting to write about each of these desirable intentions in
turn. In fact, however, they are by no means so easily separable as
that, since any given action or style of a teacher is likely to bear, for
good or ill, upon more than one of these considerations. I shall therefore discuss the methods of a liberal education under the following
three broad headings: teaching for evidence, teaching for understanding, and teaching for care.

8.2 Teaching for evidence

Knowledge properly speaking, I have said, is best conceived of as justifiable belief. To know is to have a belief that I can be reasonably sure
about because of my grasp of the evidence or warrant which justifies
the belief. Belief in itself is simply a state of mind in which I give assent
to certain propositions or to the appropriateness of certain actions.
Beliefs, as a matter of psychology, can be held with varying degrees
of strength of conviction, as Anthony Quinton has pointed out, and this
strength of conviction has no necessary connection with evidence or
justification.[2] A person is rational, Quinton reminds us, to the extent
to which his or her strength or belief is proportionate to the understood
logical justification of those beliefs. A person of strong convictions is
not necessarily a person of strong *rational* convictions.

These distinctions are connected with the idea of liberation in
education. To have a strong belief X, which is not based on an understood justification, is either not to know why I believe X, or it is to
hold the belief for some reason that does not in itself amount to an
understood justification. A common reason of this kind is to believe
X because someone else has told me of the truth of X — a teacher
perhaps. There are certain matters on which the say-so of someone else
would be quite appropriate as evidence for my belief. For example,
my belief that my wife has toothache, held on the grounds that she says
so, is a perfectly rational belief. These cases are special cases, however,
pertaining to self-knowledge which cannot be communicated in any
other way. There are other matters on which we commonly accept the
say-so of others because these others are held to be experts. These
matters might, for example, be those of law or medicine. On these
matters we assume that the knowledge — i.e. the stock of justifiable
beliefs — is greater with the experts than it is with us. We do not so
much obtain our knowledge from the experts as come to hold beliefs

on the basis of *their* knowledge. For example, my doctor *knows* that my symptoms indicate the presence of gall stones, and I believe him because I have grounds for trusting his claim to know.

Now the relationship between a pupil or student and a teacher *could* be considered to be like that between patient and doctor, or between client and lawyer, in respect of beliefs. The teacher has a stock of knowledge and the task of getting pupils to come to believe the propositions embodied in this knowledge, as the doctor and lawyer have stocks of knowledge out of which they try to get their patients and clients to believe certain things. This, however, would be a grossly inappropriate model for the teacher-pupil relationship in liberal education because of the liberal educator's duty to liberate rather than to bind students.

It is only to the extent that the knowledge I operate with is genuinely mine that I am liberated from intellectual dependency and can be autonomous. It is undoubtedly necessary, in a complex civilization, to be dependent in certain respects upon the technical knowledge of others; but there is also no doubt that to the extent I am thus dependent my autonomy is diminished. To be dependent for all or nearly all my beliefs on the knowledge of others, however, would be to live in a strange state of paradoxically civilized barbarism. The paradox arises from the fact that the knowledge might well be sophisticated and technical, the product of an advanced society, whereas the barbarism arises from the lack of distribution of such knowledge, most people holding such knowledge on the say-so of others. In this respect people would live in a similar mental state to that of primitive tribesmen relying for their beliefs on the unexamined utterances of witchdoctors and the hand-downs of ancestors.

Liberal education is not merely the exercise of letting pupils see what is known and to believe what they are told and shown, it is the exercise, as far as is possible, of getting pupils to *actually know*, and that is to get pupils to steadily expand their *own* stock of justifiable beliefs. Another way of putting this important idea is to say that obtaining beliefs from the knowledge of others, as from the doctor or lawyer, may in certain ways be very helpful but is never educative. Beliefs only become educative, at least in the sense of liberally educative, when they are taken in, assented to, in certain ways rather than others. That is to say, beliefs must be entertained and assented to on the basis of understood justification if they are to be liberating by being educative. If I understand the justification for a belief, see the point of the belief, then I am liberated from *whatever* was the source of the belief, teacher, textbook, parent or whomsoever. The liberating aspirations of a liberal education can only be met, therefore, by teaching in a way that aims at getting pupils to grasp the appropriate evidence for beliefs as well as the beliefs themselves. We might describe this as teaching evidentially, or evidential teaching.

Not only are the liberating aspects of a liberal education met most satisfactorily by teaching evidentially but so also are our concerns for respecting the pupil. It will be remembered that in 2.3 the idea of respect for persons was linked with the idea of justification in two ways. The first way was that the treatment of persons by persons always calls for justification, and the second way was that to treat someone with respect as a person must always involve treating that one as a reasoner and a justifier, i.e. as a creature for whom justification matters. The discussion in 2.3 was summed up as follows:

> Education involves the influencing of some people by others and
> therefore calls for justification; but because the subjects of
> education are persons no educational practice will *be* justifiable
> that fails to recognize these subjects as actual or potential reasoners
> or justifiers.

Now to conceive of pupils as either not to need justification for the beliefs they are required to assent to, or to conceive of them as capable of assenting to the beliefs but not capable of grasping the justifications, is exactly to fail to respect them in the sense picked out in 2.3.

It perhaps needs no demonstration to show that as well as making for intellectual liberation and respecting pupils as persons evidential teaching of course satisfies the characteristic of liberal education as involvement in the life of reason. This must be so since reason is essentially to do with believing what there is good reason to believe, and only such, and doing what there is good reason to do or at least no reason for not doing.

There is a further point about the cluster of ideas connected with knowledge as justifiable belief and the evidential teaching that goes along with it. This is a point about truth and certainty. In 5.4 I drew attention to J.S. Mill's concern that truths should not be handed on as what he called 'dead dogma' even though the teachers saw them as unquestionable truths. I take J.S. Mill as meaning by 'dead dogma' the passing on of these truths with no concern to involve pupils in the evidence supporting such 'truths', and this is quite in accord with what I have been arguing. But there is another side to the idea of 'dead dogma' which is the belief in the idea of 'truths' being sufficiently well established to be no longer questionable. What Brand Blanshard has happily called the 'rational temper'[3] would not accept that there are many areas of knowledge and understanding where such certainty is warranted. The very word 'certainty' is itself used in a variety of ways, as Quinton again reminds us.[4] At least the following four different senses of 'certain truths' can be seen in use:

   (i)   individually and psychologically indubitable beliefs,
  (ii) what everyone appears to believe,
 (iii) scientific beliefs as yet not disproved about which there appears
       to be no reasonable doubt, and
 (iv) demonstrable and unchanging logical truths.

However strongly, in the purely psychological sense, a belief is held by one or many persons this provides no grounds whatsoever for passing such beliefs on to pupils as unquestionable. It is not unknown for large numbers of people to hold false beliefs quite strongly. Although there may appear to be no presently available answer to the question 'Why is X to be believed?', nevertheless the question is very properly put. Similarly, that something is believed by very large numbers of people, whilst it properly makes me question my scepticism, is no reason for the unquestioning transmission of the belief as true.

Scientific 'truths', especially in our age, often are accepted as unquestionable once the 'truth' is allegedly demonstrated by duly qualified scientists. One does not need to be a fully convinced Popperian, however, to see that there is no logical necessity for these 'truths', that science advances to tomorrow by refuting the 'truths' of today, that final truths do not appear to be reached, and so on. No pupil could be properly introduced to scientific inquiry on the assumption that he was entering a domain of indubitable truths.

This appears to leave the area of logical truths as the only area in which a full-blown notion of certainty can be entertained. There *is* a sense in which we could say that logical truths are certain. Unless the meaning of the symbols has changed $(4 \times 7) = (30 - 2)$ is indubitably true. Even this, however, does not justify us in passing on such truths as unquestionable since we want the pupils, as well as ourselves, to see *why* such propositions are to be believed, and, indeed, why they are to be believed indubitably.

There are thus two further reasons for teaching for rationally justifiable beliefs by evidential teaching. Firstly, because in most areas of knowledge our beliefs can be no more than rationally justifiable, though they ought to be no less; and secondly, because even where truths do seem certainly established by their logical nature they will only come to be *held as justifiable* by those who come to understand the justification, those who in Mill's words come to them as 'living truths' rather than 'dead dogma'.

There are different kinds of arguments supporting the practice of evidential teaching and the bringing about of rational beliefs which are to do with the effects on liberal educators themselves rather than with the pupils. These arguments are not concerned with logical necessities but with the likely effects upon teachers of one conception of their task as compared with the likely effects of a different conception. For example, a teacher concerned to teach evidentially, with attention to the justification of the beliefs he is involving pupils in, is more likely to continually refine his own understanding of the appropriate evidence and its relation to the belief, and this continual attention to evidential structures is likely to make such a teacher a better explainer. Such a teacher will have more regard for the effect of teaching on the mental structures of pupils and be less concerned about the rote regurgitation of isolated 'facts'. Our evidential teacher, too, will have a sharper realization of the varying status of evidential claims across different kinds of knowledge and understanding, knowing that the justification of beliefs in some areas like religion, morality and politics is far less clear and agreed than in areas like science and mathematics, and vary teaching strategies accordingly. In assessing and examining a teacher concerned in this way will distrust the value of testing factual recall and strive to find other ways of getting at the more complex structures of the pupil's understanding.

There is one more consequence of teaching for rational belief rather than in some sense of conveying fixed truths. Beliefs entertained evidentially, rationally, are always in principle entertained temporarily. That is to say, they are always open to change on the presentation of further relevant evidence. The rationality of pupils, or anyone else for that matter, is to be judged by the relationship of their beliefs to the evidence that they are known to be acquainted with or that they can reasonably be expected to have been acquainted with. It is this thought, presumably, that lies behind Jerome Bruner's oft-quoted claim that any knowledge can be introduced to any pupil at any age with intellectual integrity. Many of the beliefs of earlier generations about the structure of the universe, the shape of the earth or the working of the human body were neither irrational nor non-evidential, but simply based, and often very sensibly based, on the evidence available to them at the time. We sometimes now try to take pupils beyond the evidence they can grasp and thereby force them into a rote and non-meaningful learning situation. It is sometimes supposed that Piaget has told us that children cannot reason or think evidentially until they reach the formal operations stage. This, of course, is not the case. The Piagetian claim is rather about the *nature* of the evidence that can be grasped and the impossibility, at an early stage, of children considering evidence hypothetically, or abstractly rather than concretely.

Teachers should not therefore worry unduly about the simple explanations that children must necessarily be involved in at first. As long as such explanations are reasonable and understandable, and seen by pupils to be based on certain kinds of evidence, then the procedures, though simple, are rational and evidential. For example, young children might well be trained more in applying the evidence of their own sight and hearing before they come to modify this with magnifiers, microscopes, radio and telvision and the like. They might calculate and reason themselves before seeing how calculators and computers might help to extend their skills. They might be led into inquiry about their own past and that of their family, their friends and their locality before simply being *told* about the Romans, the Napoleonic Wars, or whatever. They might be more engaged in talk about why *they* like or dislike books they read, before being told what is good and bad and why — and so on. The principle, I think, is clear. That beliefs thus formed will require modification as further things are learned and further experiences encountered will come as no shock or surprise to pupils who hold their beliefs evidentially because of appropriate teaching.

8.2.1 Indoctrination

I refer briefly to the concept of indoctrination mainly because there has been so much discussion of it in the literature of philosophy of education in recent years. Much of this discussion has been purely definitional and conceptual, addressing itself to the question: 'What ought properly to be called indoctrination?' The 'Oxford English Dictionary' gives no indication of the derogatory connotation that the word has come to have in educational discourse. The main meanings given are: to imbue with learning, to teach, and to imbue with a doctrine, idea or opinion. It would be to chance very grave misunderstanding indeed to use the word with these neutral meanings now in educational company where the word has a clear derogatory sense. Whatever else indoctrination might mean, educators seem agreed, on the whole, that it is bad. What they are not agreed about entirely is what it is about indoctrination that makes it bad.[5]

I have no intention of reviewing the semantic arguments here, but behind most of them, I believe, is the common ground, not always made explicit, that to indoctrinate someone is to get that someone to hold a belief in ways and on grounds that are non-evidential. There might be many reasons why a person would wish to do this to another, or it might be done quite unintentionally: the nature and consequences are the same, i.e. the recipient comes to hold a belief that is just 'one superstition the more' rather than to hold a rational belief. It has been suggested that the essence of indoctrination lies in the intention of the indoctrinator to implant an unshakeable belief.[6] I cannot see that the procedure is any the less indoctrinatory if there is no such intention but the teaching is none the less non-evidential; but it must be agreed that the consequences of the non-evidential inculcation of beliefs often do seem to be that the belief becomes very fixed, contrary to the relative openness of the way in which rational beliefs are held. The reason for this is not too difficult to see. If a belief is not held on the basis of supporting evidence anyway, then the adducing of evidence or argument to change the belief will hardly be of much avail. And of course it is not, as any one who has tried to combat religious or racial prejudice by rational argument will know — the word 'prejudice' simply being another name for beliefs and attitudes held non-evidentially.

The term 'indoctrination', then, is a convenient label, though by no means a necessary or essential one, for certain kinds of teaching which stand opposed to the ideal of evidential teaching urged in the previous section. This would be teaching where the teacher might be concerned that beliefs *are* justifiable but is *not* concerned to involve the pupil in that justification, either at the level of acquaintance or understanding. Much indoctrination in this sense goes on in school with no malicious or pernicious intention, but solely because of teachers' own beliefs about lack of time to involve pupils in evidence, the pressure of overloaded syllabuses, or the alleged incapacity of pupils to cope with evidential learning.

Such a widespread concept, whilst it clearly excludes evidential teaching from its meaning on the one hand, also on the other excludes — must be distinguished from — the kind of teaching where the teacher has no regard that the beliefs being transmitted are justifiable at all. This would be the teaching of known falsehoods. One hopes that this is not so common as indoctrination but it always remains a possibility, especially where, for political and other reasons, it is deemed that other considerations than truth are overriding. The appropriate term here, also with its own historical journey from neutrality to derogation, is 'propaganda'.

We have so far conceived of three broad ways in which educators might set out to bring about beliefs or to influence and change beliefs:

(i) with no concern that the beliefs are justifiable at all — i.e. lying or propaganda,

(ii) with concern that the beliefs are justifiable but no concern to involve pupils in the evidence — i.e. indoctrination, and

(iii) with concern that the beliefs are justifiable and that pupils should come to grasp the evidence that warrants the beliefs — i.e. evidential teaching.

The liberal educator, I am claiming, should practise (iii) — evidential teaching, as far as is possible with additional aspects yet to be considered.

143

8.2.2 *Training and practical activities*

Much of education is concerned with getting people to do things as well as getting them to believe things. As with believing, doing can be more or less intelligent. That is to say, the doing – the actual performance – can be more or less rooted in knowledge and understanding about what I am doing, why I am doing it, and why I am doing it this way rather than in alternative ways. It is always tempting, when trying to get another person to do something correctly, to be satisfied when the purely behavioural aspects of the performance are judged as correct by the teacher or trainer. In many walks of life this is adequate – if the lathe operator produces satisfactory turnings, the cook satisfactory pastry, the cabinet-maker satisfactory joints, then what else is there to worry about? In liberal education, however, the goals are different.

This is an important distinction having considerable bearing particularly on how we teach pupils in the so-called practical subjects in liberal education. It should be clear from all that has gone before that, whilst many practical activities will be part of a liberal education, their presence in such an education is for specific and limited purposes. These purposes might be summed up as:

(i) Instrumentally serving the intellectual purposes of liberal education: e.g. writing, using measuring devices, using purely instrumental equipment like microscopes, balances, audio-visual devices and reference equipment, and developing keyboard skills.
(ii) Engaging in practical activities in order to understand a human practice which cannot properly be understood without such engagement: e.g. painting, playing a musical instrument, singing, modelling, working with various tools and machines, dancing and acting.

Although there is a sense in which all the performances exampled above can be labelled 'skills', and a sense in which the proper development of skills involves training, there is also, however, a sense in which the word 'training' sets up a connotation opposed to the purposes of a liberal education. Many teachers feel intuitively uncomfortable in the face of modern pressures to train pupils in certain skills, and I believe this intuitive unease to be well founded. There are two reasons for this: Firstly, 'training' is most appropriately used to name an activity of specific preparation in which the trainer helps the trainee to develop skills, possessed by the trainer, and which the trainee will go on to use in some sustained way as hobby, sport, trade or profession. We thus speak quite properly of the training of boxers, jockeys and athletes, though we also talk of the training of physicists, chemists and engineers. In liberal education, whilst it is both appropriate and necessary to enable pupils to do things of the kind exampled above, it is neither appropriate nor necessary to train them in these activities in the hard sense of 'train' just indicated. Indeed there would not be time to do so given all the demands of a liberal education. Something of the feel of what I mean here can be obtained by contrasting the elements of the following pairs of statements:

He is able to sing	He is a trained singer
I am able to measure	I am a trained measurer
She can play the piano	She is a trained pianist
I can use a lathe	I am a trained lathe operator

A liberally educated person might well be able to sing, measure, play the piano and use a lathe. It would not be a function of liberal education, however, to ensure that a person became a trained singer, a trained measurer, a trained pianist or a trained lathe operator.

The second reason for supposing teachers' suspicion of training for skills to be well founded is the association of the word 'training' with some kind of unthinking performance repeated and developed by varieties of simple imitation or conditioning. The model here, presumably, is animal training which necessarily is characterized in this way; but the idea is also associated with crude forms of human training practised, in the past at least, in the armed forces and in schools. There is little doubt that large number of human beings have been induced to perform — behave — in certain ways rather than others by techniques involving force, threat of force, unpleasantness, reward, authority, conditioning or extrinsic motivation of some kind. They have, in a strictly pejorative sense of the word, been 'trained', and it is this connotation of 'trained' which fills many educators with unease, and properly so.

Now it could be argued in respect of this second reason for unease about training for skills that it is largely a historical argument having no present force. Training is not now like that, it might be said. Trainers are much more efficient and less crude and involve trainees much more in understanding what they are doing. There is no doubt some truth in the claim that these kinds of things are done better now than they were. Training in the armed forces, for example, is highly efficient and often brilliantly conceived, though it is of course very specific, intensively practised and at least likely to be used for some time in a sustained way. In schools the picture is more confusing. Attention to overt performance and unthinking obedience and compliance is still high in some places and in some activities. To the extent that it is not like this, and to the extent that pupils are involved in fitting their performances into a framework of knowledge and understanding, then to that extent we could say that liberal education *is* going on. It is also true to say, however that the extent to which such knowledge and understanding is involved is perhaps a measure of the inappropriateness of the word 'training' to name what is going on.

As with the teaching of beliefs, then, the teaching of practical activities in a liberal education should be, as it were, evidential. That is to say: the activity, the performance, the actual behaviour, should always be in a setting for the pupil such that it involves appropriate knowledge and understanding in some wide sense. The activity should also be in a context where the focus, both for teacher and pupil, is on the way in which the activity itself aims at some knowledge and understanding appropriate to a liberal education, not just at some kind of proficiency in the activity. Two examples might make the point rather more concrete.

Following the publication of the Newsom Report[7] in 1963 many schools introduced courses for young school-leavers based on motor cars. These courses could be seen as nearer to or further from liberal education on the criteria I have tried to explicate above. Those courses furthest away from liberal education concentrated on rudimentary driving skills, necessarily rudimentary because the driving was in school grounds and not amongst other traffic, and on simple maintenance like wheel-changing and attention to oil and water. To these activities was often added the rehabilitation of old vehicles which introduced the pupils to some mechanical skills connected with the repair of motor cars. The instruction on these courses was very specific and very 'cook-book' in nature − that is to say, the pupils were shown specific procedures to produce specific results. Those courses a bit nearer the liberal education ideal had more concern for getting pupils to understand things in general about motor cars with some attention to the general principles of the automobile engine, transmission systems, and so on. Other courses, yet more liberal in their educational intentions, used a study of motor cars as examples of even more general principles of mechanics, chemistry and electricity with applications well beyond the motor vehicles themselves. One course I saw even used cars and driving as focal points for moral and social problems discussed with moral and social education in mind.

What we see here is a continuum from crude training on the one extreme to general education on the other. It should be clear that from the point of view I am trying to argue (and from others also) drivers and motor mechanics are best trained in institutions other than schools of general education, and any focus on cars in such schools should only be to facilitate certain kinds of general understanding.

The rather derogatory use of the expression 'cook-book' to describe certain kinds of instruction in the last paragraph but one points readily to a further example. Cookery can certainly be taught in a liberal education sense since it properly comes into an understanding of nutrition, health and the properties of vegetable, animal and other materials when mixed, compounded and subjected in various ways to heat and liquids. Unfortunately it is by no means always taught in this kind of way but rather by the simple replication of given recipes with minimal understanding of what is going on. Successfully cooked products can, of course, be produced this way. What needs emphasizing is that it is understanding, not successfully cooked products, that is the proper aim of liberal education.

8.3 Teaching for understanding

Understanding does not always display itself quite so obviously as a cake, a meat pie or a neatly completed piece of needlework or woodwork. Perhaps more significantly, a failure to understand does not display itself so plainly as a burnt cake, uncooked meat in a pie, or uncompleted or botched needlework and woodwork. Even correctly solved mathematical problems, accurately replicated scientific experiments, correct answers to a teacher's questions and precisely recalled items of information do not *necessarily* indicate more understanding than their matched failures, or even any significant understanding at all.

The nature of understanding was discussed in 5.5. There it was claimed that all understanding involves the making in the mind of enlargements, sophistications and modifications of systems of relationships and linkages in some appropriately non-arbitrary and coherent way. From the methodological point of view it is necessary to enlarge somewhat on the two aspects of these systems of relationships only briefly referred to in 5.5.

The first aspect refers to the undoubted fact that understanding is paradigmatically a characteristic of *individual* minds. There are extensions of this idea: I can speak of the collective understanding of the government, the local education authority's understanding of the law on school attendance, or the present state of medical understanding of asthma. All these uses, however, are parasitic in the sense that unless *individual* members of the collective mentioned had individual understandings of these matters, the phrases would be meaningless. These phrases that sound as though there can be some kind of group understanding are simply shorthand expressions for individuals understanding something in the same way, or even sometimes simply agreeing to act *as if* their individual understandings were the same.

The fact that understanding has necessarily to be brought about in individual minds means that importance must be attached both to the state of understanding presently obtaining in the minds of individual pupils, which will of course vary from pupil to pupil, and the capacity to understand quickly or slowly, which will also vary from pupil to pupil. Whatever else is to be seen in the ideas of relating and linking there is no doubt that a linking must be made between what is to be understood and what is already understood by the pupil.

The second aspect refers to the kind of linkages or relationships to be made appropriately within whatever it is that is to be understood. To build, as it were, a word, an idea, a proposition, an object, into a relationship or a complex of relationships with other words, ideas, propositions, objects *is* to understand that word, idea, proposition or object.

Teachers are often aware of the significance of this second aspect of understanding, but not so much aware of the first. That is to say, teachers know that they must *explain* as clearly as possible when introducing new ideas or ideas thought to be new to the recipients: there must be a logical and connected framework of presentation; connections and links must be made plain; differences and similarities must be pointed out, and so on. What teachers often seem not to give so much importance to is the need to link all these relationships onto those already operating within the mind of a given pupil.

8.3.1 Explaining

Perhaps oddly, the word 'explanation' appears frequently in the indices of books on the philosophy of history, the physical and the social sciences but far less frequently in those of education, even of philosophy of education. For example, an Open University reader, 'Conceptions of Inquiry'[8], has over twenty-five references to 'explanation' in a book of 334 pages, whereas the 'Second Handbook of Research on Teaching'[9], unhelpfully, has one reference only, and that misnumbered, in a work of 1,400 pages.

The fact that there can exist 'explanations' of matters which can be deemed right or correct in some sense quite independent of any particular person's grasp of them, and which will be appropriately discussed under headings like scientific explanation, historical explanation or explanation in the social sciences, can lead to odd conclusions in the literature of pedagogy. For example, we find Thomas F. Green saying, in his generally very helpful book on 'The Activities of Teaching'[10]:

> It is an important fact, however, that whether an explanation is good or adequate can be decided without considering whether anyone learns from it. In other words it can be assessed independently of its consequences for learning. An explanation will be a good one if it accounts for what is to be explained. If it is well constructed and without logical faults, then it is a good explanation even when it is

not understood by anyone except its author . . . . Whether reasons are good or adequate to support a certain belief depends upon the logical properties of the relation between the belief and its reasons, and not on the psychological fact that someone happens to accept the reasons. Therefore, an explanation or demonstration of a certain belief may be a good explanation or demonstration even though, unfortunately, no one learns from it.[11]

Green, of course, is not foolish enough to consider that this is all there is to teaching. The teacher *must* be concerned to bring about learning and this involves, for Green, considerations of strategy as well as of logic.

Now there is certainly some truth in all this if we allow the meaning of 'explain' to be monopolized in the way used by the philosophers of science and history. But this is by no means the only justifiable way, as the 'OED' well demonstrates. The natural home of the concept of explaining does seem to be in the context of a person explaining to one or more other persons; and in *this* context an explanation could not be considered adequate unless grasped, understood, by the recipients. Rather, therefore, than thinking of an adequate explanation which is somehow not understood, like those successful operations where the patient nevertheless dies, it seems preferable to suppose an adequate explanation to satisfy two conditions: firstly, the coherence, consistency and logic internally manifested by the explanation in relation to what it seeks to explain; and, secondly, the satisfactory resolution in the mind of the recipient of the explanation of the puzzlement or lack of understanding which necessitated the explanation. In other words, the teacher as explainer needs to know both his subject and his pupil. Yet another way of considering this is that where a teacher explains something to a pupil there could be two appropriate judges of the adequacy of the explanation: one could be an expert authority on the subject, that is, on the logic of what is to be explained; and the other, importantly, must be the pupil himself, for only he can know, in one sense of 'understand', whether he has understood or not.

I say that in *one* sense of 'understand' the pupil is the only appropriate judge. This is the sense, given in 5.5, where 'understand' contrasts with 'not-understand'. It is in this sense that only the pupil knows whether he has established a meaningful pattern of relationships in his own mind about the object of the explanation, or not. There was, however, another sense of 'understand' given in 5.5 which contrasted with 'misunderstand'. In this sense what is important is whether the pattern of relationships formed in the pupil's mind is not only meaningful but correct. A constant complaint of lecturers, teachers and writers, is not so much that *no* sense is made of what they say and write, but that the wrong sense is made − not the sense they intended. In this

149

sense of 'understand' the pupil is *not* likely to be the best judge of his own understanding and some kind of assessment or judgment would have to be made by a teacher or other authority. It should be noted, however, that what constitutes a correct understanding is not equally clear across all areas of the curriculum.

It is not very helpful to the liberal educator to suppose, as Green does, that one side of this necessary symbiosis is a matter of logic whilst the other side, the satisfactory reception of the explanation, is only a matter of psychology and therefore of teacher strategy. That a pupil fails to grasp the excellently logical explanation of the teacher, always supposing the explanation given to be so, is not sufficiently accounted for by saying it is a psychological matter. On the account so far given we can suggest two ways in which the explanation might be inadequate in this respect. Firstly, the explanation relates in no significant way to the conceptual and propositional frameworks already present in the pupil's mind. There is nothing strange about this: if I have not been successfully introduced to the rudiments of algebra it will be very difficult for even an excellently clear exposition to explain quadratic equations to me in any direct sense. There will simply not be anything relevant in my mind onto which the explanation might latch. Secondly, even if the relevant and necessarily presupposed framework does exist in the pupil's mind there might nevertheless be a lack of concern, a lack of care about the enterprise of trying to understand further; or there might be a diversion of care and concern, previously devoted to the kind of understanding the teacher was trying to bring about, because other matters are now seen as more significant or overriding. It is the second of these two causes of inadequacy that raises the problems of motivation normally considered to be psychological and to call for appropriate teacher strategies for motivating pupils. I can think of little more frustrating to the pupil than to use the motivating techniques appropriate to the second of these difficulties when the problem is simply the first: in such a case the more successful are our motivating techniques the more frustrating will be the outcome, since the pupil will be all the more concerned to understand what he cannot without the necessary prior learning.

I shall discuss more fully problems of motivation in the next section, but one connected point, well raised by John Passmore[12], is properly placed here. I most genuinely and naturally seek explanations, seek to understand, when I am puzzled by something. This puzzlement can arise because of the frustration of my everyday endeavours not essentially connected with education, and John Dewey emphasized this connection between reflective thinking and the problem-solving necessitated by real endeavours and activities.[13] Passmore, however, makes the different but surely important point:

that a teacher will often need to get his pupils puzzled in order to teach them . . . .

In general, the unpuzzled child is a child who will understand very little. And there may be nothing in his environment, outside the schoolroom, to encourage him to be puzzled. Making him puzzled is the first, essential, step towards helping him to understand.[14]

A teacher seeking to teach for understanding, then, will need to:

(i) be aware of the state of the present understandings of individual pupils being taught;

(ii) have logically adequate understandings himself of what is being taught;

(iii) be a skilful explainer of what is being taught in that
    (a) he marshalls presentations logically and coherently, and
    (b) relates them well to individuals' present understandings;

(iv) be aware of areas of understanding where correctness matters and misunderstanding is possible, and know how to assess for correct understanding; and

(v) be able to generate puzzlement in the minds of pupils when it is not already there.

There is a little more to be said about point (v). In discussing this point Passmore uses the teaching of philosophy as an example to illustrate the necessity of puzzlement. Pupils, he says, often have to be helped to become puzzled about, say, the idea of democracy, before any analysis or discussion of the concept can be fruitful. This is certainly true; but there is another consequence of this truth that Passmore does not mention but most teachers of philosophy, especially philosophy of education, will have encountered, and which generalizes to all attempts to get pupils puzzled. It is this: to be puzzled is to realize the limits of my present understanding which is incapable of solving the problem, whatever it is. If this occurs in the pursuit of my own private activities or interest my failure to understand does not, or need not, affect my self-esteem, my respect for my own understanding. I can always change my interest to something more readily understandable. But if I am a pupil, and the teacher deliberately engenders puzzlement within me, where there was none before, whilst at the same time allowing me no escape from the particular activity, then whatever ultimately follows the immediate effect is likely to be a considerable deflation of my self-esteem. This harmful effect is made much worse if the subsequent explanations of the teacher, designed to clear the obstacle he himself has planted in my mind, patently fail to do so! I am now left:

(a) more confused than I was before, and

(b) more doubtful about my own capacity to understand than I was before.

Immanuel Kant recognized the problem a long time ago, and expressed his view of the moral duty of all who, like teachers, would try to correct the errors of others:

> Hereupon is founded a duty to respect man even in the logical use of his reason: not to censure someone's errors under the name of absurdity, inept judgment, and the like, but rather to suppose that in such an inept judgment there must be something true, and to seek it out. In doing so, one should at the same time expose the deceptive semblance (the subjectivity of the grounds determining the judgment, which were held by mistake to be objective), and thus, while accounting for the possibility of error, preserve the mistaken individual's respect for his own understanding.[15]

I conclude from all this, not that we should not try to get pupils puzzled about things as a necessary prelude to developing certain kinds of understanding, only that we should be careful how we do it. Anxiety produced by puzzlement can be motivational up to a point, but thereafter it becomes counter-productive and can destroy or seriously diminish the self-respect Kant properly urges us to value. If a pupil's respect for his own capacity to understand is lost, then so far as liberal education is concerned, *all* is lost.

I have argued elsewhere[16] that certain conclusions about teaching arrangements can be drawn at least in part from the points about understanding necessarily taking place in individual minds and the inescapable variance in abilities to understand quickly or slowly. I believe there to be arguments connected with these points, with the idea of equally valuing all pupils' self-esteem, and with certain ideas of social justice, that would favour a large amount of teaching in mixed-ability groups, but would also suggest that those subjects involving individual understanding and *not* essentially involving group activity should be taught mainly by individualized learning techniques. That is to say, they should be taught by methods allowing for individual variations in rates of understanding.

8.4 Teaching for care

To care about anything is to value it and to treat or respond to it in a way appropriate to its valued characteristics. Care manifestly involves attention and interest. Although care has an affective aspect in the person doing the caring, i.e. a *feeling* of valuing something, and is therefore to some extent subjective, the notion also implies an objective *appropriateness* of treatment or response. For example, to care about a gramophone record, whilst it involves handling it gently, trying to preserve its playing qualities by keeping it dust-free and unscratched, also involves playing it from time to time and enjoying its contents thus made audible. Merely to preserve the record, in an unplayed pristine state, would not really be to care for it or value it *as* a record. To care for literature implies that one actually attends to literature, reads books and poems, tries to find out more about the techniques of literature; and it also implies that one actually *wants* to do these things. To care for a person implies that one values that person as a rational agent and treats them accordingly, doing things that respect the person as a rational agent and enhance the person's own respect for themselves as a rational agent, and to want to do so. Of course such care also involves treating the person as a living being, seeking to maintain their physical comfort and well-being; but one might do as much for a pet cat or dog and real care for a *person* must involve more than that.

If all values were subjective the connection between education and caring would be necessarily limited. It might be possible to claim that there are certain things a pupil must do in order to know what he might choose to value or care about in the future, but there would be no case for trying to *get* pupils to care about anything save in the barest of instrumental ways. My argument has taken a different path and I have argued for the *objective* value of those understandings found to be significant in human collective development. Studying these things, I have argued, is demonstrably worthwhile – pupils *ought* to study them. If this is right then it also follows that pupils ought to come to care about these understandings, to share in their significance, to value them for themselves. The liberal educator on my account therefore has a difficult job. He has not only to get pupils to know, understand and be able to do certain things, but he has to get pupils to care about these knowings, understandings and doings.

This is not a new thought in education. Subjectivism and relativism have not always been so widely assumed in education as they are now, and the fact that the objective worthwhileness of what was being taught entailed getting pupils to care about the subject was the more general assumption of the past.[17] This was not always matched, unfortunately, by methods appropriate to generating care in pupils. This kind of concern for care all too often became transmogrified into excessive and pedantic obsession with carefulness, which often meant neatness and obedience to formal and sometimes pointlessly arbitrary prescriptions having no relationship to the real value of the subject or the learning. This kind of perverse misunderstanding is nicely caught by John Passmore in his excellent chapter on these matters:

153

There once used to be teachers of English composition who were mainly concerned that their pupils should draw neat red lines at the appropriate distance from the edge of the page and that the compositions they submitted should contain no cancellations. The pupil who wrote feebly went unrebuked, the pupil who crossed out a word to substitute a better word was the victim of his teacher's wrath. Such a teacher completely failed to appreciate — perhaps because he thought of himself as training ledger keepers — what sort of carefulness was his proper concern. Neatly ruled lines, tidy pages, are extrinsic forms of carefulness in relation to the writing of good English. The choice of the appropriate word, in contrast, is an intrinsic form of carefulness. The pupil who crossed out a word to substitute a better one was the *careful* student, the pupil who let the feebler word remain was the *careless* student.[18]

Passmore is not saying, of course, that neatness of presentation is not a justifiable virtue. The important point that I am making, and I think Passmore is too, is that to care for something is to attend to its *important* characteristics, its *valued* characteristics, its *truly characterizing* characteristics, with affective conscientiousness. One cannot, for example, be a good scholar without some concern for neatness and order, both in thought and presentation, but nevertheless these are but the instruments of scholarship, they are not what scholarship *is*.

8.4.1 *Caring about reason*

One of the great underlying types of caring that teachers must engender in their pupils, because it is presupposed in most other educational endeavours of a truly liberating kind, is caring about reason. It seems to me that little attention has been paid by educators to this necessity. R.S. Peters has often made the point, in counter to claims which polarize reason and feeling, that one can be passionate about reason. This is surely true: for some people reason *matters* and such people would suffer great agony of mind if they did not do what there was good reason to do, forbear where there was good reason to forbear, and believe only what there was good reason to believe. What is perhaps not so clear is that, sadly, for many people reason does *not* much matter. Such people believe and act in spite of all manner of reasons to the contrary which they can well see. They are impulsive and, to a large extent, driven by feelings and appetites. It is important to realize that such people are not necessarily unintelligent, uninformed or bad reasoners. Being good at reasoning and *caring* about reason are not the same thing. Perhaps the worst combination of all, from the point of view of one favouring liberal education in a rational society, is the person of sharp intellect and sophistic skill who nevertheless does not essentially care about reason in any other sense than as a tool for getting his or her own way.

Care for reason is a necessary presupposition of proper knowledge and understanding, and of moral action. A person who does not care about reason will not care about the necessity of evidence for beliefs, nor see the point of following a difficult argument, of attending to trains of consequences or of bothering much at all about problems of justification.

What is fully involved in this caring about reason has been well laid out by the American philosopher Brand Blanshard under the name of 'the rational temper', and it would be a diversion to enter into further description here.[19] Two more general points, however, must be made. Firstly, it must be noted that although it is sometimes assumed that the life of reason is today's dominant mode and a greater place is urged in education for emotion and feeling, it is very doubtful whether rationality really is dominant in either education or social life generally. My own impression is that the dominant tone in politics and advertising is one of appeal to feeling and emotion, and that this sets a tone that is ·increasingly pervasive. Selling, the really dominant influence of western society, is not a facilitator of reason. This is coupled with a prevailing subjectivism and relativism which exalts individual wishes and desires and is nothing whatsoever to do with the kind of rational autonomy urged here as an aim of liberal education. Reason, at least in its widest rather than in its purely instrumental sense, is on the defensive rather than being the establishment that needs shifting. Liberal educators should be defenders of the rational temper, trying to help their pupils care about reason in a social context by no means as conducive to that kind of caring as they, the liberal educators, might like.

The second point is that as far as I know empirical research does not help us very much on the problem of why it is that some people come to care about reason and others do not. It would be helpful to know more about the child-rearing antecedents of a concern for reason. The little that we do know, and reasonable hypothesizing, must serve us for the present. Since what we are talking about is an affective concern, i.e. it is not just a matter of knowing, being told, about the importance of reason but of feeling the concern, being compelled by the concern, then we cannot expect children in school to pick up this concern simply by having the importance of reason explained to them or pointed out to them. This will do no harm and is indeed necessary, but it is not sufficient − it will not by itself do the job. Presumably what must happen is that young people must see care for reason exemplified in the actions and talk of people already in some sense loved or respected. Ideally this will already have begun to happen in the relationship between children and parents, but realistically we know that this is not always the case. Teachers of young children therefore have a heavy responsibility to provide this exemplification. Their actions, routines, explanations, expectations and arrangements must *be* rational and justifiable in themselves and the fact that they are justifiable made clear wherever possible. This is not just a matter of talking reason to the child all the time, or demanding reasons from the child all the time, but rather a matter of providing an atmosphere in which concern for reason is patently at work and can be absorbed by those operating within it. The reason, consistency and coherence of what goes on, alongside the affection displayed by the adults, the teachers, should provide affective comfort and security for the young children, and should certainly not constitute a system of threats and challenges, though there might be room for some of that later on when the care for reason has already become part of the pupil's make-up.

The idea that the teacher, as a liberal educator, should act as a respecter of reason should continue throughout education of course; but as the age of the pupil increases it will not only be a matter of how the teacher does his or her own teaching, explaining and arranging, but also of what steps are taken to positively engender a concern for reason in the pupil. Again, in the absence of empirical research we must suggest reasonable hypotheses. If reason is to be respected the pupil's attempts at reasoning must be respected by the teacher and Kant's injunction about the correcting of error, previously mentioned, must be taken seriously. When I say that the pupil's attempts at reasoning must be respected this does not mean necessarily that they must be subject to extrinsic rewards, for there are dangers in that direction, too, whereby the care is directed to gaining the reward and away from a proper concern for reason itself.

It is also reasonable to suppose that we should avoid institutional arrangements which suggest that real reasoning is only expected of some, in the higher sets or streams, and something involving less reasoning is expected of others. We should also avoid the distinction, sometimes made, between those who are to be valued as reasoners and those who are to be valued as something other than this — games player, athlete or skilled woodworker. The reason here is not only that in practice this distinction is very difficult to make since reason always enters into these other activities, but rather that reason cannot be compared with other things in quite this way. To make someone lose his respect for his own reason is to devalue him as a person, diminish his self-esteem, in a way that is much more fundamental than letting someone see that she is not a very good hockey player or cook. These ideas point to the general desirability again of mixed-ability groupings in school and to individualized learning techniques, though they are not, of course, the only considerations in deciding those matters.

8.4.2 Caring about others

There are a number of reasons why the liberal educator should be concerned to engender in pupils care for other persons. In the first place, and most straightforwardly, I have already argued that morality is one of the great human practices that pupils should be introduced to as part of a liberal education. I have also argued, however, that the involvement of the pupil in all the human practices that are the concern of the liberal educator is to be mainly about understanding those practices, and not necessarily about training within them; and in my criticism of Hirst I said that his account of moral education was peculiar because he excluded any kind of character development or moral training from a liberal education whilst including it in a more widely interpreted general education. If I now argue, as I shall, that liberal educators should positively seek to bring about in their pupils an active morality which must involve care and concern for others, then I could be open to the very criticism that I made of Hirst, namely, that something extra is being added to the content of a liberal education that is not justified in the general argument.

The justification for getting pupils to care about others is therefore more complex than the first simple reason that we have already included morality in the content, though that remains a part of the justification, if only for the reason that a proper understanding of morality, as Hare has claimed, does appear contradictory to the non-practice of morality.[20] One who cares for reason, therefore, and has come to understand morality, should care for others.

A second reason is an instrumental one, though not, I believe, a simple example of this genre of reasons. The disposition to cooperate with others was listed in 7.4 as one of the necessary dispositions counting as a serving competency. The point here is that it is difficult to see how anyone not prepared to cooperate with others in any sense could be liberally educated. The matter goes further than this because it is not just a matter of cooperating with *any* others, one's friends and playmates for example, but with *certain* others, teachers and fellow-pupils, from whom specific educational experiences can be gained. This looks like a concern for others simply because they can help you — a matter of prudence rather than morality. Such concern would be justifiable, of course, even if it is at the level of prudence. If I want someone genuinely to help me I must attend to him, consider his wishes, respect him and so on. The nature of concern for others, or respect for others, in a liberal education, is far more complex than this, however.

157

I want to claim that the respect for reason, without which liberal education is impossible, and without which one cannot enter into a justification of liberal education, or anything else for that matter, also implies respecting, caring for, those who are the only founts or origins or living embodiments of reason, namely persons. There is thus a network of concepts centred on the concept of a person in which ideas like reason, justification, liberally educating, caring, respecting and understanding all find a mutually supporting place. Thus when I say that you cannot properly liberally educate a person unless you get them to care about reason, and to care about other persons, it must be interpreted at a level more profound than that of mere instrumentality. It is saying something more like: reason and care, or reason and respect for persons, are necessary presuppositions of the idea of a liberal education. It cuts both ways: you are not properly liberally educating if you are not engendering care for reason and for others; but you cannot justify liberal education unless care for reason and care for others are presupposed. If that sounds contradictory it is only because the care for reason and others must already exist in the *adults*, who then make sure that it is engendered in the *young*.

Caring, I said at the start of this section on teaching for care, implies an objective appropriateness of treatment or response as well as an affective feeling or disposition of valuing. In the case of caring for persons this primarily involves the treatment of others as rational, autonomous agents having individual purposes and concerns. I must not treat others simply as instruments to my ends, but as autonomous agents in relationship with me. It is important to note some of the cruder deviations from this idea of the appropriateness of treatment in respect for persons. The aged, for example, are not really being respected as persons, cared for appropriately, if we rush to take away from them all kinds of decision-making and responsibility as soon as things become physically difficult for them. All too often physical existence is prolonged at the cost of a far too early destruction of real personhood. More relevant to our present concerns, children are not being respected or helped to develop as persons by being kept in a prolonged state of dependence on their parents and teachers. Here it is not so much physical dependence that is meant, but the kind of intellectual and moral dependence brought about by non-evidential teaching and by emphasis on moral conformity or heteronomy. Helping children to reason, helping them to become autonomous, helping them to retain self-esteem and respect for their own reasoning and understanding are all ways of caring for and respecting pupils.

Now this, to the careful reader, could seem like another slip in the argument. We were talking about teaching *for* care — i.e. about how to get *pupils* to care about reason and others — now we seem to be

talking about teaching *with* care and respect for pupils. The two, however, are not separable. As with care for reason it is difficult to see how
a child will develop care for others unless he grows up perceiving care
and respect manifested to him. As with care for reason nothing can be
much more destructive than a failure on the part of parents and
teachers to practise what is preached. 'Do as I say and not as I do,'
will not work as an admonition because what is to be taught here is
an affective concern – not rules of procedure. What is necessary in the
engendering of care for others has been indicated by empirical research
rather more than in the case of care for reason. I have tried to review
some of this research elsewhere[21] and a detailed account would be
inappropriate here. The conclusions that follow from this kind of work,
however, do tend to confirm what might be expected from reflection
on the nature of the characteristics and dispositions being aimed at.
The development of concern for reason and for others seems to be
dependent upon the following:

   (i) A loving and trusting relationship between the child and at least
       one, but more helpfully some, of the adults encountered in early
       life.
  (ii) The weaning away of the child, by these adults, from sensory
       dominance.
 (iii) The use of what Martin Hoffman[22] calls inductive discipline
       techniques – that is to say, discipline techniques that are firm,
       consistent and coherent and involve much explanation and the
       use of talk.
  (iv) The use of explanations which involve attention to the effects
       of one's actions on other persons, as well as on things and on
       oneself.
   (v) The use of problem-solving approaches, accounting for situations
       and happenings in terms of causes and reasons.

Much stress is laid by some researchers (cf. Hoffman) on the complex
relationship between what is cognitive and what is affective in the
development of these concerns, the important point being that either
is of little use without the other. Point (iv) on the above list is important here. The theoretical model would be something like this: the
adult, either parent or teacher of the young child, needs to have a warm
'nurturant' relationship with the child or there will be no saliency
in anything done or said by the adult. Given the warm relationship
and the consequent saliency then it is important that disciplinary
procedures, explanations and utterances are cognitively coherent,
rational and genuinely explanatory. Both the saliency and the cognitive
coherence of explanations and admonitions are advanced if explanations involve considerations of consequences for other persons: the

saliency because of a natural empathy with other persons, and the cognitive coherence because of the proper inclusion of persons, *other* persons, in the frame of reference.

At the school level, if all this is right, then educators of young children particularly would need to follow these suggestions in their methods of teaching and in their school and classroom arrangements. Although the affective basis of caring about others is probably laid in the early years: pre-school, nursery, infant and early junior school, the necessity of teaching for caring for others continues throughout schooling. In these later stages, however, the methods will be involved more directly and cognitively in the way the humanities are taught. Here, as described earlier, we are directly concerned with knowledge and understanding of the world of persons and their relationships. Here, again, it is difficult to see how the content and methodology could really be separated. To be properly motivated to care and respect others one needs to know and to understand a great deal about persons, their characteristics and their actual and possible relationships, and also to come to understand reasons for caring for and respecting others at the level of principle. This is very different from simply being conditioned in some way to care for others, if that were possible, and the child-rearing practices suggested by Hoffman, Klein and others[23] should not be seen in that light. The objective is getting pupils to care for others because they come to see that as the rational thing to do, and because they have also come to care about doing and believing what it is rational to do and believe. Thus getting children to care about reason and getting them to care about others, about persons, are intertwined, mutually supportive and necessarily related objectives at the heart of a liberal education.

8.5 Summary

This chapter on the methods of a liberal education has not been about the lesson-by-lesson techniques of liberal education. That kind of detail, though important, would be inappropriate in a work of the general nature of this one. Nevertheless I have tried to show the falsity of the claim, sometimes heard, that whilst considerations of a philosophical kind might have something to say about the *content* of an education, these have nothing to do with the *methods of teaching*, which are simply practical considerations informed perhaps by the work of psychologists. This claim is false, I have argued, because there are necessary connections between the way a liberal education and its content is characterized and justified, and the justification of the methods, strategies and intentions of those teaching it. In other words there are certain teaching methods, strategies and intentions that are appropriate to a liberal education, and there are certain others, no doubt efficient for some purposes, that are inappropriate for a liberal education and would act against such an education. I have argued that the methods of liberal education should involve evidential teaching, that is, getting pupils to hold beliefs because they, the pupils, come to see and grasp the reasons for holding such beliefs, and not merely because textbooks or teachers say the beliefs are true. I have argued that liberal educators should try to bring about understanding on the part of their pupils, where understanding is conceived of as a coherent and consistent body of relationships entering into and amending the body of relationships already existing in the mind of the pupil. I have briefly discussed some teaching approaches that would act against both of these ideals, namely, indoctrination conceived of as non-evidential teaching; propaganda conceived of as lack of concern for what is justifiable; a narrow conception of training which emphasized mere skill in performance as against a real understanding of what one was doing and why; and meaningless rote learning of isolated facts with no regard for the mental structure or conceptual and propositional framework in which such facts were to be located in the mind of the pupil.

In addition to all this, which makes great demands on the skill and sensitivity of liberal educators, I have suggested that such educators have to teach so as to bring about certain kinds of dispositions to care on the part of their pupils. Such dispositions broadly involve coming to care about worthwhile studies in their own right and not merely instrumentally. I have also suggested that the whole liberal education enterprise, at least as characterized in this work, necessitates pupils being helped to care about reason and to care about persons — themselves as persons and others as persons. I have tried to show, in very general terms, what might be involved in getting young persons to develop this kind of caring, and I have also drawn attention to the relative paucity of empirical research in this area.

Challenges to Liberal Education   part III

Introduction to part III

The account of liberal education so far given is, of course, a particular view of what should constitute the basis of the compulsory and universal education provided by a state for its young citizens at least up to the age of 16. It is possible to find completely different views of what the basis of such an education should be; and it is possible to find sociological and political analyses of the place of education in a capitalist liberal democratic state that would point to the impossibility, impracticability or even the undesirability of successfully initiating and sustaining the kind of liberal education programme that I have outlined.

These alternative views constitute, as it were, challenges to the idea of a liberal education that I am proposing and must therefore be considered, however briefly, in order to face the possible charge of failing to appreciate the threat that they constitute to ideas of a liberal education. These challenges are not from a single political direction, nor are they always very clearly articulated, though they sometimes are. Some of them present additional difficulties in that their particular challenges are rooted in complex bodies of social and political theory — Marxism, for example — in which conflicting theoretical factions engage with one another within a rule and semantic structure which is not obvious to an outsider without considerable study. One characteristic that these views have in common, despite their political and other differences, is that they turn into action through a process of simplification. That is to say, although at an academic level the theoretical nature of the view might be complex, subtle, and penetrated with arguments as to its correct interpretation, its appearance in the thought and action of a teacher on the job, or of a parent or education policy-maker, will often take a more stark and usually unqualified form. For example, complicated theories about the way in which ideologies penetrate and influence the education system become filtered into simplistic utterances like:

This isn't a school! It's a place where those kids can find out once

163

and for all what they're up against, where the ruling class says in no uncertain terms to them, 'Forget you! You ain't going nowhere! Go on and learn to tap-dance or be a jitney girl, because you ain't going nowhere!'[1]

These are words from a fictional character in a novel, but Young and Whitty suggest that most large comprehensive schools would have at least one representative of such a view on the staff. They probably exaggerate, but they provide a good example of what I mean. Similarly, and on the other side, as it were, difficult analyses of the relationship between the provision and control of education services and the economic well-being of a country can result in simplistic claims that state education should be largely instrumental, producing amenable and potentially skilful workers and consumers with a favourable view of wealth-creation, technological growth and the particular forms of political and economic management obtaining in the state.

Recent statements from the Department of Education and Science and from Her Majesty's Inspectors in England and Wales attempt to assert a view of the curriculum in which the personal development of the pupil is balanced in some way against what is often called 'the needs of society'. This straddles and confuses the issues of justification raised in earlier chapters of this work and supposes that 'the needs of society' are easily discernible and non-controversial. These statements, important because increasingly they articulate the intentions of government, lack any clear argument or support for the liberal education case and therefore leave the ground relatively uncontested for the powerful instrumental pressures to have their way.

I intend to discuss three aspects of these challenges to the idea of a liberal education laid out in this book so far. Firstly, I shall discuss the modern form of the utilitarian challenge. Secondly, I shall look at a sociological view of the nature of knowledge that would seriously question any kind of objective statement about the universal value of certain kinds of knowledge and understanding. Thirdly, I shall discuss the view, mainly Marxist, that in a capitalist state education can be no more than the reproduction of the ideology that capitalism generates for its own survival. It is suggested that these three challenges raise issues of increasing complexity and theoretical significance as we proceed from the first to the third. They also deal with increasing degrees of what one might call 'hiddenness' as we proceed in the same direction, in the sense that arguments supporting utilitarian aims for education are often quite overt, whereas the forces of ideology, by their very nature, are not.

It is perhaps necessary to make some disclaimers about this selection of challenges. I am not, for example, saying that they are logically exclusive of one another; in fact they have a good deal of interconnection with one another, but nevertheless present conveniently separable foci of treatment. Neither, of course, is this an exhaustive list of challenges, only my judgment of some important ones. Each of the challenges has already generated a considerable literature of its own, and this might make the treatment of them here seem an exercise of supererogation (if the critic is kind) or an exercise of arrogant and presumptuous superfluity (where the critic is more harsh). It seems necessary to me, however, to treat these challenges from the particular point of view of their relationship to the offered view of a liberal education. For the finer points of dispute within each of these challenges, and they are many, I must refer the reader to the references and notes.

It should be clear from what has already been written and argued that the word 'liberal' in my phrase 'liberal and general education', whilst it cannot avoid all political connotation, is not intended to have either the very direct association with any political party that includes the word 'liberal' in its title, or to be simply associated with what might be called western liberalism as against conservatism or socialism or whatever. Actual governments, of all political views, have done some things conducive to a liberal education and many things inimical to it. No political party that I know of stands overtly for or overtly against the kind of liberal education I am arguing for. The issue is nothing like as simple as that. What is to be argued is that in so far as any political view is supposed by its supporters to be rationally justifiable, then it should necessarily include liberal education in its programme; but that is likely to be somewhat cryptic without the argument of the next three chapters.

9   The challenge of economic utility

9.1 The challenge sketched

The view under consideration here takes either a purely instrumental view of education or places so much importance on the instrumental view as to seriously play down any liberal education element even when some form of balance between the two is being nominally advocated. The view has often been tacit or implicit, revealing itself most often in the criteria apparent in criticisms of the alleged shortcomings of the educational system or of its lack of relevance. For a pupil to complain that his education is not relevant to the job he wants to do, or fails to equip him to face unemployment, is to assume that education has a proper instrumental purpose that it has failed to fulfil. For a prime minister to chide the system for failing to produce the scientists and technologists the country needs is to assume that the education system has manpower provision responsibilities that it is neglecting. For a politician to complain that the education system allows pupils to leave school with unfavourable attitudes towards wealth-creation or technological growth or competition, is to suggest that there are proper attitudes for an education system to foster.[1]

In recent years, however, the demand for at least a strong instrumental element in the curriculum of secondary education has become more overt, especially from government agencies and from employers or from institutions that speak for employers. This is so much the case that a recent HMI discussion paper on teacher training could open with the statement:[2]

> It has in recent years become 'a truth universally acknowledged'
> that education should be more closely linked with the world of
> work and with the country's economic performance; and there has
> been increasing pressure on schools to assess the relevance of their
> curriculum to their pupils' future working lives.

In particular the HMI document is arguing for a revised view of teacher training. Whilst acknowledging that teachers need to instil in pupils a sound basic education and an ability to work with others, and that they need as a first priority to be able to teach their subjects well, the HMIs nevertheless go on to say:[3]

> Initial training institutions should also make positive efforts to ensure that future teachers understand the part that their subject plays in the economic and cultural life of their society, and that they have sufficient understanding on the economic foundations of that society, and the role of industry and commerce in wealth creation, to be able to pass on to their pupils both information about and respect for industrial and commercial activity.

Presumably the inculcation of respect is not seen here as indoctrinatory because of a surprisingly naive view of the value of industrial and commercial activity being non-controversial. This continues a trend developed in earlier documents. For example, a consultative document produced by the Secretary of State for Education and Science and the Secretary of State for Wales in 1977 was able to assert that an aim of schools that 'the majority of people would probably agree with' was 'to help children to appreciate how the nation earns and maintains its standard of living and properly to esteem the essential role of industry and commerce in this process'.[4] Admittedly this was only offered as one aim among eight which included aims like:

> to help children develop lively, enquiring minds; giving them the ability to question and to argue rationally, and to apply themselves to tasks;
> to instil respect for moral values, for other people and for oneself, and tolerance of other races, religions and ways of life;
> to help children understand the world in which we live, and the interdependence of nations;
> to help children use language effectively and imaginatively in reading, writing and speaking.[5]

These aims, with perhaps some qualification, are not necessarily incompatible with the aims of a liberal education. The issue is really one of emphasis: 'understanding' the economic and political structures of a country leaves open the possibility of differing critical perspectives, whereas 'respecting', 'properly to esteem' and 'appreciating' all have a normative tone indicating a clearly and overtly instrumental purpose antithetical to the idea of a liberal education.

The desire for schools to exercise an overtly utilitarian function is seen differently by parents and pupils on the one hand and by politicians and employers on the other. Parents and pupils expect schools to prepare pupils for jobs, for what the Secretaries of State refer to as working life. Politicians and employers tend to think more in terms of international or inter-firm competitiveness:

Underlying all this was the feeling that the education system was out of touch with the fundamental need for Britain to survive economically in a highly competitive world through the efficiency of its industry and commerce.[6]

In either case the view of the proper purpose of schooling as instrumental is clear, and given much more emphasis than other purposes, even though these other purposes might be adumbrated.

In documents that have followed 'Education in Schools' the tension between a broadly liberal view (generally more espoused by HMIs) and a stronger emphasis on utilitarian views (generally more espoused by the DES and by politicians) has become more marked. Two documents appearing in 1980 indicate the difference of emphasis, though it should be noted that on matters like the desirability of a compulsory core of curriculum elements there was much more overlap. A statement entitled 'A Framework for the School Curriculum', by two new Secretaries of State, after arguing for a wide range of curriculum elements continued the earlier theme:

> substantial attention should be given at the secondary stage to the relationship between school work and preparation for working life. Pupils need to acquire an understanding of the economic basis of society and how wealth is created. Close links between the schools and local industry and commerce are valuable in this context, but also have wider benefits. Particular attention should be given to the place of careers education and guidance for all pupils, including the most able and those in the sixth form . . . . Systematic careers education should begin not later than the third secondary year, and it is normally desirable that it should occupy a specific place in the timetable.[7]

The other 1980 document, however, produced by HMIs and entitled 'A View of the Curriculum', seemed much more cautious and liberal on the point of career anticipation:

> The capacity of young people to profit from whatever opportunities may be available to them beyond 16 will depend heavily on the education they have experienced up to that point. Awareness of this is an important responsibility for all concerned with the 11-16 curriculum. On the other hand, an excessively instrumental view of the compulsory period of education runs the risk of actually reducing pupils' opportunity at a later stage, by requiring premature assumptions about their likely futures — for example in highly specific occupational terms — and by narrowing the educational base on which their potential may be developed.[8]

169

Two further relevant documents appearing in 1981 continued the official discussion on curriculum matters. The Secretaries of State produced a definitive view on the matter in 'The School Curriculum', which was followed later in the year by Circular 6/81 enjoining local education authorities in England and Wales, and school governors 'to encourage their schools, within the resources available, to develop their curricula in the light of what is said in *The School Curriculum*', and claiming that: 'These views will be reflected in the Government's policies which bear on the school curriculum.'[9] 'The School Curriculum' is thus an important statement likely to influence the curriculum of schools in England and Wales for some time to come, and is worth noting in some detail. The document undoubtedly maintains but also extends and enhances the utilitarian emphasis in a number of ways. To start with the list of aims set out in 'Education in Schools' has become altered in a number of small but indicative particulars.[10] The aim of helping children to appreciate and esteem the essential role of industry and commerce has now become conflated with another aim 'to help pupils to acquire knowledge and skills relevant to adult life and employment in a fast changing world'. Language, which was in the earlier document to be used effectively and *imaginatively*, is now conjoined with number and is only to be used effectively! An early aim, 'To teach children about human achievement and aspirations in the arts and sciences, in religion, and in the search for a more just social order', is reduced to 'to help pupils to appreciate human achievements and aspirations'. Physical skills are added to those tasks that children might properly be helped to apply themselves to. These changes are slight, hardly to be noted on a first reading, and only noteworthy because they are all in the direction of sharpening up the instrumental style and because they are unargued. What is left out is imagination and social concern; what is added is further talk of effective and instrumental skills. The emphasis is even more stark in the pages dealing specifically with the secondary school curriculum. This starts with three propositions about the secondary curriculum: firstly, that it should be planned as a whole; secondly, that it should have a common core; and thirdly, that:

> education needs to equip young people fully for adult and working life in a world which is changing very rapidly indeed, particularly in consequence of new technological developments: they must be able to see where their education has meaning outside the school.[11]

No emphasis whatsoever on any humane or liberal aims of education is given in these guiding propositions, nor is this at all evident in what follows. What is to be valued is indicated in the following portmanteau of assertions:

Although choices are made, and have to be made, at the end of the third year, every pupil up to 16 should sustain a broad curriculum. The level, content and emphasis of work will be related to pupils' abilities and aspirations, but there should be substantial common elements. These should include English and mathematics, whose vital importance schools already recognize in the time and attention they devote to them. To these should be added science, religious education and physical education: in addition pupils should undertake some study of the humanities designed to yield lasting benefit and should retain opportunities for some practical and some aesthetic activity. Most pupils should study a modern language, and many should continue to do so through the whole five year period.[12]

Of marked significance here is the brief reference to the humanities, the significance deriving from the fact that this is the *only* reference to the humanities in the document. This is to be compared with a page on science, over a page on modern languages and substantial paragraphs on mathematics, micro-electronics and craft, design and technology. A long section on preparation for adult life, which *might* have been about morality and knowledge and understanding of persons and personal relationships, in fact reasserts the by now well-worn claim that:

the curriculum needs to include some applied and practical work, particularly in science and mathematics; and pupils need to be given a better understanding of the economic base of our society and the importance to Britain of the wealth creating process[13]

and goes on to advocate better and more systematic careers education and guidance. A section on English, although mentioning the word 'literature', nevertheless treats the subject as essentially to do with instrumental skills and says nothing about literature as an insight into the imaginative understanding of the world of persons.

The whole style of this important official document is an interesting but ambiguous blend of the overt and covert advocacy of the utilitarian purposes of education in the service of a particular view of the relationship between society, education and the state. The deeper and more profound mechanisms that might be operating here must await our discussion of ideology whilst we consider some further relatively overt expressions.

The other 1981 document was produced by the Schools Council and its title, 'The Practical Curriculum',[14] was perhaps unfortunate. Such a title looks as if the matter to be considered is activities like physical education, woodwork and cookery. This would be a complete misunderstanding since the work aims to discuss the whole curriculum in a practical way! The kind of curriculum advocated here is, in fact, a highly liberal one and makes little reference to the needs of society, industry and commerce so dominant in the other documents I have considered, though it does get carried away with skills talk, as I shall show.

My point so far has not been to describe these documents in detail, but only to indicate my view that there is an articulation in government statements of a specifically instrumental view of education, revealed as much by the assumptions, implications and omissions as by the more explicit utterances. It is also interesting, and perhaps encouraging, to note that where HMIs, academics and teachers themselves have produced statements ('A View of the Curriculum', 'The Practical Curriculum' and 'Curriculum 11-16', DES, HMI Working Papers, London, HMSO, 1977) the tone has been markedly more liberal. Social historians can sometimes have a happy and interesting time tracing the lines of development leading to these differences.

Another way in which recent successive governments have set up mechanisms for the penetration of schooling by a specifically instrumental view of education is to be seen in the growth and influence of the Manpower Services Commission, and especially of its Training Services Division and Special Programmes Division. These divisions of the MSC have been mainly concerned with providing industrial training schemes for young people in the 16-19-year-old age range, partly because of a declining provision of such training by industrial organizations themselves, and then increasingly because of sharply rising unemployment among young people and the difficulty of finding jobs on leaving school. Even to provide vocational training for some 16-year-olds while others of the same age were receiving a different kind of education in school threatened the continuation of comprehensive liberal education beyond the age of 16; but very recent statements have indicated an attempt to move vocational education down to the age of 14, and even to set up special schools under MSC funding if the local education authorities in England and Wales failed to make provision. The *Times Educational Supplement* reported:

> The Government wants courses to be mounted for pupils in a wide range of ability. It is not prescribing the content, or whether the courses should be provided wholly in schools or in a combination of schools and colleges. But it insists that they should lead to a recognized qualification in technical, computer or business studies, or in the manual trades.[15]

Resisting the charge that he wants to narrow down the curriculum for the non-academic pupil the chairman of the MSC, Mr David Young, a property banker, claims that his aims are just the opposite and not so different from those being put forward by such innovators as the Further Education Curriculum Development Unit. These claims are not very reassuring to liberal educators on two counts. Firstly, the published work of the Further Education Unit can hardly be said to be liberal. The influential document, 'A Basis for Choice',[16] which proposed a programme for post-16 pre-employment courses suggested that such courses should include (i) core studies, (ii) vocational studies relevant to a given sector of employment, i.e. 'building and construction' or 'hotel and catering', and (iii) job specific studies. The only one of these offering any promise of continued liberal education would seem to be core studies, but the listing of the components of such a core soon brings disappointment to anybody with such expectations:

The core as a whole should provide opportunities for the young people to develop:

— practical numeracy
— the ability to communicate
— the ability to learn from study, experience and colleagues
— social skills and understanding in a variety of contexts
— self-confidence, self-awareness and adaptability
— a variety of manipulative skills and physical skills
— their awareness of various technological, environmental, political, economic and aesthetic factors which affect their lives
— a basis from which to make informed and realistic career choices

and it should do this in (the) context of their intention to enter the world of work in the near future.[17]

It is the direct relationship to vocation that is supposed to provide the motivation for these students that courses in their ordinary education at school had allegedly failed to provide. There is, of course, something in this, but only if the training is for a job that one has at least some reasonable chance of actually doing on the completion of the training. Without that assurance the very rationale of vocational preparation and its connection with motivation surely collapses.

A large amount of the material from the Further Education Unit is orientated towards a skill training approach which appears in its turn to be heavily influenced by behavioural objectives thinking much debated in educational circles throughout the 1970s. Those supporting a behavioural objectives view believe that teaching and learning objectives are only meaningful if they are expressed in terms of directly observable performance or behaviour. It is significant that educators on the whole have been critical of this view, seeing it as limiting and restricting, while trainers of various kinds have tended to espouse the view.[18] Examples of the transfer of understandings into skills can be seen in the following from an FEU publication on 'Vocational Preparation' where it is suggested that understanding society can be assessed in these performance achievements:

— has examined what is at stake in a given issue, the vested interests and the decision-making procedures involved
— has experienced membership of a decision-making group and has observed a decision-making group in action
— has developed background knowledge necessary for general understanding of national and local government
— has identified personal legal rights, with use of reference books where appropriate, and knows how to act on them.[19]

The narrow utility tone here is obvious. These items have little to do with any genuine or profound understanding of society and certainly do not constitute a refutation of charges of narrowness. The message throughout this and other FEU documents is that a reduction of knowledge and understanding to skills is to be favoured, that function-related learning is to provide motivation, and that the important functions to provide this motivation are to be work-related ones.

The second count on which the chairman of the MSC fails to reassure a liberal educator about charges of narrowness is that we have already seen censorship of courses where there have been attempts really to develop the critical power of the students, especially where that critical power was turned onto a consideration of the unemployment position of the students or onto the nature of the courses themselves. A report in the 'Times Educational Supplement' tells us:

> The MSC district officials have been told to ensure that everyone running a YOP project understands that political education must be limited to studying and discussing institutions like Parliament and the trade unions . . . . Particular care should be taken to avoid politically and generally controversial content in any literature produced for publication by trainees.[20]

Again, later, the same reporter noted:

> Mr Philip Whitehead, a Labour education spokesman, this week confirmed claims by a Lancashire youth service team that the Manpower Services Commission had closed down its Youth Opportunities Programme Course because trainees had produced a report criticizing the programme. It was clear that the Commission was now using rules designed to avoid party indoctrination of YOP youngsters to repress the expression of the youngsters' own views on their plight.[21]

174

The important points to note here are that powerful forces, some of them governmental, are being increasingly influential in imposing a utilitarian form on the education, firstly of certain groups of 16-18-year-olds, but now of widening groups of 14-16-year-olds still within the period of compulsory education; and that in the case of the Manpower Services Commission considerable funds are being made available for this purpose over and above the funds available to the education service generally.

Two more examples of the utilitarian challenge and pressure are worthy of note before turning to more specific criticism of this particular challenge. The first of these is interesting because of the characterization of the intellectually educated person that is given, and the way in which this is opposed to a honorific description of the creative person of action and decision. The challenge comes from the Royal Society of Arts and is supported by a very large number of eminent people including, not surprisingly, David Young, chairman of the MSC. The Society is promoting what it calls Education for Capability by large notices in the educational press and by granting its recognition, and sometimes small financial grants, to institutions running courses which it favours. The manifesto of Education for Capability contains the following:

> There is a serious imbalance in Britain today in the full process which is described by the two words 'education' and 'training'. The idea of the 'educated person' is that of a scholarly individual who has been neither educated nor trained to exercise useful skills; who is able to understand but not to act. . . .
>
> This imbalance is harmful to individuals, to industry and to society. A well balanced education should, of course, embrace analysis and the acquisition of knowledge. But it must also include the exercise of creative skills, the competence to undertake and complete tasks and the ability to cope with everyday life; and also doing all these things in cooperation with others.
>
> There exists in its own right a culture which is concerned with doing, making and organising and the creative arts. The culture emphasizes the day to day management of affairs, the formulation and solution of problems and the design, manufacture and marketing of goods and services.
>
> Educators should spend more time preparing people in this way for a life outside the education system. The country would benefit significantly in economic terms from what is here described as Education for Capability.[22]

Mentioning the RSA promotion here is solely for the purpose of illustrating yet further the pressures towards instrumentality in education.

One must note in passing, however, the polemical and rhetorical style which takes the place of argument in the above statement. The idea of an 'educated person' given here is surely a caricature; the idea of the creative mind, firmly located in a liberal education by most of its exponents, is here monopolized in the service of utility and deprived of the status of an *end* in its own right; and pointless functionalism is lauded with no consideration of the ends to which it is to be directed. The kind of creativity that is here valued is technological and managerial or entrepreneurial, not the creativity of art, music, literature or drama. Understanding is disassociated from acting as though these are two different things. All human agents act, for that is what it is to be an agent; but whether a person acts out of a coherent framework of understanding or not will be determined by the extent of his or her liberal education, by the extent of what Richard Peters has called the person's cognitive perspective. Understanding the practices of mankind *must* include, among other things, understanding the necessity and desirability of appropriate action, whether that appropriateness comes from technical, prudential or moral considerations. Capability can not be judged humanistically outside a framework of liberal understanding, save in the perverted sense that Hitler, Stalin and Genghis Khan were very capable men.

The eminent signatories to the RSA statement include people from industry and commerce as well as others from the academic world. Industry and commerce have their own pressure groups, notably the organization known as Understanding British Industry, sponsored by the CBI, and working actively with teachers and teacher-trainers to propagate views with which we are now familiar: the desirability and necessity of wealth creation, the need for pupils not only to understand industry but to be favourably disposed towards it, the need to accept the inevitability of technological growth and adapt to it, the need to develop in pupils the attitudes and personality traits that will help the nation in its competitive economic struggle, and the need to adapt the education system to these ends rather than to the ends of liberal education which are characterized as narrow, academic, abstract and not suitable for the majority.

All of this, and much else like it from individual parents and employers that is more difficult to document but exists powerfully nevertheless, adds up to a pressure upon educators that is as strong and pervasive as it is unsubtle. I say 'unsubtle' partly because the assertions have become steadily more explicit and overt, and partly to distinguish this kind of challenge from the more theoretical material of the next chapter. What is going on here contains an ideology — of that there is no doubt — but it is not a debate *about* ideologies in the sense that the participants recognize it as that. It may be a clash of ideologies of a kind yet to be discussed; but the assertions are categorically made, and it is worth some attempt to counter them from the point of view of liberal education in a similarly categorical way, before entering deeper waters.

9.2 Criticism of the economic utility challenge

9.2.1 The assumptions of non-controversiality

Running through all the discussions of the economic utility model of education, as I shall now call the collectivity of views I have just been exampling, is an unspoken assumption of consensus about society, values and education. The assumed consensus is that of continually accepted technological change and development, strangely related to nineteenth-century conceptions of the undoubted good of 'progress', all taking place in the context of a competitive free market economy, and in a wider context of international competitive trade. Also assumed is the undeniable value of wealth creation, ostensibly as a necessary condition of all else that might be valued, but in fact by its emphasis seen as a valued end in itself. Education, in this model, becomes a commodity both for the individual person and for society as a whole, to be assessed like any other commodity in terms of its profitability or usefulness. The education favoured for the individual is one leading to a well-paid job; for the employer it is one producing well-disposed and capable workers and potential managers; and for the state it is one making the country strong in economic competitive power and united around simple ideas of patriotism. Some of these views are explicit in what I have been describing, but most of them are implied or taken for granted. Such a framework of assumed consensus is necessary to give coherence to all the claims and pressures.

That such a consensus exists as anything more concrete than an assumption or necessary presupposition is highly questionable. The value of continued technological growth, especially when dictated and operated by a profit mechanism, is challenged by many people. Not only does such a challenge come from the expected people: ecologists, conservationists and the anti-nuclear lobby, but also from groups like the Council for Science and Society which issued a report in 1981 entitled 'New Technology: Society, Employment and Skill'. The kind of questioning about the advance of technology I have in mind is evidenced by this comment in the CSS Report about the alleged benefits of automation based on computers:

> If we look at past experience, it seems likely that possibilities of this kind, if they can be realized profitably with the computer, will be implemented despite any protests by those concerned.

177

... To follow such a path of increasing automation usually requires an additional expenditure on capital equipment. Profitability then depends upon a reduction of employment for a given output, or at least the substitution of less-skilled, and so cheaper, labour for the more highly skilled. Both courses reduce the demands which are made on human ability, and a classical economic argument sees this as the creation of new opportunity. The human resources set free are available for other needs of society, or to increase the production of goods. Moreover, an economic mechanism will automatically ensure that this opportunity is fully used.

Yet the experience of the last fifty years does little to establish confidence in this self-regulating mechanism. The demoralising unemployment of the 1930s ended only with the beginning of the Second World War, and it is not clear that the depression would have ended without the war. The 1970s, against expectations, saw a renewed increase of unemployment. During the whole period a large proportion of those employed have done work below their capability. What is striking is that very great effort is expended upon the creation of the opportunity which unemployment or underemployment represents, and in comparison almost none upon using that opportunity.[23]

Such a lengthy quotation is necessary to show the kind of detailed critical argument about the benefits or otherwise of technological advance that is completely and naively absent from the statements of those advocating an economic utility model of education. Unemployment has, of course, become much worse since this report was written, and political commentators on unemployment consistently play down the very large technologically structural element within it, hoping instead for some miraculous upturn in international trade to remedy the situation.

The idea of the undoubted good of technological advance is not only thus questionable, it is actively questioned by many people and groups of people in technically advanced societies. Similar detail can be found in literature from the conservationist and anti-nuclear groups, represented as cranks in much of the establishment media, but actually producing complex, sustained and serious argument of a most disturbing kind for those prepared to read it.

It is no part of my present argument to claim that the views now being referred to are necessarily correct, though I believe many of them to be so. The argument here is that views about technological growth are far more controversial than could be inferred from DES documents, HMI documents and other sources referred to in 9.1. For educators to influence the minds of pupils in the sole direction of the economic utility model of education, in this and other respects, would be highly indoctrinatory and therefore inimical to the development of rational and moral autonomy which is the duty of the liberal educator.

Similarly, the background context of the free competitive market as the determinant of resource allocation is anything but a consensus view of how society should most desirably operate. The Green Paper ('Education in School: A Consultative Document), issued by a Labour Party Secretary of State, talked of the mixed economy as the normal state which education must come to terms with, as we might have expected from a government largely in the hands of the right wing of the Labour Party. Conservative politicians and most industrialists are, of course, more stridently supportive of a larger, if not total, free market element, and more directly socialist members of the Labour Party and others too far to the left to be members of that organization would want to see more, or total, central planning of the economy. The numbers of people prepared actually to vote for one or other of these positions when dressed up in various guises in election manifestos varies over time. What is inescapable, however, is the controversial nature of the issue. Politicians and employers have every right, in a democracy, to argue their case; but it does not follow from this that any of them have the right, least of all in a democracy, to impose their particular view on the education system. Such a system, in so far as it tries to bring about political and economic understanding in the minds of the pupils entrusted to it, must treat controversial matters *as* controversial matters. The late Lawrence Stenhouse realized this when asked by the Schools Council to propose strategies for teaching the humanities, but the strategy his team constructed and tried so hard to introduce into schools is still only rarely seen in action. The suppression of student opinion in MSC-sponsored courses, already mentioned, stands directly opposed to the thoughtful strategy of neutrality and impartiality advocated by Stenhouse and characteristic of all his work.

If consensus does not actually exist in these areas neither does it exist in the matter of judging the value of activities by their contribution to wealth-creation. What this kind of emphasis leaves out of account is any consideration of what wealth is to be used for and how it is to be distributed. Even nineteenth-century utilitarians made happiness and not wealth-creation the touchstone of value, and were thus concerned about how wealth was used and distributed, and contemporary political philosophers have consistently related these ideas to the justice and morality of the ends to which wealth is put and of its distribution.[24] None of these political theorists appears to believe that a society with more wealth-creation is, in any simple and unqualified way, necessarily better than one with less. It seems particularly one-sided to judge an educational system, or even particular educational practices, by the simple criterion of contribution to wealth-creation for two main reasons. Firstly, because educators must be duty-bound to introduce pupils to controversial matters *as* controversial matters, as I have already said in connection with technological growth; and, secondly, because schools of liberal education must introduce pupils to those activities and practices which can be considered as worthwhile in themselves and therefore fit to be considered as ends rather than as means. To take small but illustrative examples of what I mean here: it would be pointless to judge the value of my listening to music, reading poetry, or even doing my gardening, by assessing their contribution to wealth-creation when these things are for me intrinsically valued ends; when they are, in fact, activities on which I *use* my wealth rather than means to increase it. It is true that for some people the issue becomes confused and wealth-creation becomes an end in itself; but that is but one of the peculiar perversions of modern capitalist society, destructive of justice, morality and a proper humanity, as Erich Fromm and others have pointed out.[25] Education must be concerned with ends, and to the extent that it is so concerned it is improperly judged on the criterion of wealth-creation.

The last important controversial area in the economic utility model of education to be noted here is the emphasis on competition, both individual and national. A full discussion of the place of competition in education cannot be entered into here, but the point must be made that the place of competition, in both education and society at large, is controversial. Some people would favour a much more cooperative society and much more encouragement of cooperation in schools. Similarly some would favour much more international cooperation on trade instead of the present automatic assumptions about national competitiveness. Yet in the model I am criticizing competition is offered as a characteristic of the 'real' world, as though to question competition is like questioning the expansion of metals under heat or the necessity of moisture for growing plants; whilst cooperation for any other purpose than to defeat the other team, the other firm or the other country, is corrupting idealism, out of touch with the 'real' world. The assumption is as if Kropotkin had never written, the Cooperative Movement had never developed and fraternity had never been a political issue for which men and women had died on the barricades. Team spirit and loyalty have become transmogrified, as R.S. Peters puts it, into instruments of destructive competition instead of universal cooperation among all rational agents.[26]

9.2.2 The diversion of responsibility

This criticism of the economic utility model of education is directed to the appropriate allocation of responsibility. Certainly it cannot be denied that there must be efficient and appropriate vocational training in any community. The criticism made by the liberal educator is not against vocational training as such, only against the idea that such training is properly located in schools of general education, or that the needs of such training should dictate the curriculum content and methodologies of schools of general education.

The paradigm notion of training is to do with preparation for some activity of a relatively specific kind which, once trained for, a person will engage in for some time. Such were the reasonable assumptions, for example, of an apprentice; but apprenticeships were features of a craft-orientated economy which has now all but disappeared from the national scene. Preparing people, especially young people, for specific industrial tasks is difficult today for a number of reasons, but two are paramount: firstly, no one can guarantee that a young person will actually get a job in the task for which he or she has been trained; and, secondly, no one can guarantee that the technical requirements of a task will not change very quickly, even before the young person takes up a job. These difficulties operate profoundly at all levels, as the Council for Science and Society reports in the case of engineers:

> In the university training of engineers, the scientific content is again heavily, and increasingly, stressed. To teach the current technology and procedures of industry is more difficult and less rewarding because they evolve within industry and change rapidly. Only someone directly engaged in the activity can teach it, and what is learned will be rapidly outdated.[27]

Yet employers still complain that graduates do not understand modern industry, and that school-leavers do not understand the particular aspects of work they find themselves in – if they do find themselves in work – as if this was solely the fault of the university or school. The very users of rapidly changing technologies, even the very makers of such technologies, show little signs of grasping these particular social implications, and education policy-makers can naively say that an aim of education should be 'to help pupils to acquire knowledge and skills relevant to adult life and employment in a fast changing world'![28]

Because industry has been unable to cope with these problems itself, and because of the costs of frequently changing training needs, there have been increased demands for national patterns of training and increased blaming of schools for alleged failures to develop appropriate skills and attitudes in young school leavers. Exactly what these appropriate skills and attitudes are does not appear to have been much discussed outside the literature of the Further Education Curriculum Development Unit, the MSC, and agencies serving them. Inside that literature, however, one finds a flowering of talk about generic skills, social skills and life skills which will have a vocational bias and provide vocational motivation whilst still being (alleged'y) very wide in application. Much of this would not concern us here were it not for the fact that unemployment has brought many more 16- and 17-year-olds under the influence of these training philosophies, and because of the present government's intention to extend these techniques to the 14- and 15-year-old pupils in ordinary schools. In the next sub-section I shall look more closely at the characterization of skills in this literature. Here I am concerned to make the point that the very agencies who should tackle the problems of industrial training in the context of modern technology and rapid change, namely the government and industry, have chosen to do so largely by attacking the general education base and attempting, not to put too fine a point on it, to take that base over for purely instrumental purposes. This is a grand passing of the buck and a lamentable shedding of blame and responsibility which has an effect that is doubly disastrous: it fails to provide adequate industrial training that is directly linked with jobs on the one hand, and frustrates, confuses and belittles attempts at a genuine liberal education for all pupils on the other.

Much has been made in some recent discussions on these issues of the need for school-leavers to be very adaptable in the present-day situation. The need is genuine, but there are no magic skills for adaptability. The best basis for adaptability is a liberal education which has encouraged a wide understanding and the development of reason and autonomy, in the fullest sense of those oft-misused words, without any early prejudging of how this understanding might later be put to vocational and career use. The very rate of technological change argues in favour of liberal education for all, and not against it; and only from such an education can come adaptability, if that is what is necessary, or the critical power to work for a social control of technology as that increasingly becomes necessary. Liberal educators should be left to their logically prior task, and only after that should those properly responsible for industrial training see that it is efficiently undertaken.

9.2.3 *The characterization of skills*

It is odd to note that most of the Further Education Curriculum Development Unit teaching material that is so favoured by the MSC attempts to characterize everything in terms of skills. These are not only skills like being able to use a screwdriver or an electric drill, which would be clear and comprehensible, but much more grandly named skills like 'life skills', 'social skills', 'interpersonal skills' and even 'generic skills' which are supposed to underlie all we do. The oddity comes from the contrast between this view that all that is necessary is to equip people with appropriate skills for work, leisure and life, and the comments on skill that we find in the Science and Society report on 'New Technology: Society, Employment and Skill'. This report traces historically how the advance of technology has generally been accompanied by an *elimination* of skill:

> The historical evidence is not encouraging. Where it was possible to eliminate skill in the past, this was generally done. The opportunities which are being offered by the computer to remove skill from office work, printing, engineering design and other occupations, in general seem likely to be taken. . . . It will affect the majority of occupations up to and within the professional level. There will be a resistance to this development which will be strong and tenacious. . . . If it is unsuccessful, then the great majority of people will for the first time find themselves united in the misfortune of work which allows them no control or initiative.[29]

Of course the report notes that developing technology generates a need for new skills, but these are for a smaller number of people, usually different people, from those who are de-skilled.

We seem, then, to have two different accounts. One seems to be saying that education does not concern itself enough with skills: 'We believe schools need to make a conscious effort to ensure that their pupils acquire skills, many of which may prove to have a life-long value.'[30] The other appears to be saying that the trend of technological change is generally to make increasingly useless the skills that people have acquired.

Part of the confusion here arises from the way in which the word 'skill' is used. The Schools Council gives as examples of skills: initial reading and number skills, the ability to work alone and the ability to work with others.[31] These are among what I have called the serving competencies because they serve instrumentally the other aims and purposes within a liberal education. Whether they are appropriately called skills is questionable. Further skills mentioned by the Schools Council are: a knowledge of political processes, the ability to interpret scientific data and the ability to make judgments on environmental matters. What is gained by calling these abilities 'skills' is difficult to see. Most writers agree at a superficial level as to the components of a skill.

> A skill is more than knowing, and more than knowing how. It is action too. A skill involves the application of knowledge to achieve some anticipated outcome. It needs the capacity and the will to act, as well as knowledge. Skill without knowledge is inconceivable, but knowledge without skill has a long sad history.[32]

There are, however, interesting differences of emphasis. If the above quotation stresses the instrumentality of skills and their connection with action and the will, the following, from the Council for Science and Society report, emphasizes the knowledgeable control aspect of skill and marks off two interesting limiting conditions:

> we should prefer to stress 'knowledgeable practice', and to emphasize the element of control without which skill does not exist. . . .
>
> Because control is essential for the exercise of skill, it follows that there can be no skill where everything is completely predictable. Screwing a nut onto a bolt demands at most dexterity, not skill. In a large measure, therefore, skill is a response to the unexpected and unpredictable. The blacksmith so places the red-hot iron on the anvil, and strikes it with such a sequence of blows, that its shape converges to the horse-shoe he desires, even though his actions will never be the same on two occasions.
>
> . . . On one side skill is marked off from more trivial accomplishments such as dexterity or 'knack'. On another it is distinguished from activities which are intended to affect people rather than things . . . 'managerial skill' has a manipulative sound if it is applied to the leadership of people. The 'skilled negotiator' or the 'skilled advocate' seem to contradict this rule, but reflection will show that both operate in situations where human contact is circumscribed and manipulation is sanctioned.[33]

The suggested limiting conditions set in this quotation are, it seems to me, sensible ones which accord with our normal usage of the term 'skill'. On the one hand it accords with our intuitive idea that skills are never *merely* manual and always have a strong cognitive determination which is sometimes almost entirely determinant, as in the doctor's skills of diagnosis which cannot be disassociated from his knowledge and understanding of anatomy, physiology and pathology, as Ruth Jonathan points out.[34] On the other hand the limiting conditions accord with our unease when morality, personal relationships and even certain features of communication are characterized as skills. People *can*, of course, be skilfully manipulated by others. The point is that this has usually been seen as a perverted side of human relationships, to be spoken of in derogatory terms, and having nothing to do with those humanistic aspects of morality, personal and social relations which should be the concern of liberal educators.

These concerns for life, persons and society are, however, complex and are only to be understood by the prolonged study of the kind of content discussed in 7.5.1. The advocates of a skill approach are obviously attracted by a simple view of skills which they then project into matters too complex to make the appellation appropriate. They seem to want the advantages of simplicity which lend themselves conveniently to precise statements of objectives and easily manageable assessment and monitoring:

> In specifying the type and level of skill they intend their pupils
> to acquire teachers come near to setting themselves precise aims.
> Schools need to decide and state exactly what skills they do hope
> to develop in each of the main areas of experience they are
> concerned with. They could use statements of this kind as a basis
> for self assessment.[35]

Yet at the same time this simplicity and precision must be injected into complex areas like 'verbal skills as vehicles for thought, feeling and imagination'[36] because the more complex realms of human action and reflection are clearly the most important and valuable.

Perhaps the fallacy of thinking that these complex areas can be characterized as skills arises from the fatal slip from the properly adverbial or adjectival to the improper substantive which is so ready a temptation of language. Because a person can be a thoughtful politician or an imaginative architect it is tempting to think that there are reifications like 'thought' or 'imagination' which can be readily identified, isolated and trained for. Similarly, because it *is* meaningful to talk of someone being a skilful thinker, or expressing their feelings skilfully, we are tempted to believe that there is a 'skill' to be identified, isolated and trained for. This reaches its maximum absurdity in notions like 'life skills', 'social skills' and 'generic skills', as if it were meaningful to think of people as skilful at life, in society or in some universal generic sense. These conceptions are either vacuous or pretentious names for isolated and relatively trivial abilities that might in some sense be subsumed under such titles, in the sense that blowing one's nose efficiently or cutting one's toenails adequately are 'life skills'. Ruth Jonathan puts it very well:

> It begins to look as if we have only to dub any desirable capacity
> or area of experience a 'skill' in order to suggest it can be easily
> identified and acquired. Advocates of the teaching of 'life skills'
> or 'surivival skills' either have something utterly trivial in mind
> (like the ability to change plugs or walk through doorways), or
> something hopelessly vague (like the ability to be innovative or
> to work cooperatively) or are simply proffering glib new labels for
> the old educational aims of moral autonomy, rationality and
> aesthetic discrimination. If we are serious about the desirability of
> such goals we must look for advances in epistemology, psychology
> and ethical argument and be prepared to apply these insights in

education, rather than following the blind alley of a behaviourist-inspired skill-based approach.[37]

Other people are wary of the skills approach. Bernard Davies, writing for the National Youth Bureau, defends what he sees as a 'social education' orientation of youth workers against the pressure to go over to a skill-based approach. He rightly locates social education in the broad tradition of liberal education:

> advocates of social education who wish to resist the drift to social
> and life skills training may need to be looking for alliances with all
> those other educators now trying to defend the liberal and
> personalised traditions of education generally.[38]

He also shares my view, or appears to do so, of the importance of justifying and substantiating a liberal education philosophy if one is to be in any position to resist the encroachment of a crude skills approach:

> youth workers, teachers and others involved in social education
> need to regain their nerve — their conviction that some of the person-
> centred, critical and creative goals to which they have been
> committed are still valid.
> ... If they cannot re-assert what is distinctive about the theory,
> philosophy and practice of their specialist field of work, they cannot
> hope to resist, still less to influence, the cruder, often highly
> mechanistic and behaviourist forms of social and life skills training
> now being foisted on so many young people.[39]

It was noted in the previous sub-section that only one immersed in the practice of a skill, properly so called, can train another person in that skill. This was the long-standing basis of apprenticeships and many other less thoroughgoing types of on-the-job training. If we are speaking of the skills of operating a lathe, a computer, a sailing dinghy or anything where particular processes and performances are to be explained and demonstrated by one person to another who then practises the processes under the eye of the expert, then this is an important part of the paradigm of skills. If it is, however, then even more doubt is cast on the idea of life skills, social skills, moral skills and the like. Who are those arrogant enough to claim the necessary expertise to *train* others in these areas? What qualifications should they possess and what experience should they have had? What is their ongoing practice of the expertise which trainees watch and then practise for themselves? What is the rationale of their explanations? How does it escape the controversy found in these fields for thousands of years by philosophers and other reflective persons? Perhaps it is simply ignorance of all these problems, arising from prolonged immersion in action and the assertion of the will.

I must end this sub-section, and lead into the next, with what after all is the liberal educator's main complaint about the emphasis on skills. This is to do with the way in which any emphasis on skills divorces the instruments from their purposes, separates means from ends. Logically, of course, skills are not separable from purposes and ends. It is the characterization of particular purposes that helps us to see the use of a particular skill — ball control in football, say — and there is no performance that is just a skill in any isolated sense. To make this point, obvious though it may seem to be, is immediately to diminish the importance of instrumental skills relative to other considerations like being able to *choose our ends* in some understanding and informed way; like entering into an understanding of the *values* involved in different ends; like considering the *morality* of certain means rather than others, even when the ends are determined; and like *understanding* the varied and multitudinous practices of humankind which might or might not come to be valued ends for us. Ruth Jonathan again makes the point crisply when she says that 'education must logically equip children to make these choices before it equips them to carry them out.'[40] Later in her paper she makes this point more fully:

> Formerly, individuals were either educated or trained. As social divisions became slightly more blurred, the vast mass of young people found themselves at the end of formal schooling neither educated nor trained. The answer does not lie in replacing education by training for all, but in acceptance that all young people require a general education which will open to them as many options of an intellectual, aesthetic and moral kind as they are capable of entertaining and society is able to support, followed by an appropriate period of generic training — not in imitative and obsolescent motor skills, but in the appropriate fundamental principles and general skills of particular technologies, whether industrial, commercial, scientific or service. The more specific our skills the shorter their useful life.[41]

With perhaps some room for negotiation as to where the former ends and the latter begins, few liberal educators would quarrel with that.

9.2.4 The belittling of knowledge and understanding

Knowledge and understanding, I have claimed, are proper terms for what a liberal education is trying to develop in pupils. These, however, are the very characterizations belittled by exponents of the economic utility model of education, in favour of characteristics like 'skill',

187

largely of course because of the active and instrumental connotation of the latter as compared with the apparent passivity of the former. Part of the technique of advocating the utility model, whether used deliberately and consciously or not it is difficult to say, is to give false, Aunt Sally, conceptions of knowledge and understanding: 'able to understand but not to act', or 'knowledge without skill has a long sad history'. This polarity supposes there to be a kind of knowledge and understanding disconnected from action and purpose, and therefore easily characterized as 'useless' with all the derogatory force of that word in a mainly instrumental, acquisitive and materialistic society. I want to argue that the polarity is a false one. Not only can you not have skills, properly speaking, without knowledge and understanding, which seems to be grudgingly admitted by those who attack liberal education, but it is also nonsense to suppose there to be *any* knowledge and understanding that does not involve the appropriate exercise of skills. These skills may indeed be mental rather than physical in some, though not all, cases; but then so mainly are the skills of engineers, lawyers, doctors, politicians, business executives and other 'practical men and women'. The point is that to come to know and understand anything in the rich evidential sense I have been arguing for is anything but a passive and purely recipient business. To know and to understand in this sense is to be able to follow and to practise particular kinds of investigative procedures, weigh evidence, make judgments and decide what to believe and what not to believe; to decide how to see things and how not to see things. Being able to explain things to oneself in this kind of a way, with attention to consistency and coherence, is the first step to being able to explain them to others. Seen like this it is not at all surprising that the *leaders* of industry and commerce and their related services usually come from those who have had a rich liberal education, rather than from those who at an early age have been cut off from such an education and directed into narrow vocationalism emphasizing mainly motor skills.

The first complaint, then, against the attempted belittling of knowledge and understanding, is that these ideas are wrongly characterized. The decision-making that is so valued by the exponents of the utility model and by the 'capability' proponents is in fact both a necessary part of knowledge and understanding and would be pure unguided will without them.

The second complaint, also following directly from arguments made earlier in this work, is that only knowledge and understanding on a wide base can liberate a peson from the particular restrictions of birth, social class and geography. Without such a base any choices are bound to be restricted because of the limited perspective brought to bear on them. To think that choices of career or life-style can be made solely on the basis of necessarily limited work experience, factory visits and similar experiences to be found in careers education courses, is clearly wrong. The number of places visited, the types of work experienced, the life-styles sampled, would need to be enormous for the choices to be made on 'that basis. The supposition that the evidence on which choices are made becomes more 'real' because of this kind of experience is a fallacy which might be dubbed the 'concrete fallacy'. Having a broken leg, being stuck in a front-line trench or being unemployed are *not* necessarily the best ways of gaining any extensive *understanding* of bone injury, war or unemployment; neither is working on a conveyor belt, learning to use a lathe or to prepare hotel meals the best way of getting an understanding of the so-called 'world of work'. The direct experience may well be sharp and penetrating, but because it is necessarily of such a limited aspect of what is to be understood its very force becomes a handicap rather than an asset. The emotive impact of an experience is no necessary measure of its contribution to understanding. The very detachment, lack of passion, and abstractness of much of the knowledge and understanding handled in a liberally educative way, which it is now so fashionable to attack, are essentials of a balanced, wide and liberating understanding.

A third complaint against the diminution of the extent of knowledge and understanding in a compulsory education, and its replacement by cruder training elements, is that such diminution reduces the liberating influence of education by reducing the pupil's opportunity to develop a critical framework of thinking. To be capable of critically viewing one's own position, one's own perspective, the demands being made upon one and the opportunities provided or not provided, it is necessary to be able to make comparisons and contrasts against a wide background of actual, possible and imaginable different conceptions of things and of how things might be. This kind of comparative complex is only to be gained by a reasonably extensive study of human practices as delineated in Section 7.6.1. These practices included those that manifested themselves in economic, commercial and industrial institutions, and in art, craft and design; and the point was made that understanding these practices would necessarily involve some active participation, but that such participatory activities were to be directed to the end of understanding the practices and not towards training for a future in them. For example, I claimed that a pupil engaged in art at a school of general and liberal education is studying and practising with a different purpose from that of a student in an art school. In a school of liberal education we are not trying to produce an artist, but a human being who has some understanding of the arts as a great and pervasive human practice. I should add here that another characteristic of the place of art, or anything else, in a liberal education is that the particular

189

practice is to be seen in the light of, and as shedding light on, all the other practices studied. What R.S. Peters called 'cognitive perspective' is an important aim of liberal education but does not seem to figure very largely in the economic utility model of education. To foreclose too soon on this process of a widening of cognitive perspective through an individual's growth of knowledge and understanding is to limit the growth of critical power which is a necessary part of individual autonomy.

It is perhaps wrong to claim that exponents of vocational training or emphasis within the period of compulsory education are deliberately seeking to curb critical power and attitude, though the references to MSC course censorship already made would lend weight to such a claim. Nevertheless, the result is the same whether deliberate or not, whether wished for or not. Those who seek to devalue knowledge and understanding, as compared with training, and those who seek to reduce the time involved in school concern for knowledge and understanding as against training, are devaluing the concern for developing the rational autonomy of the pupil which constitutes the main justification for compelling children to be in school at all.

9.3 Conclusion

In this chapter I have given a sketch and a criticism of what is perhaps the most overt and immediately pressing challenge which faces the view of liberal education that I have outlined in earlier chapters. What I have sketched here is also, of course, an attack on the education system as it stands in this country today. It is important not to be confused here, since an attempt to develop a genuine liberal education for all pupils up to at least the age of sixteen would *also* be an attack on the system as it exists today. To defend my view of liberal education against alternative conceptions giving emphasis to training and to vocational preparation is *not* to defend the present system. Conversely, arguments pointing to defects in the present system, in schools as they actually exist today, and they are many, are not necessarily arguments against the view of liberal education presented here. I happen to believe that a good deal of what goes on in our schools *is* liberally educating; but not enough of it is. There is not enough concern for evidential teaching and teaching for understanding; there is far too early a narrowing of curriculum spread; there is too much concern for relating the curriculum to career choice and there is too much emphasis on competition and not enough on collaboration. An exponent of the economic utility model of education that I have tried to characterize and criticize would no doubt turn these criticisms of the status quo on their head, claiming there to be too much concern about understanding and not enough concern about the 'realities' of competition, careers and the creation of wealth. Neither of us totally approves of the present system, but we would improve things in totally opposed ways. The debate is a real one.

At this historical moment (late 1983) there is little doubt that the economic utility model, supported by the government and the Manpower Services Commission as well as by powerful agencies of industry and commerce, is winning the power struggle if not the debate. The reason it is winning is mainly to do with the strength and alignment of political forces, but a powerful subsidiary factor is the failure of professional educators to first articulate, and then defend, a coherent view of liberal education.

There are those who would say that what is happening is no more than forces already and always at work in a capitalist democratic society becoming open about what they are always trying to do. The liberal education I am advocating would never stand a chance, these critics would say, because it could not be divorced from the productive and social relationships obtaining in a capitalist society. These critics raise profound problems about the relativity of knowledge, and about the relationship between knowledge and ideology, and to these difficult questions we must now turn.

10

The challenge of relativism, ideology and the state

10.1 Introduction

In this chapter I shall consider some challenges to my view of liberal education that group themselves around the idea of the relativity of knowledge and its relationship to political, social and economic interests. This is to consider arguments at once more complex than, and different in kind from, those considered in the previous chapter. Those people holding what I there called the economic utility view of education do not set out to challenge the taken-for-granted view of knowledge. They hold the same view of knowledge as most other people but suppose, quite overtly, that some knowledge, especially technological knowledge characterized in terms of skills, is much more useful than other more abstract knowledge and understanding, and ought to be the main consideration in schools. The challenge of those I shall now refer to as 'relativists' is more profound in that all knowledge is presented by them, to a greater or lesser degree, as arbitrary systems of meaning, and opposed to absolute and objectivist views of knowledge which they suppose to characterize the way knowledge is presented to and received by pupils in schools. To this extent the challenge is an epistemological one about the nature of knowledge, and can be met, at least in some measure, by reminders about how I have characterized knowledge and understanding earlier in this work. The challenge of the relativists is more complex even than these epistemological differences and hypothetical characterizations of knowledge, because grafted onto the relativistic epistemology is a theory, or a body of alternative theories, seeking to account for the dominance and institutionalization of certain systematizations of meaning, albeit arbitrary and problematic, by socio-economic or political explanations of the dominance of social or political groups.

As if this was not already difficult enough there is a third powerful layer of consideration to weave into the challenge. This is the concept of ideology, with its attendant problems of whether ideologies are consciously or unconsciously manifested; whether ideologies can be recognized as such and resisted; and how ideologies arise, are maintained and how they might be distinguished, if at all, from knowledge.

Within the challenge of relativism we thus have three vast territories of thought contributing: a specific view of epistemology, though not without variant; a sociology of knowledge, sometimes offered as neutral analysis, but often with a prescriptive purpose like the favouring of 'open' or 'integrated' curricula; and a view of the relationship between education and ideology. Each of these topics has generated a literature of its own, and this makes it a daunting task to consider the entire nexus in one chapter. Yet to ignore such a powerful challenge would leave a very large gap in what is supposed to be a general theory of liberal education. A sketch of this challenge, with some suggestions as to how it might be answered in a way which leaves the general theory intact, must therefore be attempted.

10.2 Epistemological relativism

In this and the next sub-section I shall be referring extensively to papers in the collection 'Knowledge and Control', published as an Open University set book in 1971.[1] This work attempted to change the direction of sociology of education from its erstwhile focus on the relationship between social class and access to education, and on education as an agency of social mobility. The 'new sociology of education'[2] was to concern itself more with the curriculum and the knowledge handled within the school system, especially in terms of the 'legitimation' of this knowledge – that is to say, the way in which certain kinds of knowledge are considered worthy of transmission in schools and others not. The technique used was to consider all knowledge, pedagogical arrangements and methods as 'problematic'. To consider something problematic is the opposite of taking it for granted, as absolute or simply as given. To approach, say, the teaching of science as problematic is to consider both scientific knowledge and the teaching of it as questionable. This is to claim not only that science need not be taught, but that there is no absolute necessity to view the world scientifically. The same can be said, of course, about any kind of knowledge that happens to feature in schooling, science being mentioned here only as an example.

If school knowledge is viewed as problematic in this way, then explanations of a sociological kind can be sought both as to the mechanism of knowledge legitimation and, more specifically, why certain kinds of knowledge and pedagogical styles or methodologies become dominant in certain socio-political environments at certain historical times. Explanations can also be sought for paradigmatic shifts in curriculum content and practice analogical to the shifts in the framework of scientific understanding claimed by Kuhn.[3] There is much concern in 'Knowledge and Control', especially in papers by Bernstein[4] and Esland[5], about shifts from a strictly subject-based curriculum to an integrated curriculum of the kind much under discussion in the late 1960s and into the 1970s, and interesting things are said about both the possible causes and likely effects of such a shift.

In so far as all this is in the style of neutral sociological analysis it does not in itself constitute a challenge to my ideas of liberal education. After all, there *is* a sociological account to be given of, say, why certain ideas of an educational kind get established or do not get established at a certain time, which stands quite apart from accounts of whether the ideas are coherent, consistent and justifiable or not. In this sense a sociologist would be proceeding *as if* knowledge and pedagogy were problematic because the question of justification was simply not relevant to his proper enquiries. There would be some sense in this since the justification of a practice is never a sufficient explanation of the presence of a practice, any more than the presence of a practice is sufficient evidence of its justifiability. When discussing beliefs earlier I made the point, following Quinton, that the strength with which a belief is held has no necessary connection with the justification of the belief. There are always psychological and sociological accounts that can be given of people's beliefs. There are also questions as to the justification of beliefs and these are separate from the psychological and sociological accounts, or so I shall claim.

The writers of the papers in 'Knowledge and Control', however, would not accept this distinction, for to talk of justification in the way I am doing supposes there to be what they would call 'absolutes' — that is, certain categories of logic, reason and argument by which issues of justification are to be decided, and absolutes are to be denied because their use is also problematic.

Now this is a much more serious, much more prescriptive, and much less purely a sociological matter. The 'as if' technique, a matter of characterizing sociological procedure, has now become an epistemological assertion about the total relativity, the total social construction of all knowledge, especially as treated in schools. The treatment of the problematic nature of knowledge is not always clear in the papers. Sometimes it does seem as though the 'as if' style *is* being adopted:

> If the sociologist is able to suspend, in his enquiry, the taken for granted moral and intellectual absolutism of the teacher, who in his everyday situation has no such alternative, then the phenomena of the classroom and the school can be studied for what they might mean to the participants; such distinctions, then, as right or wrong,

strict or slack, interesting or dull, which might be used by either teacher or taught, become phenomena to be explained.[6]

At other times, however, the prescriptive tone appears, as here where Michael Young is making the point that philosophers of education, like Hirst and White, have tried to criticize certain curriculum developments like topic-based work and special 'Newsom' courses on the grounds that they fail to provide a proper education in terms of the forms of knowledge:

> The problem with this kind of critique is that it appears to be based on an absolutist conception of a set of distinct forms of knowledge which correspond closely to the traditional areas of the academic curriculum and thus justify, rather than examine, what are no more than the socio-historical constructs of a particular time. . . . . The point I wish to make here is that unless such *necessary* distinctions or intrinsic logics are treated as problematic, philosophical criticism cannot examine the assumptions of academic curricula.[7]

The argument here seems to be that absolutist conceptions of knowledge are to be considered bad or unhelpful because they do not help us to 'examine' the assumptions of the academic curricula. There is a number of things wrong with this passage, but let us simply note the prescriptive argument for the moment.

Geoffrey Esland is much more clearly prescriptive. He sets up what he believes to be the presently dominant characteristics of 'knowledge' and then claims that sociology of knowledge has challenged the *epistemological* sufficiency of such an account. The characterization must be given at length because of the many assertions within it. The quotation gives both the message and the assertive style:

> Knowledge is usually considered and referred to as a set of abstract structures with intrinsic natures − as particular classifications of problems, data and verification procedures conforming to assumed patterns of coherence. Thus the naming which confirms the separation between zones of knowledge in a curriculum − called 'subjects' or 'projects' − is thought to represent certain ontologies, essences of human experience. In other words, it is assumed that zones of knowledge are objects which can be considered to have meaning other than in the minds of the individuals in which they are constituted, irrespective of their human realization.
>
> This is the objectivist view of knowledge. It is the view represented in the traditional epistemology and analytic philosophy. It is also how knowledge is conceived in the reality of everyday experience where the taken for granted nature of the world is rarely questioned. . . . Knowledge is thereby detached from the human

195

subjectivity in which it is constituted, maintained and transformed. Such a view implicitly presents man as a passive receiver, as a pliable, socialized embodiment of external facticities. He is represented not as a world-producer, but as world-produced. We have, therefore, a reified philosophy in which objectivity is autonomized and which does not regard as problematical for the constituency of the object its constitution in the subjective experience of individuals.[8]

The particular sociology of knowledge that Esland believes challenges the 'epistemological sufficiency' of this account of knowledge derives in part from Hegel and early Marx but also from more recent writers like Schutz, Husserl and Schleger in the tradition of phenomenology, and more recently still from the works of Berger and Luckman,[9] C. Wright Mills[10] and Kuhn[11]. Although there is some feeling of all these writers being treated as grist to Esland's particular mill, it is no doubt true that they are all talking about the social construction of knowledge in one way or another. There are, however, weak and strong theses about the social construction of knowledge and reality, as I shall try to show later. Esland characterizes his view like this:

> The essential feature of this tradition . . . is that human sociation is a dialectic phenomenon. Man externalizes himself through physical and mental activity in the process of objectivation. The products which he has created then become his subjective world, a reality which confronts him and is available to the definitions of others. This is subjectively appropriated, and the objective structures are transformed into subjective consciousness. The interpretative architecture of the mind is at once an active and a passive agent in the construction of meaning and significance. . . . The individual biography is, therefore, both a subjective and an institutionalized history of the self: the one acts on the other.
>
> Because this view emphasizes man's active construction of experience, there is a clear challenge to the static, analytic conception of knowledge. . . . The focus, therefore, is now diverted from how man absorbs knowledge so that he can replicate it to how the individual creatively synthesizes and generates knowledge, and what are its social origins and consequences.[12]

These characterizations, contrasted here by Esland, constitute the epistemological basis for much of the argument in 'Knowledge and Control' and are to that extent important. We must be clear, however, as to what is being argued or asserted. This is not simply an 'as if' technique. Esland is not saying, 'Let us look at this problem of knowledge through two different hypothetical models, the objectivist model and the sociology of knowledge model, and see what is illuminated.'

He is asserting, as far as I can see, a number of direct propositions as true, but not actually arguing for or demonstrating their truth. These propositions – the main ones at least – are:

(i) Knowledge is usually construed as objectivist in the manner described.

(ii) This view of knowledge dominates traditional epistemology and analytic philosophy.

(iii) This view is 'firmly embedded in the norms and rituals of academic culture and its transmission'.

(iv) The objectivist view of knowledge, as described, is a wrong view.

(v) A more correct view is the social phenomenological, or sociology of knowledge, view as described.

(vi) Only this view will enable us to make correct critiques of educational arrangements and practices.

(vii) Education based on the phenomenological view of knowledge would be a better, more humanizing, more liberating education.

To move to a criticism of this view, I believe only proposition (iv) to be wholly true. There is some truth in proposition (iii), especially as 'firmly embedded' leaves us room to suppose that other versions have some room to grow in the system as well. Similarly, there is some truth in proposition (v) in the sense that the phenomenological view contains some useful insights and emphases on the nature of knowledge. It does not, however, contain the whole truth in this polarized way. Propositions (i), (ii), (vi) and (vii) I believe to be false. I shall make some brief comments on these claims before going on to consider how this all bears on the theory of liberal education.

(i) Knowledge is *not* usually construed as objectivist *in the manner described*. An objectivist view might be said to dominate a simplistic view of scientific knowledge and a good deal of everyday knowledge about the physical world where, incidentally, it seems to serve our pragmatic purposes quite well. People have different views, however, about other types of knowledge – knowledge of persons, morality, historical knowledge, aesthetic knowledge and values generally are widely held to have either cultural or individually relativistic elements and subjective dimensions.

(ii) The objectivist view of knowledge, *as described*, does *not* dominate traditional epistemology or analytic philosophy. Within those traditions the issues of relativity and subjectivity continue to be debated.[13] I know of no philosopher, of education or otherwise, who believes that the naming of subjects in the curriculum, or even Hirstian forms of knowledge, represents 'certain ontologies' or 'essences of human experience'. About subjects, nothing of an epistemological, metaphysical or ontological kind has ever seriously been claimed by

197

anybody. What has been claimed about a form of knowledge is that it is 'a distinct way in which our experience becomes structured around the use of accepted public symbols.'[14] There is nothing ontological or essentialist about such a claim. Indeed, Hirst sees himself as specifically rejecting 'the doctrines of metaphysical and epistemological realism with which it (liberal education) has been historically associated'.[15] Similarly, I know of no philosopher, of education or otherwise, who believes that 'zones of knowledge are objects which can be considered to have meaning other than in the minds of the individuals in which they are constituted'. That both meaning and knowledge are features of minds is widely acknowledged and certainly not an exclusive discovery of the sociology of knowledge. Certainly many people would accept something like Popper's World Three, in which knowledge is objectified in the coding of material substrates and theoretical systems[16], but this is a necessary feature of the social nature of knowledge whereby the products of individual minds become available for sharing with other individual minds. Without contributors and users World Three could not exist *as* knowledge. Many people, dialectical and other materialists among them, believe intuitively in some stuff or matter or 'things in themselves' existing in some sense apart from our knowledge of it or them, but this must not be confused with what they suppose *knowledge* to be.

(iii) There is some truth in proposition (iii). It is true in the sense that many teachers *do* treat knowledge in the dead dogma way that I have described in Chapter 5. That is to say, they consider that they have truths to dispense to pupils and do this in a way that does not involve pupils in the appropriate evidence held to justify the beliefs they are transmitting. This has the effect of making the pupils view knowledge in something like Esland's objective sense: external collections of verities to be released by teachers who are the custodians and gatekeepers, the selectors and legitimators. Active pupil engagement and understanding are belittled in favour of passive reception, mystification and consequent alienation or uncritical acceptance of received doctrine. That all this happens is, I believe, true. It does not, however, happen all the time with all teachers or with all pupils. Some teachers try actively to teach evidentially, probably more now than used to. Many new teaching syllabuses and schemes devised by Schools Council groups and others are constructed with evidential teaching in mind, and the training of teachers in recent years is more likely to make them realize the need for this kind of teaching. Some pupils, too, even when taught in a dead dogma, non-evidential fashion, nevertheless develop a critical awareness of the part they can play in the development of their own knowledge. I suspect that this is partly because the very *content* of some school subjects, and the *competencies* involved in them, develop a resistance to dogmatic limitation. You cannot teach a child to read, for example, encourage her to read novels and plays, and then expect her awareness to be confined only to the texts specifically given. You cannot teach mathematics and science, even badly, and then guarantee that *no* concern for evidence and proof will be engendered, perhaps to turn against the very system itself. If there is no mechanism or dynamic like this operating there is a difficult explanatory task in showing how a dogmatic education system produces as many critical thinkers as it undoubtedly does. Of course much education goes on outside the system, but to suppose that critical power is only generated outside the system, whilst passive acceptance is all that is generated within it, would be grossly to oversimplify.

(iv) The objectivist view of knowledge, as described by Esland, is a wrong view of knowledge indeed; but, as I have tried to show, it would be very difficult to find anybody who subscribes to it. What is wrong in the characterization of knowledge given by Esland is firstly the ontological and essentialist account of the suggested sub-divisions of knowledge, especially if these are supposed to be indicated in the naming of school subjects; and, secondly, the externalization of knowledge as object outside human minds. The view of knowledge that *does* have wide adherence, though admittedly with many variations, among modern philosophers in the analytic tradition is that knowledge is justified true belief: that is to say, a claim to know must involve a belief that is held to be true because of the grounds, evidence or warrant offered for its support.[17] I have discussed this conception of knowledge properly so called in 5.3.3 and cast some doubt on the truth condition in 5.4, and I shall not recapitulate the accounts given there. The present point is simply that whilst Esland is right in rejecting the view of objectivist knowledge that he sets up, this does not help us very much because his attack does not engage with modern mainstream epistemology.

(v) The social phenomenological, or sociology of knowledge, view of knowledge as described by Esland is by no means unilluminating. It casts a good deal of light on matters affecting the knowledge and beliefs people come to have and the way in which such knowledge and belief is held or entertained. It provides, properly, a phenomenology and a sociology, even in some of its forms an anthropology, of knowledge. It overreaches itself, however, in claiming to provide a superior epistemology. It cannot do that because it does not provide an epistemology at all. In particular the view described gives no account of how we might distinguish between those beliefs justifiable enough to count as knowledge and those beliefs not so justifiable, or any other account of what it is that makes some beliefs knowledge and others not. Surely these are the central epistemological questions?

It might be argued, though it is not done so clearly in the work being discussed, that the whole point of the phenomenological account is *not* to distinguish between beliefs that are knowledge and beliefs that are not. On this view there would simply be beliefs, interesting problems about their origins, developments and consequences but no concern about their justification unless it was a matter of the alignment of certain beliefs with certain political commitments: e.g. certain beliefs facilitate exploitation of the working class and certain other beliefs facilitate the liberation of such a class. This view would be incoherent since it leaves no justification for considering the exploitation of the working class to be *bad*. There would have to be some justifiable beliefs of an ethical or other kind to make this possible, which is perhaps why some of the Marxists to be considered later *do* want a distinction to be drawn between ideology on the one hand and knowledge or science on the other.

(vi) The problem of justification enters, too, into questions of what particular stance enables us to best examine and criticize existing institutional systems like schools. Hirst's views, as I showed in a quotation above, were seen as inadequate for a base from which critical examination of certain curriculum proposals could be made. Surely the reverse is true. No examination based on the problematicalness of *everything* can yield a criticism of *anything*, if by criticism we mean showing some proposals or practices to be bad compared with others considered to be more desirable. In order to prescribe – that is, in order to say that what is going on in education should change, or be defended from change, in any particular respect – there must be some appeal to justificatory argument and evidence that is, if not absolute, at least a widely enough agreed set of assumptions or long-lasting conventions for meaningful argument to take place between conflicting views. Some criteria, some points of reference, must be considered at least for the time being as non-problematic. Young appears to be saying that only if we dispense with all such absolute or near-absolute presuppositions can we critically examine the assumptions of academic curricula. Perhaps he only means that the existing curriculum divisions in certain types of school should not be taken as given; but if that is what he means we all agree, and to suppose that Hirst was taking such divisions as given is simply (but seriously) a misunderstanding.

It is worth making a few comments on the general idea of the social construction of knowledge and what is called the social construction of reality. I said earlier that there were weak and strong theses in this area of speculation. The weak thesis, undenied as far as I know by anybody other than those of certain religious views attributing all knowledge to God, is that without minds and without social interaction of minds there would be no knowledge. An elaboration of this idea is the thought that if all minds vanished from the world then knowledge and understanding would vanish as well because these are properties of minds now vanished. The materials left behind in the form of books, micro-fiche, films, tapes, records and computer programmes would not in themselves constitute knowledge, being simply artefacts awaiting the decoding of minds.

Building upon this simple, but profoundly true and widely agreed base, many much more controversial extensions have been claimed. Some are to do with how human beings come to have this knowledge. The part played by language, itself a property of mind and society, has been widely discussed in relation to thought and understanding.[18] Marxists have tended to emphasize the part played by human labour and the social relationships attendant upon it. Much of the consideration arises from different views on the materialist presupposition that there is some matter or stuff, a real existing universe, to be known and understood in some sense. Kant's claim that knowledge and understanding were of phenomena and not of any stuff or matter or 'thing in itself', whilst making plain the separation between whatever might actually exist on the one hand and knowledge of it on the other, also paved the way for much stronger idealist views about the nature, not just of knowledge, but of reality. An extreme idealist view would be that the only 'reality' lies in the knowledge and understanding within minds, thus doubting, discounting or even ruling out altogether the materialist presupposition.[19]

Intermixed with these complicated and contentious debates about the relationship between knowledge and 'reality', which bears particularly on the nature and possibility of scientific knowledge of the physical world, are other traditions inquiring into the nature of our knowledge of persons and of personal and social relationships, and extending into our knowledge and characterization of ethical, political and economic knowledge. In this area, of course, theorists have been on a much safer ground in pointing out the generally conventional and problematic nature of such knowledge and understandings. It is much more difficult to claim any social 'reality' that is anything more than what is temporally and locationally supposed to be the 'reality', when what we are talking about is social conventions and relationships which demonstrably have historically changing characteristics. Even in this area, however, we have debate as to whether the problematic and conventional nature of social knowledge means that the ideas of the politically, socially or economically *powerful* necessarily hold sway; or whether even within these ideas there is room for holding that some ideas are more *justifiable*, as distinct from being held by the powerful, than others.

Some recent sociologists and social philosophers have concentrated on explaining the nature of everyday knowledge, described by Schutz as:

> the reality which seems self-evident to men remaining within the natural attitude. This reality is the everyday life world. It is the province of reality in which man continuously participates in ways which are at once inevitable and patterned. . . . Only in the world of everyday life can a common, communicative, surrounding world be constituted. The world of everyday life is consequently man's fundamental and paramount reality.[20]

The reminder that the level at which we share most with our fellows is at the level of everyday assumptions is an illuminating reminder, especially perhaps for academics of all persuasions; but the everyday life world is also changed and penetrated by second-order attempts to characterize and understand it, just as the everyday characterizations of personhood have become changed by the oversimplified downward penetration of ideas from people like, for example, Freud, Sartre and D.H. Lawrence. The problem, as always, is to determine the bearing of all these kinds of enquiry on the practical and theoretical questions of what to do and what to believe, whether the questions, as here, are about what to do and to believe about education, or about one's own personal and social life.

10.3 Epistemological relativism and liberal education

I believe the theory of liberal education already laid out to be not greatly disturbed by the relativistic challenge. This is partly due to the confused nature of the challenge and partly to do with the characterization of the theory of liberal education itself. The theory of liberal education argued in this work does *not* rest on the objectivist view of knowledge set up by Esland, though it does assume that knowledge can be characterized in terms of justifiable belief. The theory allows for the fact that what counts as justification in some areas of inquiry will not be the same as in others and, in particular, it allows for the fact that the *status* of some evidential reasoning, especially in the area of human practices, will be among the things to be studied. In respect of methodology the theory argues specifically against treating information and knowledge as simply given, as dead dogma, in favour of teaching evidentially, even where this leads to recognizing the frailty of evidence offered in support of some conventional and superstitious beliefs. All this imports into the theory of liberal education some of the insights of the relativistic position − what is truly problematic is to be seen as such, treated as such, and not offered as categoric knowledge.

On the other hand, the theory of liberal education offered here rests very much upon assumptions regarding the necessary presupposition of justification, logic, rationality and reason generally; together with all the principles and characteristics like consistency, coherence, impartiality, sufficiency and necessity that are attendant upon, and indeed constitutive of, the notion of reason; and together with such moral notions as can be derived from such presuppositions. This avowed dependence is by implication a rejection of the excessive relativism of 'Knowledge and Control', which would throw rationality into the melting-pot along with everything else. Young argues that just as feudal, clerical and market ideas were dogmas which have become questionable and thus replaced:

> Today it is the commonsense conceptions of 'the scientific' and 'the rational', together with the various social, political and educational beliefs that are assumed to follow from them, that represent the dominant legitimizing categories. It therefore becomes the task of sociological enquiry to treat these categories not as absolutes but as constructed realities realized in particular institutional contexts.[21]

In case we might misunderstand what Young means here by 'the rational', he cites C. Wright Mills with approval later on and makes the point clear:

> Mills (1939) makes the significant point that what we call 'reasoning', 'being logical', or validating the truth of an assertion, all involve a self-reflection or criticism of one's own thoughts in terms of various standardized models. These models will necessarily be sets of shared meanings of 'what good argument is, what is logical, valid etc. . . .' . . . like all shared meanings they can be treated as problematic and become the objects of enquiry . . . . the rules of logic, whether practical or academic, are conventional, and will be shaped and selected in accordance with the purpose of the discourse or the intentions of the enquiry.[22]

Young then goes on to note that if logic, good reasoning and justification are all to be treated as problematic then shortcomings on the part of a pupil need no longer be considered as 'wrong', or 'poorly argued', but simply as deviance. In one sense there is no problem here if all that is being said is that it might be more useful and revealing to an educator to look at the causes of a pupil's 'deviance' rather than to harp on the pupil's wrongness or lack of logic. But one cannot resist the feeling that much more than this is being said. Reason and logic are being offered as part of the legitimating apparatus of the ruling power of the dominant economic system, presumably monopoly capitalism. Similar arguments can be found in Marcuse where 'reason' seems to be limited to an instrumental, means-end, interpretation.[23] It is this conception of the problematic nature of reason and rationality and their associated cluster of concepts, principles and techniques that the theory of liberal education rejects.

Of course logic and reason are conventions; of course they constitute shared systems of meanings; of course they involve standardized models and of course they would not exist without minds. Systems of logic are not immutable: Aristotle did not work out all the possibilities of the propositional calculus; he did not envisage the complexities of symbolic logic; nor did he see the controversies within modal logic that modern logicians concern themselves with. Of course systems of logic, to some extent, can be shaped and selected to suit different discourses and purposes. Having said all this, however, the status of logic and reason as *necessarily presupposed* in serious discourse and serious enquiry remains. Human beings do not *have* to engage in serious discourse or enquiry in any absolute sense, whatever that might mean; though human life would be very different and the species potential would be much more circumscribed if they did not. But *if* they do *then* reason and logic are necessitated since without them it would be meaningless to talk about believing or doing one thing being any better than believing or doing another. Writing books like 'Knowledge and Control' which seek to assert bodies of propositions as preferable to other propositions that could be considered, would be quite pointless enterprises, as would any kind of argument or discussion. When people claim this kind of necessity they are not claiming reason and logic as objective physical presences which cannot be avoided, but they *are* claiming the necessity of presupposing certain things (concepts, principles or techniques) if we want to engage in certain other things (argument, discussion, proof, justification). To say that you *only* need to subscribe to certain conventions, say passing the after-dinner port and madeira in a certain direction, *if* you want to value certain high-table society is true if trivial. To say that you *only* need to attend to reason and logic *if* you want to have meaningful discourse and to engage seriously in justificatory questioning, is not so clear since nobody could utter or entertain such a proposition unless they were already committed to such discourse and such enquiry. That is to say: they could not utter or entertain such a proposition meaningfully, or with any point, unless so committed; nor could they have any way of indicating the truth of such an assertion without commitment to accepted procedures of justification connected with reason and logic. The *tu quoque* argument, in short, can always be turned upon anybody who tries to *demonstrate* or *argue* the dispensability of reason: in order to make the case such a proponent must necessarily presuppose not only the use of reason but its value.

The theory of liberal education rejects this extension of relativism to rationality itself. Indeed, the arguments of the theory have all been in the other direction: that is to say, they have started with the necessary presupposition of reason in asking justificatory questions about education and have tried to work out the extensive implications of such necessary presuppositions. If our most fundamental justificatory principles are not to be rooted in the very necessities of justificatory enquiry it is difficult to see where else they might be located. The point at issue here is an extremely important educational and political one. To suppose, for example, that working-class youngsters need not engage too seriously in reason and logic because these are merely the instruments and legitimations of those who exploit them, would be seriously to betray working-class youngsters. If this became a seriously prevalent view, instead of merely an academic one, then working-class youngsters could, as it were, be betrayed from two sides: one side saying that a liberal education is not necessary because it has no economic utility, and the other side saying that a liberal education is not necessary because it is merely a body of capitalist legitimations. My argument is that liberal education, properly understood, liberates precisely because of its dependence, in content and method, on the only resource we have for arbitration between conflicting calls to belief and action, namely our reason. Sociological accounts of the kind I have so far mentioned go a long way in describing forces acting against the use and development of reason, just as Freudian accounts attempt to explain different kinds of distortions and aberrations of such development; but both go too far if they claim that there is *nothing* but an arbitrary area of conflict in which all we can do is make blind and meaningless commitments.

In these two sections I have tried to deal with the challenge of what I have called epistemological relativism on a front admittedly limited by my present purposes, and taking the work of Esland and Young in 'Knowledge and Control' as reasonably clear exemplars of such a challenge. Since the publication of 'Knowledge and Control' the challenge of relativism has widened and much more has been written about the way in which social forces affect the content and methodology of education. Much of this work has clustered around the idea of ideology, and to this I must now turn in rather more detail.

10.4 Ideology

A great deal of sociological writing on education at the turn of the decade and into the 1980s is centred around the concept of ideology, and the discussion here is at once complex, interesting and challenging to the ideas of liberal education I have outlined. The discussion is complex for a number of reasons. There is, to start with, no immediate and authoritative definition of 'ideology' that can be given, part of the debate always being to do with what ideology *is* and whether or not its illocutionary force is to be taken as pejorative or not. A further complexity is that discussions of ideology are inevitably political, not least because the concept is a key one for theorists in the Marxist tradition of political and cultural analysis. It is therefore difficult to avoid being caught up in the many debates within Marxism itself between humanistic, classical and neo-Marxists as to the nature of ideology, its relation to the state, the ruling class and the working class, and the possibility or impossibility of transcending the influence of dominant ideologies.

The discussion is interesting because, in my view, considerable light is thrown on human belief and understanding, and educational attempts to facilitate the development of these characteristics, by considering them in the context of ideology. Notions that have concerned philosophers of education, like 'indoctrination', 'justifiable beliefs', 'living truths and dead dogmas', 'knowledge' and 'understanding', which have already figured in my account, have obvious connections with concepts like ideology and can only gain in sharpness of characterization by being considered together with that concept.

For some writers education in a capitalist society is nothing more than the socialization of pupils into the particular ideology of such a society. If this is an accurate description of education in a capitalist society, then claims that liberal education was going on would be mere pretensions; and claims that liberal education as I have characterized it *could* go on would be countered by a demonstration of the dependence of prevailing ideologies on the existing capitalist mode of production and the social relations necessarily entailed by such a mode of production. On such a view a genuinely liberating education could only follow the liberation from domination and oppression consequent upon the destruction of the capitalist mode of production and its attendant social relations. In this way, certain analyses of education in capitalist societies, involving the notion of ideology, constitute a serious threat and challenge to ideas of the desirability and possibility of liberal education spelled out earlier in this work, in that so far they seem to have ignored the forces of ideology with which they have to contend.

It will be helpful, I think, to state my thesis on this before I go on to attempt its demonstration and justification. This will at least help readers to see where I am heading for through some admittedly confusing territory. I shall argue that ideology is a meaningful and useful concept, and that the term does name a force acting in culture generally and in education particularly. Further, I shall argue that it is also meaningful to talk of dominant ideologies that are related to political and economic structures, as picked out in certain uses of the concept of hegemony. On the other hand I shall claim that the distinction some-times drawn between science and ideology is confusing and leaves an epistemological gap to do with the justification of other human practices than science. Finally, I shall claim that ideologies, in so far as they are basically of limited rationality to those living them, can be transcended by the necessity of seeking consistency, coherence and justification in one's life, and a liberal education, properly conceived, is the facilitator of this transcendence. Liberation from the tyranny of the present and the particular is, in part, liberation from ideology.

'Ideology' was originally a word connected with the study of ideas, and it retains that connotation to some extent still. Most writers using the term today, however, use it to name a framework not just of ideas but of actual practices, institutions, engagements and interactions that *embody* ideas in some way. This wider connotation is important to keep in mind, since it helps to establish the notion that ideologies are not just theoretical structures or propositional frameworks but lived experiences in which the 'bearers' of the ideologies, those living them, have no conscious awareness of bearing or living an ideology. A sophistication of the idea of ideology is that an individual's own percep-tion of self is created within and by the ideology within which he lives, and that this is not entirely at the level of reason, cognition and con-sistent awareness. Indeed, among some Marxists there has been a revival of interest in Freudian ideas of the unconscious which attempt further explanation of the penetration of ideologies below the level of conscious awareness.[24]

As characterized so far, of course, there could be any number of ideologies within which different people live. Most of the views I wish to consider, however relate the idea of ideology to political and econo-mic structures. The idea here is that people live within a *dominant* ideology generated by the relations of production in a mainly capitalist market economy. It is not that such an ideology (incorporating ideas of ownership, management and labour, the profit motive and rationale, the separation of public, private and political, and so on) is conceived theoretically and accepted *as* dominant. It is rather that it becomes dominant by being lived in as natural and inevitable, a characteristic as it were of human nature. It is not that the features of such an ideology are not allowed by anyone to be questioned, it is simply that for most people they are not even conceived of as questionable. Yet, of course, the claim of Marxists and others is that such an ideology serves the interests of those members of a capitalist society who rule that society by owning and controlling the means of production, and therefore helps to perpetuate conditions of oppression and exploitation of which the victims, in any full sense, are unaware. It is a further part of this characterization that education constitutes one of the major (for some *the* major) institutional apparatuses for involving each rising generation into the dominant ideology. As Althusser puts it:

> I believe I have good reasons for thinking that behind the scenes of its political Ideological State Apparatus, which occupies the front of the stage, what the bourgeoisie has installed as its number one, i.e. as its dominant ideological State apparatus, is the educational apparatus, which has in fact replaced in its functions the previously dominant ideological State apparatus, the Church.[25]

and, as one of the crudest exponents of the view puts it:

> Education, then, in a capitalist liberal democracy, is a deliberately systematic process that aims to get people to perceive the world in a certain way that favours the ruling class, while at the same time having them believe that they are seeing the world 'objectively'.[26]

Many Marxists would want to say that this last quotation makes the matter sound too deliberate and conspiratorial. What the idea of ideology picks out is something far more complex than mere propaganda. It is not the manipulation of ignorant pupils by skilled servants of the ruling class, all knowing what they are about. It is rather that *all* are caught up in the ideological framework: pupils, parents, teachers and even individual managers, employers and members of the ruling classes themselves. The capitalist mode of production itself, and the social relations it produces, necessitates a framework of thought and practice, of assumptions and institutions that, whilst taken for granted, make the whole set-up coherent and matter of fact. Althusser even describes how he believes the education system provides adaptive perspectives of the ideology to fit subsequent roles in the capitalist mode of production: some pupils being 'ejected' at about 16 years of age into 'production' as workers, whilst others go on gaining different aspirations and attitudes and become:

> small and middle technicians, white collar workers, small and middle executives, petty bourgeois of all kinds. A last portion reaches the summit, either to fall into intellectual semi-employment or to provide . . . the agents of exploitation (capitalists, managers), the agents of repression (soldiers, policemen, politicians, administrators, etc.) and the professional ideologists (priests of all sorts. . .),[27]

the point here being that *all*, not just the workers, are directed and role-determined in an appropriate way by the ideology carried by the education system.

I am still at the stage of briefly characterizing the concept of ideology as it appears in the literature, and anxious to convey the pervasiveness, the taken-for-grantedness, the all-incorporating idea that the more sensitive Marxist writers have in mind, as well as the dependence of the notion on the actually existing mode of production and its necessary social relations. Of course we can still imagine a believer in the virtue of a free market economy actually and *overtly* trying to match education to his ideas, as perhaps some of the advocates of skill-based vocational training are doing, but this would not in itself be an example of ideology at work. More controversially we may imagine a person coming to understand the forces of ideology and resisting them. The extent to which this is possible, or whether it would be just one ideology combating another, we have yet to consider. It is the vast area of taken-for-granted, everyday lived experience — unquestioned, relatively unexamined, yet relatively coherent and sense-making, not a mere illusion or fantasy, yet not the truth or the whole truth — that is the domain of ideology; and school, it is claimed, is the purveyor and reinforcer of it.

Now there seems little doubt to me that this idea, in its more carefully expressed forms at least, conveys a good deal of truth. Schools as they actually exist in democratic capitalist societies do convey, in a taken-for-granted way, much of the value-attitude-thought structure that is conducive to the maintenance of such a society. They tend to favour and institutionalize competition; they favour individual acquisition *against* other individuals; they encourage conformity, often blind conformity, to authority; they relate knowledge status to occupational hierarchy status; they screen in relation to a required occupational hierarchy in a way not unlike that claimed by Althusser; and in spite of much lip-service to the contrary their practices do not always appear to place much emphasis on critical thought, either in teaching methods or in assessment. This is not an inclusive nor an exhaustive list of what schools do, but I believe they do all these things. In so far as they *do*, then the picture of schools as ideological apparatuses is not too difficult to draw.

Whether this, even if true, is to be seen as bad, is a further question. Marxist writers vary; some, like Kevin Harris, manage to convey, if not actually to state, a picture of undiluted capitalist wickedness![28] Others, perhaps Marx himself, and certainly Antonio Gramsci, much more convey the idea of the *necessities* of certain stages of historical development. On this view no wickedness is entailed whatsoever: it is simply the case that certain modes of production will evolve certain sense-making ideologies and the institutional apparatuses to further them. Interestingly, though, and strangely neglected in some contemporary Marxist writing, it is also the case within classical Marxist theory, that historial stages contain within themselves the very contradictions that will bring about their transformation, and these contradictions can exist not only in the material productive base, but in all that is superstructurally co-existent with that base – in other words within the ideology itself. I shall explore the dialectic fruitfulness of that idea later. For the moment there are two ways in which we could say that if schools *are* purveyors of ideology in the way described then it is bad and they should not be. The first is political, and some Marxists would agree with it. The second is educational and most Marxists, though perhaps not Gramsci, would shudder at the separation!

The first argument, then, would say that the prevailing ideology is bad because it tends to support the exploitation and oppression of the working class. I would make two comments on this. The argument only works if you *do* believe the democratic capitalist society to be exploitative and oppressive. For believers of this claim, and the Marxist theories of value that underlie it, then ideology provides a ready answer for why most people fail to see that they are exploited. If you do *not* accept the charge of exploitation, then what is being called 'ideology' could be seen as simply an appropriate inculcation of the young into the values, attitudes and knowledge appropriate to their citizenship in a liberal democratic state – which is exactly how some teachers *do* put it. My other comment is that if ideology is only wrong because it facilitates the exploitation and oppression of the working class, it *seems* to follow that an ideology that did not do that would be all right. Indeed, some writers have seemed to indicate that teachers should encourage the ideology or culture of the working class as a kind of counter-culture or counter-ideology. School then would be seen as a site for conflicting ideologies to, as it were, battle it out for supremacy.[29]

The second argument for considering that ideology is bad is a different one and more closely related to my conception of a liberal education. This argument would be that *any* inculcation of values and beliefs which was not on a basis of reason and evidence, not concerned with issues of justification, would be bad because it fails to respect the pupil as an actual or potential rational agent. This argument, of course, supposes there to be beliefs that are more justifiable than others, more objective than others, and that access to such objective knowledge is possible even in the face of ideological pressure and mystification. I must return to a discussion of this important possibility, but at the moment I am concerned to maintain the meaningfulness of talking about ideology as mediated and reinforced by schools, and the justification for assuming such mediation to be bad.

A further conceptual tool for discussing these notions is to be found in the idea of hegemony. The notion of hegemony, as used in Marxist analysis, combines the idea of a strong and pervasive ideology with that of class dominance. For Raymond Williams, for example, hegemony is:

> the central, effective and dominant system of meanings and values, which are not merely abstract but which are organized and lived. That is why hegemony is not to be understood at the level of mere opinion or mere manipulation. It is a whole body of practices and expectations; our assignments of energy, our ordinary understandings of the nature of man and of his world.[30]

and he is clear that: 'The educational institutions are usually the main agencies of the transmission of an effective dominant culture.'[31] Williams is also concerned, however, to emphasize the complexity, the pervasiveness, and what he calls the 'selective tradition', in the operation of hegemony:

> the way in which from a whole possible area of past and present certain meanings and practices are chosen for emphasis, certain other meanings and practices are neglected and excluded. Even more crucially, some of these meanings and practices are reinterpreted, diluted, or even put into forms which support or at least do not contradict other elements within the effective dominant culture.[32]

Like other writers Williams emphasizes the enormous penetrative power of hegemonic ideology so conceived:

> If what we learn . . . were merely an imposed ideology, or if it were only the isolable meanings and practices of the ruling classes, or of a section of the ruling class, which gets imposed on others, occupying only the tops of our minds, it would be — and one would be glad — a very much easier thing to overthrow.[33]

Now such a force as is picked out in the notion of a hegemonic ideology, or what Williams calls an effective dominant culture, certainly constitutes a challenge to liberal education as a feasible possibility. Some Marxist writers appear to reject the liberal education possibility out of hand — Kevin Harris, for example:

> On the one hand there are fine ideals continually expressed by people who would sincerely and seriously wish to see those ideals manifested in schools and other institutions. On the other hand, there is the capitalist society which requires vast numbers of people to undertake menial instrumental tasks (and to remain unaware of, and powerless to criticize, their real relations in and to the world). Education, as an instrument of society, is thus powerless to practise what it preaches, for it is characterized by the contradiction that

it cannot produce the products it theoretically desires and ostensibly strives for within the society that it is charged with reproducing.[34]

Althusser even 'asks the pardon' of those teachers who he believes try to work against the prevailing ideology:

> They are a kind of hero. But they are rare and how many (the majority) do not even begin to suspect the 'work' the system (which is bigger than they are and crushes them) forces them to do, or worse, put all their heart and ingenuity in performing it with the most advanced awareness (the famous new methods!). So little do they suspect it that their own devotion contributes to the maintenance and nourishment of this ideological representation of the School, which makes the School today as 'natural', indispensable — useful and even beneficial for our contemporaries as the Church was 'natural', indispensable and generous for our ancestors a few centuries ago.[35]

The challenge is thus clear. Since ideology operates below the level of any awareness that it *is* an ideology, and because it is determined by the necessities of the mode of production in a capitalist society, no education in such a society is likely to be liberal in the sense I have been trying to describe and to justify, or so it would seem to follow.

There is another consideration to add to the power of a dominant ideology which has a particularly topical force, and this has to do with the relationship between education and the state. If state power is seen as basically an instrument of the ruling economic class, as Marxists see it, then the rise of state education systems in the late nineteenth century in liberal democratic capitalist states raises interesting explanatory problems. On the one hand extensive, even universal and compulsory, education seemed to turn the coercive power of the state *against* those who would exploit children by employing them for long hours in factories, farms or mines. On the other hand, however, state provision of education made it more possible for schooling to be part of the dominant ideology in two ways. Firstly, by making ostensibly less necessary, and in some cases impossible, the distinctively working-class provision of education in institutions like the socialist Sunday schools — the providers of an alternative vision.[36] In other words the occasion for a class-based working-class education diminished as state-provided education increased. Secondly, of course, the provision of state education made more possible the direct state influence on the *type* of provision and on curriculum content. It thus becomes possible to argue as Rachel Sharp does:

> Although running the risk of overgeneralization the thesis seems plausible that in the course of the nineteenth century the ruling

class gained effective control over a crucial instrument for establishing its dominance: the form and content of schooling. This process facilitated therefore, the increasing management of knowledge in the service of the technical problems generated by the accumulation process and the requirements of maintaining hegemony.... Education for most no longer involves the transfer of sweetness and light, the initiation of the young into a broad and general humanistic curriculum.... the emphasis is on training pupils in those specific instrumental skills required by a differentiated workforce through a range of practical ideologies which serve to reinforce and legitimize the social relations of production.[37]

Similarly, but more generally, Nicos Poulantzas refers to 'the capitalist state's take-over of education and its regimentation of the culture domain in general'.[38] There appears to be some confusion here between what a particular government might advocate and seek to advance as a matter of overt policy – the kind of thing we considered in the previous chapter – and the generally prevailing ethos in which what the state does seems to be in the service of a generally accepted consensus about how things should be. The power of the state is great in either case; but it is more insidious, and more truly ideological, in the latter. Whether state power can be used to advance a truly liberal education system, even in a society still correctly described as capitalist, most Marxists would seem to seriously doubt. Not all of them, though, and I shall return to this debate in my critical section.

Marxist writers, in their complex but illuminating analysis, make use of another notion which we must consider at least briefly before turning to a criticism of their case and a defence of the liberal education ideal against it; this is the notion of *incorporation*. The idea of incorporation picks out the characteristic of a hegemonic ideology to absorb into itself ideas which initially seem to be threats or challenges to it. For example, ideas constituent of liberal democracy, like individual freedom, equality, universal suffrage, freely elected legislatures and responsible cabinet government are, it is alleged, absorbed and metamorphosed into the dominant ideology without altering the basic social relations attendant upon capitalist modes of production. Freedom comes to refer to certain freedoms necessary for capitalist production and the operation of the market; equality comes to refer to equality 'before the law' but not to actual equality in terms of wealth, or it becomes changed into equality of opportunity rather than actual equality; and the conditions of elections require political parties to constrain their programme proposals within the dominant ideology because of the necessity to win votes. The actual ability of liberal democracy to effect change, therefore, is limited to the change that is possible within the parameters established by the capitalist mode of production, change beyond these parameters being seen as 'revolutionary' and destructive of 'society itself'. To the extent that incorporative strategies successfully enable the hegemonic ideology to embrace change whilst still leaving economically determined social relations relatively untouched, to that extent there is little need for the full coercive power of the state to be used. As in so many other aspects of ideology an important agency of incorporation is held to be the school, not only in the reinforcement given to the assumptions of liberal democracy, but also the instrumental assumptions built into curricular structure and practice:

> ways in which the curriculum field supports the widespread interests
> in technical control of human activity, in rationalizing,
> manipulating, 'incorporating', and bureaucratizing individual and
> collective action, and in eliminating personal style and political
> diversity.[39]

It would be a mistake, however, to imagine that incorporation, and other phenomena discussed above, succeed in creating a monolithic and uni-directional dominant ideology. Force can be great, indeed mighty, while still falling short of being absolute — and that is important. Much of the incorporation enables a number of contradictory and alternative positions to operate and be tolerated, as in the case of parliamentary politics, as Raymond Williams points out. Importantly, too, Williams reminds us that *not all* residues of previous cultures, not all aspects of what he calls emergent forms, are incorporated into the dominant culture.[40] Both of these perceptions can serve us in criticism, to which I shall now turn.

10.5 Ideology and liberal education

In turning to a criticism of ideology seen as a challenge to liberal education it is important to make, and to bear in mind, some significant distinctions. The first distinctions to make concern what is under challenge. The first possibility here is that it is education and schooling as it is at present to be found in western capitalist societies that is actually challenged by a characterization of ideology. Kevin Harris is a clear exponent of this view, though not the only one, when he speaks of the overt assertion of liberal and civilizing aims of educators in capitalist states who fail to see that their aims are not, and cannot be, realized because of the dominant ideology within which they work. Since I am *not* claiming that schools at present operate a curriculum or practise the methods of liberal education as outlined earlier in this work, I am not concerned to defend present practice, though I do believe the claims of Harris, as similarly the claims of Althusser, to be somewhat exaggerated if they are to be considered as empirical claims. I also believe, however, that present practice falls considerably short of the ideals of a liberal education that I have tried to spell out, and that part of the cause of this is pressure from a dominant ideology. There is a strong, though far from perfect, match between the ethos of schools and the ethos of capitalist market economies, as I indicated earlier; there are powerful pressures, some covert but some quite overt, to make this match even more marked; and there is a professional failure to articulate a clear conception of liberal education which can be defended against these pressures.

The challenge of ideology is not only directed against liberal education as a name for present practice. The challenge is also clearly one to the ideas of this work. But even here a distinction must be made, for there can be both a hard challenge and a softer challenge addressed to two different objects.

The hard challenge is addressed to the very conception of a liberal education as here expounded. It involves the assertion of the complete impossibility of escaping from or transcending ideology and, in particular, of escaping from or transcending the dominant ideology. I call this challenge the hard challenge because it is of the nature of a logical challenge, though this is never quite clear, it being the logical impossibility of transcending ideology that appears to be asserted. I shall deal very briefly with the hard challenge for two reasons. Firstly, it is not very clear whether anyone actually makes the challenge in quite this form: even Kevin Harris, who comes quite near to it, usually falls somewhat short of making the claim a purely logical and theoretical one. Secondly, as a logical claim the rebuttal seems to me fairly obvious. Nevertheless it is important to consider the possible potential of the logical challenge, partly to set limiting conditions to the argument, and partly to be alert if the strength of the logical challenge is being claimed when the actual argument is somewhat weaker − a strategy not unknown in educational discussions.

The rebuttal does seem plain: if it is impossible to transcend ideology what credence can be given to the accounts claiming to characterize ideology in all its complexity and subtlety? It is much more reasonable to suppose that to understand ideology, to be able to characterize it, is at least to begin to recognize and to escape from it. Further, if some people can give very full accounts of ideology then it is reasonable to assume there to be a continuum, with complete and unconscious absorption at one extreme and relatively conscious liberation or autonomy at the other, with all kinds of intermediate positions with people conscious of some kinds of ideological pressures but ignorant or unconscious of others. The quantitative and qualitative distribution of populations on such a continuum, or more likely on a mesh of continua, could be the subject of empirical enquiry, albeit a very difficult one. These things at present cannot be shown; but what *is* demonstrable is the contradictory nature of asserting the impossibility of escape from ideology, since that proposition can have no force, and barely any meaning, unless considered as itself extra-ideological. This must apply, too, to any statements claiming to embody justifiable beliefs of any kind about ideology.

Marxist writers appear quite often to acknowledge the truth of this in various ways, though the significance of such an acknowledgement often appears to be missed. Two contemporary Marxists, Reynolds and Sullivan, have no doubts that at least Marx himself escaped:

> Marx himself clearly believed that intellectuals such as himself
> could transcend the relativism that results from class position and
> generate accurate accounts of the social world and its nature.
> Marxist theoretical formulations were therefore presented in testable
> form together with the evidence that generated them,[41]

and they assume, as I have done, that if Marx can do it so can at least some others; and they argue, like Gramsci, for the possibility of doing this even on the basis of the curriculum as it exists in capitalist social formations — but that is to run ahead. Reynolds and Sullivan appear to reserve the capacity to transcend ideology for intellectuals, but, as Gramsci reminds us:

> *homo faber* cannot be separated from *homo sapiens*. Each man,
> finally, outside his professional activity, carries on some form of
> intellectual activity, that is, he is a 'philosopher', an artist, a man
> of taste, he participates in a particular conception of the world,
> has a conscious line of moral conduct, and therefore contributes
> to sustain a conception of the world or to modify it, that is, to
> bring into being new modes of thought. . . . All men are intellectuals,
> one would therefore say: but not all men have in society the
> function of intellectuals.[42]

A common distinction made in Marxist terminology is that between science on the one hand and ideology on the other. 'Science' here, of course, does not refer to the physical sciences alone but also, and indeed particularly, to the possibility of social, political and economic science: systematic, evidential and logical enquiries of which Marxism would, presumably, constitute a paradigm. Science, on this account, reveals inherent contradictions leading to constant reappraisals, whereas ideology presses constantly towards coherence, cohesion and consensus:

As opposed to science ideology has the precise function of hiding
the real contradictions and of *reconstituting* on an imaginary level
a relatively coherent discourse which serves as the horizon of agents'
experience; . . . its social function is not to give agents a *true
knowledge* of the social structure but simply to insert them as it
were into their practical activities supporting this structure.[43]

For Poulantzas to make these kinds of oppositions, of course, he
must be supposing a genuine possibility of discerning and justifying
accounts of 'real contradictions' and 'true knowledge of social structure'. He must be so supposing not just because he asserts them as
possible, but because he is himself giving a supposedly justifiable
account of how things are as concerning ideology and science. Other
Marxists have noted the difficulty of presenting Marxism itself as
credible unless its own valuative and epistemological claims can be
tested. Rachel Sharp, for example, claims that:

It follows logically from a Marxist theory of language and of
ideology that it is both possible and politically necessary to make
judgments about the adequacy of one's thought, otherwise the
grounds for Marxism itself and its epistemological validity
disappear.[44]

Sharp shows the same concern for rational justification when she
argues that a rational debate does not involve the withholding of one's
own substantive point of view:

What it does entail is that the stance adopted is itself open to
rational scrutiny, the basic assumptions exposed for critical appraisal
and the sequences in the discourse examined for their logical
consistency.[45]

Though perhaps it is more akin to faith than the rational temper when
she so firmly claims:

Historical materialism has little to fear in this respect. Precisely
because it is a superior mode of analysis, it can withstand rational
appraisal and be confident when juxtaposed with other systems of
thought.[46]

Rational humanism reasserts itself, and liberal educators might prick
up their ears, when she says:

even within capitalist societies themselves there are moments of
transcendence which, whilst often reflecting capitalist societies'
contradictions, point to the possibility of moving beyond them,
in literature, art and music, in love and friendship and in the
spontaneity, free from ideology, of very young children.[47]

One might add: *and* in science, in mathematics and logic, or in biology and geography — but this is to run ahead again. The point at the moment is to show that not only do Marxists as a matter of fact go beyond ideology, but that the very integrity and justification of Marxism rests on the presupposition of a framework of reason, logic and empirical testing that must be assumed to be relatively free of ideology. Knowledge, or science in its broad sense, rests upon the idea of *justifiable* belief, where 'justifiable' has a much stronger sense than 'legitimated'. A liberal education, in my conception of it, would be essentially concerned with justifiable beliefs, and therefore essentially concerned with diminishing the influence of ideologies, as of other superstitions and mystifications. I have tried to show, so far, that this is at the least a logical possibility. The hard challenge, therefore, is not a threat to my conception of a liberal education.

The softer challenge is of a different kind and accords more with what most Marxist writers are actually saying. This challenge, called softer here because it is not a matter of logical necessity, addresses itself to the *empirical possibility* of practising a liberal education and achieving the kind of liberation from ideology that I have said to be logically possible. Here it is as if a Marxist critic were to say, 'All right, I am not claiming that the liberal education you describe, or the liberation to be achieved by it, is *impossible* to achieve in a capitalist society, but I am saying that success is highly unlikely and that the great majority of people will remain trapped in ideology.' One point that must be made immediately is that although this challenge is addressed to empirical possibility it is not suggested that the issue can be settled empirically. What is going on here is still a matter of judgment as to the forces with which a liberal educator must contend and the possibility of overcoming them to some degree. Neither challenger nor defender can actually set up empirical tests here since the arena for such testing must eventually be history. Nevertheless the judgments we make are important, since they affect our striving to influence history in one way rather than in another. They are particularly important judgments for teachers to make. What could be more demoralizing for a teacher than to come to understand ideology and believe him or herself powerless against it?

I have already cited both a French Marxist, Althusser, and an Australian Marxist, Kevin Harris, as claiming that teachers try to be liberal educators but without much chance of success because of the system and the ideology within which they operate; and the first step in a critical response to this challenge must be to admit the strength of the force acting against the chances of successfully implementing a liberal education policy. As detailed in the previous section ideological forces *are* both strong and pervasive, they tend increasingly to be supported, sometimes overtly, by agencies of the state, and subtleties of incorporation go massively unnoticed. Instrumental and increasingly technical approaches to educational aims and curriculum content, as well as to teaching techniques and assessment procedures, undoubtedly all act against the ideas I would wish to see practised. All this I do not deny.

Agreeing that this is the case, however, and that it is a situaion to be deplored, the next step is to seek the most justifiable countervailing strategy. I say the most *justifiable* strategy, rather than simply the one most likely to succeed, because it is no good freeing people from an ideology, even partly, if what replaces that ideology is as bad or worse. Let me consider briefly two possible countervailing strategies that are not, in my view, justifiable. The first is the naive view, which Murdock and others appeared to hanker after in the early 1970s, that all might be improved if schools recognized a working-class culture as well as a middle-class culture and adapted the curriculum to it, or at least broadened the cultural possibilities of the curriculum. The trouble with this argument is that it is very difficult to point to features of working-class culture, in any distinctive sense, that are not either trivially irrelevant (darts, football, brass-bands, pigeon-fancying), or themselves features of cultural entrapment and ideological exposure (restricted language codes, over use of television, work and neighbourhood-based social relations). It is easy enough to give base and superstructure or other sociological explanations of why working-class cultures are as they are, and why middle-class cultures have distinguishing features. It is also possible to show why the embourgeoisement of the working classes, which some predicted would accompany a rise in working-class living standards, has not taken place. The more interesting point for our present purpose, is that middle-class, and to some extent petit-bourgeois, culture, for whatever cause, appears to have more genuinely liberating (ideology-transcending) possibilities in it than does working-class culture; and this possibly explains why we find so many middle-class Marxists trying to tell workers how exploited they are, from Marx and Lenin onwards to more recent products of the lycée, the gymnasium and the grammar school and the university! What would have to be shown on the 'more working-class culture' argument, is that such a culture contained more liberating or ideology transcending elements within it. I simply do not believe this to be the case. For reasons that are not too difficult to spell out, mainly concerned with privileged access to knowledge and understanding that is more universal and humanistic, the opportunities for liberation among the middle classes are greater than among the working classes, and this has been recognized in campaigns for more equal access to liberal and universalistic education. In one sense it is, of course, misguided to claim that middle-

219

class culture is *better* than working-class culture — it is simply that the former has more access to a liberating universal culture. There appears to be some evidence that mainstream Marxists in England recognize this, as Entwistle reports:

> English Marxist educationists, for example, have put their energies into a campaign for structural reform of the system along comprehensive lines and have not dismissed the traditional curriculum as bourgeois and irrelevant to working class children . . . except for the new radical Left (and some conservative educationists, e.g. G.H. Bantock in Britain) there has historically been no insistence from Marxists upon replacing the traditional subject curriculum with one focused upon 'working-class culture', whatever that might be.[48]

Another variant of the argument, which avoids the concept of working-class culture, is to emphasize the alleged problematic nature of knowledge and the consequent equal validity of pupils' own common-sense knowledge with what Nell Keddie calls 'classroom knowledge'. Keddie's paper[49] is essentially a study of the link between teachers' categorization of pupils and the rigid conceptions of knowledge and ability held by teachers; but implicit in her arguments is the assumption of the equal validity of alternative perceptions, beliefs and classifications of knowledge, and this in turn reflects the general phenomenological position of the 'new sociology of education' of the mid-1970s. Reynolds and Sullivan, claiming to speak as traditional Marxists, strongly contest this view, which appears to ignore the problem of ideology altogether:

> Intellectuals have a role for Marxists in pointing out that many individuals' common sense understandings or constructions of reality are invalid, erroneous beliefs that are especially damaging if they prevent people from seeing, through false consciousness, the nature and causes of the social reality around them. The primacy and importance given to actors' explanations within the new sociology of education is, then, a thoroughly unsocialist method of analysis.[50]

Not only do Reynolds and Sullivan, as classical Marxists, appear to be valuing certain elements of a normal capitalist education system because it can produce intellectuals capable of transcending ideology, but because of its possibilities for working-class children in linking them with historically evolved, universalistic, and liberating humanistic cultures. In this they call in both Gramsci and Lenin as allies:

> Antonio Gramsci echoes Lenin's warning that a working-class culture is 'theoretically wrong and practically harmful' in pre-

socialist, Fascist Italy. He argues that a working-class denied access to the *humanistic rationality* of the traditional scholastic mode itself reinforces the ideology and political hegemony of the ruling class by its incapacity to perceive that the social and economic relations of capitalism can be transcended.[51]

My own rejection of the possibilities of either working-class culture or individual phenomenological views of knowledge effectively or justifiably countervailing dominant ideologies, whilst not Marxist, coincides with the views of these writers. No learning is likely to take place in a completely ideology-free environment, that would be too much to expect; but some curricula, some teaching strategies and methods, will have more possibilities of intellectual liberation than some others. This is precisely the liberal education claim.

If working-class culture and individual phenomenological approaches do not offer much hope against ideology, neither does what might be called 'counter-indoctrination'. To counter the indoctrinatory elements of ruling-class ideology with indoctrination in support of working-class aspirations might be acceptable if the issue were merely one of politics or the class struggle, though even here the ultimate justification would be dubious. From my own point of view such a strategy would be unacceptable because one set of mental chains is simply exchanged for another set, with no *real* liberation taking place at all. It might indeed be the case that to see the school as only a place in which the dominant ideology operates is grossly to oversimplify, and a much more realistic account might be that the school is a site of conflicting ideologies and indoctrinatory pressures, some of which, for working-class children, come from the very conditions of working-class life outside school. That this might be a source of counter-hegemony can give the liberal educator no satisfaction unless the possibility of escape from *all* ideologies, *all* false consciousness, *all* mystification is somehow increased. A better hope probably lies in the idea that if the pupil is exposed to several conflicting ideologies the chance of him coming to see them *as* ideologies is, perhaps, increased.

Unless we are completely cynical, and see education as never more than a tool of those in power or those trying to obtain power, we should try to see how education can become a genuinely liberating force. The liberation would in the first place be a liberation from what we might call a genuine and undistorted ignorance, that of primitivism or childhood. This is what a commonsense view of education has always been, and only the cynical or those with vested interests will insist that this view is entirely naive. People *can* be prisoners of simple ignorance, and education *can* release them. In our own time, however, education can liberate us from the additional and more sophisticated forms of

221

anti-knowledge as well. If we admit all the possibilities and likelihoods of indoctrination, and if we acknowledge the prevailing and dominant ideologies of capitalist states, then we must also recognize that there is no escape from these distortions of the mind unless we pay heed to the genuinely fundamental, the truly evidential and justifiable, and the real requirements of reason and morality that I have claimed should shape our approaches to a liberal education. Ideology trades on the force of the present and the particular; liberal education draws, or should draw, on the longer memory and the wider imagination, on the universal and the humanistic, on the genuinely intellectual advances in knowledge and understanding properly to be shared by all humankind.

There are at least four reasons important enough to note for supposing the liberating benefits of liberal education to be achievable even in an undeniable ideological context.

Firstly, we must note the impossibility of limiting the effects of the very studies necessitated by the instrumental purposes of a capitalist economy. What I mean here is that to teach pupils to read and to compute, to teach them even distorted history and selectively emphasized geography, to teach them the methodology of the physical and the life sciences, to introduce pupils to even conformist views of morality — to do all this, even within all the restrictions of the constraining ideology, is nevertheless to sow the seeds of liberation. Reading skills can be applied anywhere and readers can browse beyond the directed texts; proofs requiring at least some logic can give a taste for reasoning and questioning; the demonstration of historical or geographical 'facts' can show the possibility of alternative views; practical science can rouse the enquiring mind; and the pressures of authority to ensure conformity to its wishes can engender rebellion and questioning for justification. Yet these skills, these attitudes and this knowledge are all required to achieve the purely instrumental purposes, the preparation for work and citizenship, in a capitalist society. In short, you cannot train people in the sophisticated knowledge and skills necessary to function and to maintain the social relations of a capitalist economy and its accompanying political system, without at the same time generating the very skills, knowledge and understanding that can be turned critically and reflectively inward upon the system and its ideology.

Secondly, we should note that this ought not to surprise any Marxist who espouses a dialectical view of historical development, for the idea that forces for change are generated by the inherent contradictions of a system is central to that view. The idea that certain modes of production and the social relations consequent upon them give rise to certain educational needs, and that the satisfaction of these needs has the further consequence of generating critical and countervailing ideas that will in time act against the system, is almost a classical example of dialectical materialism at work. Such an idea explains the fact, otherwise difficult to explain, that critical minds *do* emerge from capitalist education systems, and gives hope and support to those who seek to liberate their pupils from ideologies and other mystifications. Such an idea suggests that the views of Kevin Harris and Louis Althusser, mentioned earlier, are unduly pessimistic and fail to take account either of the dialectics of change or of what Geoff Whitty calls 'the empirical reality of schooling'.[52]

Thirdly, it must be emphasized that if these possibilities appear to exist even within existing practice in capitalist schooling, they would exist much more strongly within a system of liberal education as argued for in earlier chapters of this work. The reason for supposing this to be the case is precisely because those rational concerns which are engendered as it were reluctantly, half-heartedly and accidentally, in existing practice, would become the very *raison d'être* of liberal education as here characterized. Reason, evidence and critical reflection would no longer be the subordinate necessities of instrumental functioning, but would become the essential components of the liberating understanding that a liberal education aims at.

Fourthly, a liberal educator can take some comfort from the idea that Raymond Williams has fed into the debate: namely the view that what he has called residual and emergent forms of culture are not always incorporated into the dominant ideology and provide lacunae within which potentially liberating and transcending notions can lodge and multiply.[53] There are many illustrations of what Williams means here. Literature admittedly contains many forms supportive of the dominant ideology, giving an oversimplified view of married family life, romance, heroism in war and generally exalting wealth acquisition and financial success. But it is also the case that literature is the great medium of the universal questioning of the human condition, the exploration of the possibilities of human life and of the variety of human relationships. To help a child enter the world of literature is to help him or her move away from the present and the particular to the wider imagination and the greater variety of possibility. Precisely because children and young people read the literature of the past they are put in touch with residual elements of culture which help them to question the dominant assumptions of the present. The same can be said about drama, and to a lesser extent about music and art. Activities of an aesthetic and creative kind reinforce a universal concern for activities worthwhile in themselves and generate a questioning of the dominant utilitarian ideology. Potters, sculptors, painters and art historians may appear to pose no threat to the dominant ideology, and therefore escape the worst of incorporation, but in the way I have indicated they are avenues of escape and transcendence and focal points of questioning and subversion of establishment ideas: witness the part played by writers and artists in revolutionary activity.

Emergent cultures may be seen in the present range of private hobbies and interests, always ahead of and distinct from the apparatus of the state and the school. It is perhaps more correct to say that most of these hobbies and interests have both emergent *and* residual elements: they often embody traditions but their followers are alert to new technologies which the market provides in response to the interest-generated demand — gardening would be a good example of this. In the case of interest in electronics, computers and micro-processors it might be more correct to speak of genuinely emergent cultures, though whether the market leads or follows here might be more debatable.

The significance of the growing influence of private hobbies and interests goes much further than their exemplification of residual and emergent cultures. The phenomenon demonstrates a concern for activities valuable in themselves rather than for instrumental or wealth-gaining reasons. Such interests are often foci of clubs and collectivities where reason, autonomy, imagination and creativity are fostered and rewarded by significant fraternity that is outside the dominant ideology. Most significantly these interests continue many elements of a universalistic liberal education that would have no outlet in the paid occupations of most people. I do not subscribe to the simplistic forms of the 'education for leisure' lobby, but there is promise in the idea that if technology can reduce the need for labour then we might have more time for educated and civilizing pursuits of intrinsic worth, rather than having to spend long times in the diminishing, de-skilling and crudely utilitarian context of the factory, office or shop. Such arrangements, of course, cannot grow on the basis of a simple division between the employed and the unemployed; but even here the hope of social arrangements to deal justly with diminishing labour need must come from the pressures of a broadly educated population capable of imagining radically different possibilities.

For all these reasons a truly liberal education remains the best hope against both primitive ignorance with all its accompaniments of prejudice and superstition, and against the more modern forms of anti-knowledge, embodied in ideology, that we have been considering. The existence of dominant ideologies *is* a threat and a challenge to the possibility of a liberal education, but this must be seen as a challenge to liberal educators to make education genuinely liberating. This is precisely what my earlier chapters have been about.

All the foregoing might understandably be seen as an attempt to persuade those of a socialist or Marxist viewpoint to see my account of liberal education as the best and most justifiable countervailing force against capitalist ideology, apart from direct political action within or outside parliamentary forms. To some extent that is exactly the direction of my argument, which is against the counsel of despair to be found in some left-wing writings. The argument, however, is on a broader front and on more general principles than that. This is for two main reasons. Firstly, the argument says to the left-wing view not only that liberal education stands as a countervailing force to capitalist indoctrination, but that it also stands against any attempt at left-wing indoctrination, because it acts against *all* non-evidential, non-rational, non-universalistic forms of education. Secondly, the liberal educator says to those of other political persuasions: you have nothing to fear from liberal education if you genuinely believe your views to be justifiable and rational. We would state this as a principle that has wide application, since it applies not only to political but to religious groupings: to the extent that a political or other view is held by its supporters to be rationally justifiable its supporters should have no reason to fear liberal education. Indeed, to the extent that any particular group, party or sect does fear liberal education and its connection with reason and autonomy, then the views of that group, party or sect must be suspect as to their justification.

It is now necessary to look more closely at what might be called the providers of liberal education. I shall limit myself to some fairly brief observations about the part of the state in the concluding section of this chapter, and then consider the position of the liberal educators themselves, the teachers, in the final chapter.

10.6 The state and liberal education

I make no attempt in this section to give a full analysis of the relation between the state and liberal education. My purpose is the more limited and purely prescriptive one of asserting briefly what such a relationship *should* be, given that the state claims to be democratic and the type of education we are considering is the liberal general education characterized and justified in earlier chapters. The questions here are of two broad kinds: firstly, what is the justification of the state providing and in some sense controlling education, as against other claims to deny to the state such power and influence? Secondly, what are the limits to state control of education? It will be seen that the answers to these two broad questions are very closely connected.

We have already noted that the state has increased its power over educational provision and policy in this country, and is now increasing its power and influence over the content and methodology of education. We have also noted that this can be a mixed blessing which on the one hand has undoubtedly made education more widely available, but on the other hand has tended to make education more monolithic and more likely to serve ideological hegemony. All this is matter of fact, but I am now more concerned with what ought to be the case. Should the state have such power over education, or is there something to be said on behalf of the counter-claimants?

The two main counter-claimants, though not entirely forming two clear camps, are those who claim rights for parents to send their children to entirely private (independent) schools financed out of fees or in other ways independent of public finance, and those who call themselves 'de-schoolers' and seek the abolition of schools in the normal sense altogether. Both of these counter-claims rest to a greater or lesser extent on the alleged rights of parents, though this is more explicit in the former than in the latter. I shall not give expositions of the two views here, since the arguments are familiar to most people and can be easily read elsewhere.[54] The position I am maintaining is as follows: rights are extremely difficult to characterize and to uphold, and in any case are often contradictory. For example, if parents can be said to have rights, then so can children, and some of the children's rights could be held to be rights *against* parents, as Bruce Ackerman argues.[55] It is less confusing to argue the case in terms of duties. Parents, it is true, have certain duties and responsibilities towards their children. The collective adult community, the state in its collectively sovereign sense, also has duties and responsibilities towards all the young of the community. These duties, those of parents individually and of all adults collectively, include on my account the moral responsibility of ensuring that all youngsters are helped towards a moral and rational autonomy, because to do anything other is to foreclose on some possibilities of choice and therefore to fail to respect youngsters as persons or potential persons. The *duties* of the state, and the *duties* of parents are thus the same in respect of education. Because of the practical difficulties on the one hand, and the possibilities of inequality and injustice on the other if there were no central provision or control of education, there is some justification for the state in its executive aspect acting as agent for the state in its collective, adult community, sovereign aspect, in providing and to some extent controlling education for all the young of that country. This, however, does not give the state, in its executive aspect, unlimited rights. The duty is a clear one, that is to provide, maintain and support a general, liberal education of something like the kind I have described, or of some other form that can be justified in terms of liberation, rationality and autonomy. The state must provide what Entwistle has happily called 'disinterested schooling'. Entwistle refers to Gramsci's argument that the school should be basically disinterested:

> By this he (Gramsci) seemed to have at least two things in mind.
> First, that the schooling of children should not be vocational in the

sense of providing technical or professional training . . . thus the school should be disinterested as to the future occupational destiny of the child. But, second, the humanistic culture of the school should enshrine the traditional academic values of objectivity, pluralism . . ., rationality — the disinterested pursuit of knowledge.[56]

To the extent that the state fails to provide *this* kind of education, or actively promotes some other kind — say, vocational training or political indoctrination — to that extent its rights in the matter are abrogated, its justification for commanding obedience collapsed.

It might be argued, as against the view just outlined, that provided a government is properly elected its powers cannot be limited in the way described, and that it could claim a right to control or to de-control education in any way that the electorate did not object to by turning the government out of office. This may have force in constitutional law, but little in logic or morality. The force of a majority mandate has been much exaggerated in modern conceptions of democracy, and can lead to considerable tyranny, as Hayek has pointed out.[57] It is much more reasonable to suppose that a government elected to office within democratic forms is bound to uphold the presuppositions of those forms, namely, certain assumptions about the autonomy of individuals, reason, freedom of inquiry and debate, and the proper adherence to argument rather than to force. These presuppositions are more important than the temporary will of the majority, since they underpin — give coherence to — any particular representative arrangements; and they should therefore provide the limits necessary to prevent a tyranny of the majority. To put this another way: both democracy *and* liberal education presuppose the same respect for persons and for reason. It would therefore be inconsistent and incoherent for a democratically elected government to impose a form and content of education which was not based on the development of rational autonomy in some full and plain sense. For any particular democratic government to recognize an obligation to provide and defend liberal education, therefore, does not rest upon any majority mandate, but rather upon the much more profound and fundamental roots of the political forms of which it is but a temporary part.

On this argument the executive state might allow other agencies to run schools if they too were run on genuinely liberal education lines, and this necessarily would require inspection and the satisfying of certain standards of content and methodology. Whether the state *justifiably* allowed such private and independent ventures in education, even if genuinely liberal, would depend upon other aspects of government policy concerning economic and social equality; but this raises issues beyond my present intentions. What would not be justifiable, on my account, would be to allow the provision of schools of a religious denominational kind where the pupils were to be educated and trained into a predetermined set of beliefs and attitudes, simply because these were the beliefs and attitudes of their parents. The right to provide such schools, or even to have them provided, is sometimes claimed on the basis of tolerance and pluralism; but this again is a confused point of view since the toleration appealed to is to be extended to the parents who then impose a rigid and intolerant control over the future of their children. Any believer in tolerance, like any believer in democracy, must favour the provision and protection of a liberal education. To favour or allow other kinds, whereby some youngsters are excluded from liberal education, is to subvert the very roots of democracy and tolerance.

In order to exercise the function of providing and defending liberal education the state must employ administrative officials and, of course, liberal educators — that is to say, teachers who see themselves and are seen by others to be liberal educators. My final chapter will be concerned with the role of such teachers.

11   Teachers, assessment and accountability

The theme of this my concluding chapter is a simple one. It is to argue that teachers in a system of state-provided general and compulsory education should owe their major professional loyalty to the ideals of a liberal education as laid out here, and have the capacity, training and education to practise the methods and strategies of liberal education. It is, secondly, to claim that examinations, assessments and other testing procedures in schools should primarily be to monitor and evaluate the general achievement of the objectives of liberal education, and to serve the diagnostic purposes of such an education, rather than to serve the selective purposes of employers and higher education. Thirdly, the chapter will argue that a moral accountability model which stresses the autonomy of the teacher is appropriately applied to teachers as liberal educators, rather than a conception of accountability in which teachers are seen as employed simply to serve the needs of society as perceived variably from time to time by governments and other providing agencies.

11.1 Teachers as liberal educators

For reasons which are not always made clear in any general sense people employed as teachers are often expected to engage in tasks which impossibly extend their role. To list only the more important areas of competence expected from teachers, apart from that of teaching, is most revealing. Teachers to start with (I take the British case throughout) must be collectively responsible in a school for the general management of the school and for the organization, discipline and control of the pupils. So much is this taken for granted that to list it as my first *addition* to the role of the teacher will surprise most readers. Nevertheless it *is* an addition, and it is a function which generates many difficulties in the way of liberally educating and many diversions from it. A teacher has no sooner demonstrated his or her excellence as a teacher, for example, than much of that teacher's time and energy is diverted into responsibilities of an organizational or managerial kind which do not need teaching expertise to carry out. Further to this, the confusion of teaching role with control and custodial roles spreads to the understanding of the pupil. The more successful the teacher is, as a liberal educator, in achieving aims of neutral and evidential exposition, concern for the pupil's autonomy, and so on, the more this will clash with the teacher's exercise of authority as organizer, controller and manager. One has only to work with teachers on in-service courses to hear how often this kind of role conflict is a source of genuine worry and debilitating tension. In initial training the first fear of student teachers is not whether they will be able to *teach* children anything, but whether they will be able to *control* their pupils. Head teachers, those in charge of schools, need to be financial and public relation experts, problem consultants, fund-raisers, personnel managers and employment agencies — so much so that it is not surprising if the claims of liberal education are seen as almost hopelessly idealistic to them as compared to their control and managerial functions. All these problems have undeniably increased as the size of schools has increased and as pressures of economy and financial stringency have appeared on the scene with every sign of staying there.

I state the problem here because of my concern with its effects on the possibilities of a liberal education, not because I have instant solutions. I am inclined to think that we are wrong to try to solve this problem by extra courses for 'upper and middle management' and by providing class teachers with better control techniques. My own reasoning is all in the direction of leaving good teachers free to teach, recognizing teaching as important and rewarding it accordingly. At the moment we tend to attach further organizational responsibilities to promotion possibilities and career advancement, almost as though being a good teacher was considered insufficient. This is to devalue the most important and central competency of the liberal educator.

Nor is this all, since ordinary class teachers are expected to do many other things besides teaching. Counselling and what is now popularly called 'pastoral care' are expected of all teachers, again without any very convincing reasons as to why this should be so. Confusion of role abounds again in this area. Of course pupils must be cared for in schools, and of course they must be appropriately advised. The appropriate care and advice that teachers might be expected to give, however, is limited both by the expertise and by the purposes of teachers, and very rightly so. It is ironical that nowadays teachers are expected to give advice on all kinds of personal and social matters, on career choices, on health, on personal relationships and family life-styles and leisure activities, yet seem not really expected to have either individual or collectively professional views on the nature of the education they are providing. An expertise appears to be expected of teachers in all kinds of areas in which they are not trained and could not possibly be trained, whilst any claim to expert knowledge about the nature, content and methodology of a compulsory and universal education is greeted with suspicion against the claims of government, employers and parents. As a recipe for confusing and demoralizing teachers and imposing a pre-determined amateurism and incompetency on them, little more harmful could have been devised.

Teachers, as liberal educators, badly need a narrowing of focus and the will to resist extensions of role and dilutions of purpose. Their job is to liberally educate the nation's young people. To do that teachers need to be free to get on with the job within a framework largely determined by themselves acting collectively as liberal educators. Managing, organizing, counselling, career advice and many aspects of in-school caring, necessitated or merely made convenient by the presence of large numbers of young people in one institution, could and should be carried out in very large part by other people, specially trained and able to form appropriately different relationships with young people from those appropriate to teachers and their pupils.

What I have said here should not be pushed to *reductio ad absurdum*. Of course teachers must do such organizing, managing, advising and caring as is a necessary part of and accompaniment to teaching. It is because this is the case that all the extensions of role that I have been criticizing have found such ready and willing subjects. Teachers should have a sharp sense, however, of the limits of their professional purpose and competence; and they should be sensitively aware of the point where the role extensions take over and the time, energy and thought devoted truly to the purposes of liberal education start to be diminished. Nor should we be too much impressed by what some few persons of exceptional energy, will and intellect can achieve across all these broad areas. Their achievements are positively harmful if it is supposed that all teachers of average competence can emulate them. That way lies frustration and failure for many who on a narrower front could have been reasonably efficient.

Even if teachers are left free to teach, as I am advocating, there is still the question of what they teach. Not all that can be taught is taught for the purposes or in the style of liberal education. Little need be said here about this matter since earlier chapters have discussed it. I have said that liberal education need not be all that goes on in a school, and this remains true. There is room for all kinds of voluntary activities which schools can conveniently provide, both for their pupils of school age and for adults in the community; and within the bounds of morality and safety I see no reason why this provision should not be based on demand and the available skills and facilities. The major task of the teachers, however, is to provide as full as possible a pattern of liberal education for pupils of compulsory school age, and this demanding task will take most of their time, their thought and their energy.

The two main temptations likely to divert teachers, in terms of content and method, away from their proper liberal education task are those of instrumentality and specialism. The temptation and pressure of instrumentality has already been discussed but little has so far been said about specialism. In a way specialism is itself a form of instrumental or vocational preparation because the unstated assumption is that the pupils will themselves become teachers or researchers in the subject area. The content and style of such teaching looks less narrowly vocational because the subject looks liberal − i.e. it might be history, literature or physics. Nevertheless the assumptions behind the teaching are that the students are aspiring to be historians, literary critics or physicists, that they will take public examinations in those fields, go to universities, and in due course either work to extend knowledge of the particular field or, by teaching, initiate others into these lines of inquiry.

Specialism is, of course, necessary to a cultured and civilized society. We do need people to carry on the specialized study and teaching of discrete areas of knowledge and inquiry. It does not follow from this, however, that there is any public obligation to train all young people as specialists, or even very large numbers of them; the general justification of the provision of a universal and compulsory system of liberal education does not extend to this at all, and different justifications would be needed to determine what training should be provided, for whom, and at whose expense. This all goes beyond my present concerns and arguments, but a second point about specialism is more pertinent.

People who have themselves been trained as specialists in subject areas often become teachers in secondary schools of liberal and general education. Because of their background, training and personal interest they often find it difficult to think of themselves as liberal educators, seeing themselves rather as having a major loyalty to mathematics, literature, history or whatever. Pupils are then taught, in terms of content and method, as though they too are future specialists, the teaching of the multitude who will not go on to university being largely determined by the requirements of those who will. Thus the specialist training appropriate to post-compulsory education gets pushed down into the compulsory period to the detriment of liberal education. Again the complaint must not be misunderstood. Specialist teachers are needed in schools of liberal education in the sense that teachers with specialist knowledge are needed. Such teachers, however, must also be liberal educators. They must see their subjects in the light of liberal education, that is to say:

(i) as illuminating and being illuminated by other subject areas,
(ii) as serving the methodological purposes of a liberal education in terms of evidential teaching, concern for reason, and the development of and respect for pupil autonomy, and
(iii) as not making exclusive claims to 'proper' knowledge or making excessive claims on pupils' time and energy in the light of the wide demands of liberal education.

In other words, within the period of compulsory education at least, though teachers may need to be specialists they should not be trying to turn their pupils into specialists. Their first duty is to liberally educate.

11.2 The functions of assessment in liberal education

Examinations and assessments at present perform a great variety of functions in British education, few of them to do with the purposes of a liberal education. The three common public examinations: GCE 'O' level, CSE and GCE 'A' level, are widely used by employers and by .universities and other institutions of higher and further education for selection purposes. In the case of employers any relationship between the achievements indicated by the examination results and the aptitudes, knowledge and understanding required by the employers is usually remote. Internal examinations in schools are often, though not exclusively, practices for the public examinations or indicators of suitability for them, and thus modelled largely on them. This pattern broadly dominates the examination system. It is norm-based, essentially competitive, and compares pupils with other pupils rather than indicating anything at all precise or informative about the pupil's understanding.

The present examination system also encourages the early specialization into a narrow range of subjects that is so inimical to a broadly based liberal education. It is of course true that many pupils at age 16 take a broad and humane mixture of 'O' level or CSE subjects, and it is also true that pupils study subjects other than those they are taking for examination purposes. Nevertheless, the very importance of examination success forces some pupils to concentrate on a smaller number of subjects than would be advisable in terms of liberal education; and the very same importance tends to devalue in the minds of pupils and teachers any studies not leading to examinations. At the Advanced GCE level the range is usually quite narrow and attempts to revise the system to encourage a wider range of studies between age 16 and 18 has been constantly resisted by the universities.[1]

There is another way in which the present system does not well serve the purposes of liberal education. This is in the actual nature of examinations, which in spite of many attempts at reform remains largely that which rewards memory and the regurgitation of material acquired from school courses and textbooks. Again because of the importance of the examinations, and the way success in them is assessed, many teachers will claim that they simply do not have time to nurture in pupils the qualities of evidential thinking, imagination and independence that should be the hallmarks of the liberally educated. Indeed, the examination system is especially pernicious in its effects upon parents and pupils, who are quick to argue that if a course of study does not prepare the pupil either for a job or an examination then it cannot be worthwhile, and who are suspicious of any teaching methods or learning methods likely to complicate the readiness of an approved response.

It is perhaps too much to claim that the present system of examination and assessment is wrong in any absolute sense. It seems to satisfy the universities and employers, though I am inclined to think that far too heavy a price is paid for that satisfaction. My more modest complaint, serious enough in this context, is that the present system does not and cannot serve the purposes of the liberal educator.

Such purposes do have monitoring, evaluating, assessing and diagnostic implications. Whenever aims and intentions are given, as they are in any clearly thought-out and accountable system of liberal eduction, then teaching and learning must be monitored in some way to see whether the aims are being met and the intentions carried out, both in general and in the case of individual pupils. The purpose here is nothing to do with the rank ordering of pupils, and nothing to do with grading or declaring some pupils to have passed and others to have failed. It has everything to do with finding out, over given content areas, whether and to what extent pupils are coming to appreciate evidence, use argument, make and extend cognitive and conceptual relationships and care about reason, other persons, and for what is worthwhile. The point, in any given pupil's case, is not how the pupil compares with others, but how the pupil compares with what he or she could understand, know, reason about, imagine, care about or create a month ago, a year ago or whatever. The general point is the range of such cognitive and dispositional advance that we are able to achieve over the total number of pupils. The criteria are personally dynamic, not interpersonally comparative.

As in other things I have discussed, it should be the task of those who need to select — employers, universities, institutions of higher and further education, grant awarders, and so on — to devise their own tests and procedures to select efficiently in terms of what they need to satisfy *their* purposes. Liberal educators should then be free to tackle responsibly the task of efficiently monitoring their own achievements on their own criteria, without the constant difficulty of using instruments of selection and comparison to guide educational purposes.

Most textbooks on the curriculum[2] seem to agree that educational assessment and evaluation should relate to educational purposes, not other purposes, and they offer a simple model in which educational aims are evolved from which objectives are determined and learning-teaching experiences designed to achieve such objectives. The learned outcomes are then assessed and the aims, objectives and particularly the teaching modified if necessary in the light of the evaluation. This is correct in its location within the purposes of education but over-simplified in a number of respects. Teaching and learning arrangements cannot be seen simply as means to the achievement of certain desirable outcomes, at least not in a liberal education, because the teaching and the learning must themselves satisfy certain criteria of the kind des-scribed in Chapter 8. The whole procedure cannot be one in which only outcomes are judged, especially if the outcomes are to be characterized in behavioural or performance terms. The purposes of liberal education are far better served by something like Lawrence Stenhouse's insistence on all procedures satisfying certain criteria and standards implicit or explicit in the general educational purposes.[3] Simple behaviourism will not serve liberal education with all the latter's emphasis on what goes on in the mind of the pupil.

Though perhaps more difficult to construct and less familiar than ordinary examinations, it is possible to assess against the criteria required by liberal education. Changes in attitudes and dispositions can be measured;[4] it is possible to come closer to the revelation of a person's real understanding than conventional examinations do;[5] imagination and creativity are assessable;[6] and the use of evidence, reason and argument can certainly be judged. Instruments for the careful diagnosis of individual difficulties in reading and elementary mathematics are well established and exist in other learning areas as well. Because of our insistence on the individual nature of understanding and on the importance of individualized learning techniques there is a great need in liberal education for a wide development of individual diagnostic testing methods which guide both pupil and teacher in the best next step forward to enhanced understanding.

Above all, and to use the current terminology, testing for liberal education purposes needs to be criterion-referenced and not norm-referenced.[7] That is to say, pupils and teachers in liberal education do not much need to know how a pupil compares with other pupils. Rank orders, standard scores, percentiles and the like offer no real aid to liberal educators and their pupils. What they need to know, in the case of pupil Jane, say, is what Jane knows and understands; how Jane reasons, uses evidence and argues; and what Jane cares about.

All this needs to be known against criteria of what is understandable and knowable in certain areas of inquiry; against established criteria of reasoning, the use of evidence and argument; and against judgments of the appropriateness and worthwhileness of certain kinds of caring and of certain objects of caring.

11.3 Teacher accountability and liberal education

It has become a matter of growing concern, as the importance of education and schooling has grown in people's minds, that schools and teachers should be accountable in some way. This has sometimes been taken to mean that teachers should be seen to be doing what others would have them do. For example: that they should teach a core curriculum laid down by an agency of government; that they should turn out products capable of satisfying the country's manpower requirements; that they should help pupils adapt themselves to a technological society; or that they should persuade youngsters to come to terms with our particular version of the mixed economy. Others, of course, have seen a different location of accountability, not to central or local government authority so much as to the local community, where this is seen in terms of the wishes of local parents and employers.

A theory of liberal education must accept the general idea of the accountability of teachers, but it cannot accept an oversimplified version of accountability in which all is satisfactory if teachers are seen to be doing what they are told to do by others. The reason for the inadequacy of this view for the liberal educator should be apparent. A liberal educator must be accountable only in the sense that he or she is acting professionally *as* a liberal educator, and cannot be held accountable for not satisfying aims, or not achieving objectives which are themselves inimical to the purposes of a liberal education.

The conception of accountability to be argued for here, therefore, is that of the relatively autonomous teacher, actively involved as a liberal educator, and accountable as a professional expert in the field of liberal education. Such a teacher would be accountable in the main to his or her own informed conception of the role of liberal educator. The only, but important, sense in which accountability extends and is characterized beyond this are, firstly, the sense in which the teacher should explain to others − pupils, parents, employers and government authorities − what he or she is trying to do and why; secondly, the sense in which it should be shown publicly that what is attempted is being achieved; and, thirdly, the sense in which professional consensus should be sought and reasonable cooperation maintained with professional colleagues. These conditions of an accountability appropriate for liberal educators might conveniently be listed as:

  (i)   the moral autonomy condition,
 (ii)   the explaining and justifying condition,
(iii)   the public evaluation condition, and
 (iv)   the professional cooperation condition.

It is perhaps worth noting here the similarity of this description of accountability to our normal sense of moral responsibility. To be morally responsible I have to be basically autonomous, self-governed, but I am also expected to give reasonable explanations and justifications of my actions, to show that I *am* doing what I say I am doing, and to engage in reasonable cooperation with my fellows. Moral action is accountable action; professional action is accountable action; but accounts of both only make sense where the agent is considered to be autonomous, and neither make sense where the agent is considered as simply doing what others tell him. Accountability necessarily involves and does not contradict autonomy. What it does contradict is a refusal to give an account of one's actions or to cooperate with others.

To be autonomous in the sense intended here is to be governed by oneself rather than by others. It has sometimes been made to sound as if 'autonomous' meant doing simply and selfishly what one felt like doing, instead of being governed at all. It cannot be emphasized too strongly that no serious advocate of the importance of autonomy has ever meant this. What governs the autonomous person is not feeling but reason.[8] This is particularly important when it is teacher autonomy that is at issue. An autonomous teacher would be governed in his professional decisions by the professional exercise of his own reason, not by whim, impulse or feeling. Such a teacher would take proper advice, heed the needs and concerns of pupils and other appropriate people and take into account relevant knowledge and research. He would do all these things because that is what it would *be* to exercise reason in the making of decisions. What an autonomous teacher could not do, and retain autonomy, would be to consider the teacher's role simply as that of agent for someone else's decision-making, especially where such another was not a professional educator.

This is not to say, of course, that the autonomous teacher would necessarily be opposed to authority or the rule of law. Neither of these, however, can be overriding for an autonomous teacher, since both must be subject to justification and a framework of consent, whether we are talking about the law of the land or the framework of rules and authority within a given institution such as a school or an education system. How things are decided in a school, for example, makes a great deal of difference as to whether a teacher can exercise and develop professional autonomy without frustration.

Autonomy, moral or professional, depends to a considerable extent upon knowledge. An autonomous teacher would try to resist the pressures of political and other groups in so far as they appeared to be unreasonable. This could only be done with awareness of, and understanding of, such pressures. Similarly, the autonomous teacher would not follow the promptings and urgings of a non-rational and unconscious id or super-ego in so far as these seemed incompatible with what it appeared reasonable to do. Autonomy requires the existence of a strong and healthy autonomous ego, in Freudian terms, where reason can flourish relatively unhindered and undistorted.[9] This, too, would depend upon the knowledge and understanding of the existence and power of non-rational forces within the self. Thus teacher autonomy requires knowledge, both in the basic sense of understanding the forces acting against reason, socially and individually, and in the more particular sense of professional knowledge, understanding and skill. All this emphasizes the links — the necessary links — between morality, rationality, autonomy and liberal education which have been the themes of this work. Liberal education is seen here as a rational and moral enterprise where those already at least relatively autonomous help others gain the knowledge and understanding they need in order to become as autonomous as possible themselves.

The possibility of autonomy increases as the opportunity for observing and imagining alternatives increases, since to be autonomous in decision-making a person must be able to imagine alternative courses of action and choose between them. This is an extremely important consideration for those who educate and train teachers. A teacher rigidly trained in a narrow conception of what it is to teach will find great difficulty in making autonomous decisions and adjustments in a rapidly changing social and technological environment.

Another way to approach the problem of teacher accountability is to note the ambiguity surrounding the words 'accountability' and 'responsibility'. The ambiguity arises because of the bi-polarity of reference the two words have. One can be responsible or accountable *for something* and/or *to somebody*, and confusion arises because of a failure to indicate which significance is to be given emphasis. In normal usage the emphasis of either significance can be implied. A soldier might be responsible *to* his immediate superior in the sense that he is required to do exactly as the superior says. At the other extreme I can be considered responsible *for* my actions in a moral sense with no clear indication of being responsible *to* anyone for them. Not only are these differences of emphasis, but they oppose one another because the more responsible I am *to* another person in the sense of working strictly to that person's orders, the less I am morally responsible for my actions in any other sense than that of simple obedience. The converse also obtains: the more I am morally responsible or accountable for my actions the less it is reasonable to expect me to be responsible or accountable *to* anyone else in the sense of simply obeying them; though it might indeed be reasonable to expect me to give an account of, explain or justify my actions, if only to show publicly that I am acting in a morally responsible way.

The view taken here, then, is that indeed teachers within liberal education must be accountable, but this accountability should emphasize the 'responsibility *for*' significance of the term. Such teachers are responsible *for* the liberal education of their pupils. They are responsible *for*, and therefore accountable *for*, helping pupils to become more generally rational and autonomous, with all the connotations of involvement in knowledge and understanding that this entails. To do this liberal educators must rely on their own professional knowledge and education. The criteria they bring to bear upon their own actions and those of their colleagues must derive from their own understanding of what it is to involve others in a general and liberal education. The responsibility and accountability to be exercised here is clearly more of the moral kind and less of the obedience kind; more of the accountability *for* kind and less of the accountability *to* kind; more dependent upon a preparation for autonomous teaching and less dependent upon a preparation in specific skills approved of and decided by others.

Accountability in this sense clearly presupposes that the person to be thought of as accountable is also to be thought of as autonomous. A person not autonomous cannot be accountable in this sense. More correctly, since autonomy is not an all or nothing characteristic but rather a matter of degree, the more autonomous a person is the more accountable in this sense that person can be, and the less autonomous a person is the less accountable that person can meaningfully be. Only relatively autonomous teachers can logically be called upon to explain, justify or give an account of their actions, since if they are not autonomous it is their directors who must give an account, explain and justify. Only relatively autonomous teachers need submit themselves to reasonable evaluation, since if they are not autonomous it is the commands of their directors that need evaluation. Only relatively autonomous teachers can seek agreement by reasonable cooperation with their peers, their professional colleagues.

Teachers with these kinds of loyalties, understandings and dispositions will only be produced, of course, by appropriate kinds of professional education and training, and I have tried to give an account of what is desirable here in another place.[10] It is perhaps worth ending this attempt to construct a theory of liberal education, however, by emphasizing the importance for liberal education of teacher training and education. Even in an ideal situation, where there is consensus about the need for liberal education and adequate monetary and material provision for it, and where no inappropriate assessment system distorts the purposes of liberal education, the skills, knowledge, understanding and attitudes of teachers would be of crucial significance in the successful pursuit of the purposes of liberal education. In the actually prevailing situation, where the politically and socially dominant attitudes seem inclined to instrumentally directed education rather than to the liberating form advocated here, where the provision of money and resources is far from generous, and where examinations and incentives all pull away from liberal ideals, the situation is far worse. Here only teachers trained and educated themselves in the justification, content and appropriate methodology of a liberal education are likely to defend those elements of such an education to be found in the existing system and to work and argue for an extension of liberal content and methods. Without convinced teachers nothing much can be done about liberal education even in a favourable climate. Where the teachers are convinced liberal educators, however, much may be defended, and much developed and expended even where political and social climates are generally unhelpful; and from such committed teachers, from their work and their attitudes, can come a change of view in society at large, which surely cannot live on instrumentality alone for ever. Such at least is the hope.

Notes and references

Chapter 1 Introduction — theory and education

1 K.R. Popper, *Conjectures and Refutations: The Growth of Scientific Knowledge*, London, Routledge & Kegan Paul, 1963 and later editions.
2 P.H. Hirst, Educational Theory, in J.W. Tibble (ed.), *The Study of Education*, London, Routledge & Kegan Paul, 1966, p. 48.
3 P.H. Hirst, op.cit., p. 55.

Chapter 2 Education and its justification

1 A. Quinton, *The Nature of Things*, London, Routledge & Kegan Paul, 1973, p. 144.
2 S.I. Benn and R.S. Peters, *Social Principles and the Democratic State*, London, Allen & Unwin, 1959, ch. 15.
3 See T.K. Abbott's translation of Kant's *Critique of Practical Reason*, London, Longmans, 1909, p. 69: 'In the order of efficient causes we assume ourselves free, in order that in the order of ends we may conceive ourselves as subject to moral law . . . freedom and self-legislation of will are both autonomy.'
4 For a clear exposition, see B. Magee, *Popper*, London, Woburn Press, 1974, ch. 4.
5 R.S. Peters, 'Aims of Education — A Conceptual Inquiry', in R.S. Peters (ed.), *The Philosophy of Education*, Oxford University Press, 1973.
6 R.S. Peters, op.cit., p. 55.
7 See, for example, comments by J. Woods and W.H. Dray in R.S. Peters (ed.), op.cit.

Chapter 3 Types of education

1 Ministry of Education, *Half Our Future: A Report of the Central Advisory Council for Education (England)*, London, HMSO, 1963, para. 100.
2 P.H. Hirst, *Knowledge and the Curriculum*, London, Routledge & Kegan Paul, 1974, pp. 30-53.
3 P.H. Hirst, 'Liberal Education', in L.C. Deighton (ed.), *The*

Encyclopedia of Education, vol. 5, New York, Macmillan and Free Press, 1971. For Aristotle see *Politica*, trans. B. Jowett, Oxford, Clarendon Press, 1921, Book VII, cc. 13-17 and Book VIII, cc. 1-7.

4 E. Fromm, *The Sane Society*, London, Routledge & Kegan Paul, 1956, p. 69.
5 R.S. Peters, 'The Justification of Education', in R.S. Peters (ed.), *The Philosophy of Education*, Oxford University Press, 1973.
6 P.H. Hirst, *Knowledge and the Curriculum*, op.cit., pp. 30-53.
7 For an expansion of these ideas see Jonathan Bennett's excellent little monograph, *Rationality*, London, Routledge & Kegan Paul, 1964. See also C. Bailey, 'Morality, reason and feeling', in *Journal of Moral Education*, vol. 9, no. 2, 1980, pp. 114-21.
8 P.H. Hirst, *Knowledge and the Curriculum*, op.cit., p. 22.

Chapter 4 The justification of liberal education

1 B. Blanshard, *Reason and Goodness*, London, Allen & Unwin, 1961, p. 427.
2 P.H. Hirst, *Knowledge and the Curriculum*, London, Routledge & Kegan Paul, 1974, p. 43.
3 M. Wertheimer, *Productive Thinking*, New York, Harper, 1945.
4 B. Blanshard, op.cit., ch. 5.
5 P.H. Hirst, op.cit., p. 43.
6 Ibid., pp. 42-3.
7 B. Crittenden, *Education and Social Ideals*, London, Longmans, 1973, p. 49.
8 H.J. Paton, *The Moral Law*, London, Hutchinson, 1961, p. 88 and p. 96.
9 I. Kant, *The Metaphysical Principles of Virtue*, trans. James Ellington, Indianapolis, Bobbs-Merrill, 1964, p. 108.

Chapter 5 Some preliminary ideas

1 A. O'Hear, *Education, Society and Human Nature*, London, Routledge & Kegan Paul, 1981, p. 116.
2 R. Barrow, *Common Sense and the Curriculum*, London, Allen & Unwin, 1976, p. 147.
3 Department of Education and Science and the Welsh Office, *The School Curriculum*, London, HMSO, 1981, p. 2.
4 T. Devlin and M. Warnock, *What Must We Teach?*, London, Temple Smith, 1977.
5 For examples of philosophical analyses of the concept of knowledge, usually with more emphasis on the truth condition than I have given, see I. Scheffler, *The Conditions of Knowledge*, Glenview, Illinois, Scott Foresman, 1965; A.D. Woozley, *Theory of Knowledge*, London, Hutchinson, 1949; and K. Lehrer, *Knowledge*, Oxford, Clarendon Press, 1974.

6   J.S. Mill, *Essay on Liberty*, (ed. R.B. McCallum), Oxford, Basil
    Blackwell, 1946, pp. 30-1.
7   Ibid., pp. 38-9.
8   M. Boden, *Artificial Intelligence and Natural Man*, Brighton,
    Harvester Press, 1977.
9   There are many convenient accounts of Piaget's work. A good
    one is J.H. Flavell, *The Developmental Psychology of Jean Piaget*,
    Princeton, Van Nostrand, 1963.
10 For accounts of the idea of coherence, see N. Rescher, *The
    Coherence Theory of Truth*, Oxford, Clarendon Press, 1973,
    pp. 31-40. Less technically in B. Blanshard, *The Nature of
    Thought*, London, Allen & Unwin, 1939, vol. 2, pp. 264-9.
11 B. Blanshard, op.cit., p. 266 footnote.

Chapter 6   Three accounts considered

1   P.H. Hirst, *Knowledge and the Curriculum*, London, Routledge &
    Kegan Paul, 1974, p. 43.
2   Ibid., p. 41.
3   Ibid., p. 39.
4   Ibid., p. 40.
5   Ibid., p. 39.
6   Ibid., p. 40.
7   Ibid., p. 64.
8   Ibid., p. 66.
9   Ibid., p. 85.
10 Ibid., p. 46.
11 Ibid., p. 46.
12 Ibid., p. 46.
13 Ibid., p. 51.
14 P.H. Hirst and R.S. Peters, *The Logic of Education*, London,
    Routledge & Kegan Paul, 1970, p. 63.
15 P.H. Hirst, op.cit., p. 86.
16 Ibid., p. 87.
17 Hirst and Peters, op.cit., p. 63.
18 Ibid., p. 64.
19 Hirst, op.cit., p. 66.
20 For the debate mentioned, see P.H. Hirst, 'Literature and the
    Fine Arts as a Unique Form of Knowledge', in *Cambridge Journal
    of Education*, vol. 3, no. 3, 1973, and 'Reply to Mr. Peter
    Scrimshaw', in *Cambridge Journal of Education*, vol. 4, no. 1,
    1974. Also P. Scrimshaw, 'Statements, Language and Art', in
    Cambridge Journal of Education, vol. 3, no. 3, 1973.
21 Hirst, *Knowledge and the Curriculum*, op.cit., p. 87.
22 J.R. Martin, 'Needed: A New Paradigm for Liberal Education', in
    J.F. Soltis (ed.), *Philosophy and Education*, 80th Year Book,
    NSSE, University of Chicago Press, 1981.
23 Hirst, *Knowledge and the Curriculum*, op.cit., p. 96.

24 For a brilliant critique of various stages in the development of the verificationist theory of meaning, see B. Blanshard, *Reason and Analysis*, London, Allen & Unwin, 1962, ch. 5.
25 L. Wittgenstein, *Philosophical Investigations*, trans, G.E.M. Anscombe, Oxford, Basil Blackwell, 1967, pp. 11e-12e.
26 M. Heidegger, *Being and Time*, trans. J. Macquarrie and E. Robinson, Oxford, Basil Blackwell, 1978, p. 209.
27 M. Heidegger, 'The Origin of the Work of Art', in D.F. Krell (ed.), *Martin Heidegger: Basic Writings*, London, Routledge & Kegan Paul, 1978, pp. 143-88.
28 P. Phenix, *Realms of Meaning*, New York, McGraw-Hill, 1964, p. 21.
29 Ibid., p. 21.
30 Ibid., p. 21.
31 Ibid., p. 25.
32 Ibid., p. 25.
33 Ibid., p. 25.
34 Ibid., p. 24.
35 Ibid., p. 252.
36 Ibid., p. 25.
37 Ibid., p. 28.
38 Ibid., p. 277.
39 P.H. Hirst, *Knowledge and the Curriculum*, op.cit., p. 62.
40 Ibid., p. 61.
41 Ibid., p. 62.
42 P. Phenix, op.cit., p. 7.
43 P.H. Hirst, *Knowledge and the Curriculum*, op.cit., p. 63.
44 Ibid., pp. 63-4.
45 P. Phenix, op.cit., preface.
46 Ibid., preface.
47 Ibid., p. 5.
48 Ibid., p. 7.
49 Ibid., p. 7.
50 Ibid., p. 270.
51 J.P. White, *Towards a Compulsory Curriculum*, London, Routledge & Kegan Paul, 1973.
52 J.P. White, *The Aims of Education Restated*, London, Routledge & Kegan Paul, 1982.
53 P.S. Wilson, *Interest, Discipline and Education*, London, Routledge & Kegan Paul, 1971.
54 J.P. White, *Towards a Compulsory Curriculum*, op.cit., p. 20.
55 Ibid., p. 21.
56 Ibid., pp. 21-2.
57 Ibid., p. 22.
58 Ibid., p. 21.
59 Ibid., p. 23.
60 Ibid., p. 26.
61 Ibid., pp. 27-9.

62 In connection with the issue of compulsory competitive games, see
    C. Bailey, 'Games, Winning and Education', in *Cambridge Journal
    of Education*, vol. 5, no. 1, 1975.
63 J.P. White, *Towards a Compulsory Curriculum*, op.cit., p. 35.
64 Ibid., p. 55.
65 Ibid., p. 57.
66 J.P. White, *The Aims of Education Restated*, op.cit., 1982, p. 52.
67 Ibid., p. 124.
68 Ibid., p. 122.
69 J. Kovesi, *Moral Notions*, London, Routledge & Kegan Paul, 1967,
    ch. 5.

Chapter 7 The content of a liberal education

 1 M. Oakeshott, 'Education: the Engagement and its Frustration',
    in *The Proceedings of the Philosophy of Education Society of
    Great Britain* (now the 'Journal of Philosophy of Education'),
    vol. 5, no. 1, 1971. As will be seen I have made much use of the
    illuminating ideas of Michael Oakeshott in this chapter. He, of
    course, bears no responsibility for the use I have made of his ideas,
    which he himself might well consider a misuse.
 2 M. Oakeshott, *On Human Conduct*, Oxford, Clarendon Press,
    1975, pp. 12-13.
 3 Ibid., p. 55.
 4 Ibid., p. 59.
 5 Ibid., p. 59.
 6 See, of course, the many works of Piaget himself. Those not familiar
    with these might consult J.H. Flavell, *The Developmental
    Psychology of Jean Piaget*, Princeton, Van Nostrand, 1963, and/or
    M. Boden, *Piaget*, Brighton, Harvester Press, 1979.
 7 A brief summary and convenient bibliography of Edward de
    Bono's work is to be found in his *About Think*, London, Jonathan
    Cape, 1972.
 8 The basic ideas are to be found in J.S. Bruner, *Towards a Theory
    of Instruction*, Cambridge, Massachusetts, Harvard University Press,
    1966; but all Bruner's writings contribute greatly to the ideas of
    liberal education.
 9 M. Oakeshott, *On Human Conduct*, op.cit., p. 5.
10 For the thrust of the views I am opposing here see P.S. Wilson,
    Interest, Discipline and Education, London, Routledge & Kegan
    Paul, 1971, and M. Bonnett, 'Authenticity and Education', in
    Journal of Philosophy of Education, vol. 12, 1978.
11 For a discussion of possible approaches to political education see
    B. Crick and A. Porter (eds), *Political Education and Political
    Literacy*, London, Longman, 1978. There has been much, perhaps
    overmuch, discussion of indoctrination in the literature of
    philosophy of education. See, for example, I.A. Snook (ed.),
    Concepts of Indoctrination, London, Routledge & Kegan Paul, 1972.

12 For a recent report on the teaching of mathematics see the Report of the Committee of Inquiry into the Teaching of Mathematics in Schools under the Chairmanship of Dr W. H. Cockcroft, *Mathematics Counts*, London, HMSO, 1982.

13 For suggestions of a liberal view of moral education see C. Bailey, 'Moral Education', in R. Whitfield (ed.), *The Disciplines of the Curriculum*, New York, McGraw-Hill, 1971. A slightly revised version is to be found in C. Bailey, 'Moral Education in a Pluralistic Society', in *Epworth Review*, vol. 5, no. 2, May 1978.

14 For a good recent advocacy of the importance of the arts in schools see the report of an advisory committee under the chairmanship of Peter Brinson, *The Arts in Schools*, London, Calouste Gulbenkian Foundation, 1982.

15 C. Bailey, 'Games, Winning and Education', in *Cambridge Journal of Education*, vol. 5, no. 1, 1975.

16 M. Oakeshott, *On Human Conduct*, op.cit., p. 13.

17 Interesting thoughts concerning man's relationship to his technology are to be found in, for example, E.F. Schumacher, *Small is Beautiful*, London, Sphere Books, 1974; and in a more complex way in M. Heidegger, 'The Question Concerning Technology', in D.F. Krell (ed.), *Martin Heidegger: Basic Writings*, London, Routledge & Kegan Paul, 1978. For the two examples of proposals for science content mentioned in the text see R. Ingle and A. Jennings, *Science in Schools — Which Way Now?*, University of London Institute of Education, 1981, Appendix 5.1: and Department of Education and Science, *Curriculum 11-16*, London, HMSO, 1979, pp. 28-9.

18 P.S. Wilson, op.cit.

19 M. Bonnett, op.cit.

Chapter 8 The methods of a liberal education

1 See this work, section 4.5.

2 A. Quinton, *The Nature of Things*, London, Routledge & Kegan Paul, 1973, ch. 6.

3 B. Blanshard, *Reason and Goodness*, London, Allen & Unwin, 1961, ch. 15.

4 A. Quinton, op.cit., pp. 143-9.

5 For a feel of the recent debates see I.A. Snook (ed.), *Concepts of Indoctrination*, London, Routledge & Kegan Paul, 1972.

6 See J.P. White, 'Indoctrination and intentions', in I.A. Snook (ed.), op.cit.

7 Ministry of Education, *Half Our Future*, London, HMSO, 1963.

8 S. Brown, J. Fauvel and R. Finnegan, *Conceptions of Inquiry*, London, Methuen in association with the Open University Press, 1981. Apart from the reference I have made this is a most useful book for liberal educators.

9 R.M. Travers (ed.), *Second Handbook of Research on Teaching*,

Chicago, Rand McNally, 1973.

10 T.F. Green, *The Activities of Teaching*, New York, McGraw-Hill, 1971, ch. 7.

11 Ibid., p. 7.

12 J. Passmore, *The Philosophy of Teaching*, London, Duckworth, 1980, p. 210.

13 There is a helpful selection of Dewey's writings in F.W. Garforth (ed.), *John Dewey: Selected Educational Writings*, London, Heinemann, 1966.

14 J. Passmore, op.cit., p. 210.

15 I. Kant, *The Metaphysical Principles of Virtue*, (Part II of 'The Metaphysics of Morals'), trans. James Ellington, Indianapolis, Bobbs-Merrill, 1964, p. 128.

16 C. Bailey and D. Bridges, *Mixed Ability Grouping: A Philosophical Perspective*, London, Allen & Unwin, 1983, esp. chs 3, 4 and 5.

17 This emphasis on caring for what is worthwhile is well caught in the writings of R.S. Peters. See especially his 'Education as Initiation', in R.D. Archambault (ed.), *Philosophical Analysis and Education*, New York, Humanities Press, 1965, p. 110:

> To be educated is not to have arrived at a destination; it is to travel with a different view. What is required is not feverish preparation for something that lies ahead, but to work with precision, passion and taste at worthwhile things that lie to hand.

Also in his 'Aims of Education — A Conceptual Inquiry', in R.S. Peters (ed.), *The Philosophy of Education*, Oxford University Press, 1973, p. 18:

> A hallmark of a good school is the extent to which it kindles in its pupils a desire to go on with things into which they have been initiated when the pressures are off and when there is no extrinsic reason for engaging in them.

18 J. Passmore, op.cit., p. 184.

19 B. Blanshard, op.cit., ch. 15.

20 R.M. Hare, *Language of Morals*, Oxford, Clarendon Press, 1952, and *Freedom and Reason*, Oxford, Clarendon Press, 1963.

21 C. Bailey, *Theories of Moral Development and Moral Education*, unpublished Ph.D. thesis, University of London, 1974, chs 10 and 12.

22 M. Hoffman, 'Moral Development', in P. Mussen (ed.), *Carmichael's Manual of Child Psychology*, New York, John Wiley, 1970, vol. 2, pp. 261-360.

23 J. Klein, *Samples from English Cultures*, London, Routledge & Kegan Paul, 1965, especially vol. 2, *Child Rearing Practices*.

Introduction to Part III

1 M. Young and G. Whitty, *Society, State and Schooling*, Barcombe, Falmer Press, 1977, p. 11.

Chapter 9 The challenge of economic utility

1 Mr James Callaghan, then Prime Minister, made such charges in his speech at Ruskin College, Oxford, on 18 October 1976. The charge that schools pay insufficient attention to respect for industry and wealth creation was made by Mrs Shirley Williams, then Secretary of State for Education, in 1977 and more stridently by Conservative politicians and by groups like Understanding British Industry ever since.
2 Department of Education and Science, *Teacher Training and Preparation for Working Life*, HMSO, 1982, p. 1.
3 Ibid., p. 1.
4 Department of Education and Science, *Education in Schools: A Consultative Document*, London, HMSO, 1977, p. 7. For a criticism of this publication see C. Bailey, 'A Strange Debate: Some Comments on the Green Paper', in *Cambridge Journal of Education*, vol. 8, no. 1, 1978.
5 DES, *Education in Schools*, p. 7.
6 Ibid., p. 2.
7 Department of Education and Science, *A Framework for the School Curriculum*, London, HMSO, 1980, p. 8.
8 Department of Education and Science, HMI Series: Matters for Discussion 11, *A View of the Curriculum*, London, HMSO, 1980, p. 15.
9 Department of Education and Science, Circular No. 6/81, 1 October 1981.
10 Department of Education and Science, *The School Curriculum*, London, HMSO, 1981, p. 3.
11 Ibid., pp. 12-13.
12 Ibid., p. 13.
13 Ibid., p. 18.
14 Schools Council, Working Paper 70: *The Practical Curriculum*, London, Methuen Educational, 1981.
15 Report by Mark Jackson, *Times Educational Supplement*, London, 19 November 1982, p. 6.
16 Further Education Curriculum Review and Development Unit, *A Basis For Choice*, London, HMSO, 1979.
17 Ibid., p. 23.
18 A consistent critic of the behaviourist view was Lawrence Stenhouse. See particularly his *An Introduction to Curriculum Research and Development*, London, Heinemann, 1975, chs 5, 6 and 7. For a particular criticism of skills approaches in social education see B. Davies, *From Social Education to Social and Life*

Skills Training: In Whose Interest?, Leicester, National Youth Bureau, 1979.

19 Further Education Curriculum Review and Development Unit, *Vocational Preparation*, London, HMSO, 1981, p. 36.

20 Report by Mark Jackson, *Times Educational Supplement*, London, 3 December 1982.

21 'Times Educational Supplement', 10 December 1982.

22 'Times Educational Supplement', 18 February 1983, p. 13.

23 Council for Science and Society, *New Technology: Society, Employment and Skill*, published by the Council, London, 1981, pp. 7-8.

24 To confirm this brief assertion readers might look at: J. Rawls, *A Theory of Justice*, Oxford, Clarendon Press, 1972; A. Gewirth, *Reason and Morality*, Chicago, University of Chicago Press, 1978; and B. Ackerman, *Social Justice in the Liberal State*, New Haven, Yale University Press, 1980.

25 E. Fromm, *The Sane Society*, London, Routledge & Kegan Paul, 1956.

26 R.S. Peters, *Ethics and Education*, London, Allen & Unwin, 1966, pp. 225-226.

27 Council for Science and Society, op.cit., p. 89.

28 DES, *The School Curriculum*, p. 3.

29 Council for Science and Society, op.cit., p. 77.

30 Schools Council, op.cit., p. 22.

31 Ibid., p. 22.

32 Ibid., p. 22.

33 Council for Science and Society, op.cit., pp. 23-4.

34 R. Jonathan, 'The manpower service model of education', in *Cambridge Journal of Education*, vol. 13, no. 2, 1983, p. 9.

35 Schools Council, op.cit., p. 23.

36 Ibid., p. 23.

37 R. Jonathan, op.cit., pp. 8-9.

38 B. Davies, op.cit., p. 11.

39 Ibid., p. 10.

40 R. Jonathan, op.cit., p. 8.

41 Ibid., p. 9. The whole of Ruth Jonathan's paper is an excellent case against the trends criticized in this chapter. For another form of criticism against skills approaches see P. Atkinson, T.L. Rees, D. Shore and H. Williamson, 'Social and Life Skills: The Latest Case of Compensatory Education', in T. Rees and P. Atkinson (eds), *Youth Unemployment and State Intervention*, London, Routledge & Kegan Paul, 1982.

Chapter 10 The challenge of relativism, ideology and the state

1 M.F.D. Young (ed.), *Knowledge and Control*, London, Collier-Macmillan, 1971.

2 A label used by many following the publication of *Knowledge*

and Control; see for example D.A. Gorbutt, 'The New Sociology of Education', in *Education for Teaching*, November 1972.

3   T.S. Kuhn, *The Structure of Scientific Revolutions*, Chicago, University of Chicago Press, 1970.

4   B. Bernstein, 'On the Classification and Framing of Educational Knowledge', in M.F.D. Young (ed.), op.cit.

5   G.M. Esland, 'Teaching and Learning and the Organization of Knowledge', in M.F.D. Young (ed.), op.cit.

6   M.F.D. Young (ed.), op.cit., p. 7.

7   Ibid., p. 23.

8   Ibid., p. 75.

9   See P.L. Berger and T. Luckman, *The Social Construction of Reality*, Harmondsworth, Penguin, 1967.

10   See C.W. Mills, *The Sociological Imagination*, Harmondsworth, Penguin, 1959; and I. Horowitz (ed.), *Power, Politics and People: The Collected Papers of C. Wright Mills*, London, Oxford University Press, 1969.

11   T.S. Kuhn, op.cit.

12   M.F.D. Young (ed.), op.cit., p. 77.

13   On general philosophical issues of subjectivity, objectivity and relativism see: B.R. Wilson (ed.), *Rationality*, Oxford, Basil Blackwell, 1970; R. Trigg, *Reason and Commitment*, Cambridge University Press, 1973; M. Hollis and S. Lukes (eds), *Rationality and Relativism*, Oxford, Basil Blackwell, 1982; and J.W. Meiland and M. Krausz (eds), *Relativism, Cognitive and Moral*, Notre Dame and London, University of Notre Dame Press, 1982.

14   P.H. Hirst, *Knowledge and the Curriculum*, London, Routledge & Kegan Paul, 1974, p. 44.

15   Ibid., p. 92.

16   See K.R. Popper, *Objective Knowledge*, Oxford, Clarendon Press, 1973, especially chs 3 and 4.

17   See almost any recent work on mainstream epistemology; e.g. K. Lehrer, *Knowledge*, Oxford, Clarendon Press, 1974; and R. Nozick, *Philosophical Explanations*, Oxford, Clarendon Press, 1981, chapter on Knowledge and Skepticism.

18   A classic is B.L. Whorf, *Language, Thought and Reality*, edited with an introduction by J.B. Carroll, Cambridge, Massachusetts, MIT Press, 1956. A useful and more recent work with an extensive bibliography is R. Needham, *Belief, Language, and Experience*, Oxford, Basil Blackwell, 1972.

19   For a proper expansion of this over-simple summary see F. Copleston, *A History of Philosophy*, London, Burns Oates, 1963, vol. VII, part I, Post-Kantian Idealist Systems.

20   A. Schutz and T. Luckman, *The Structures of the Life-World*, trans. R.M. Zaner and H.T. Engelhardt Jnr, London, Heinemann, 1974, p. 3.

21   M.F.D. Young (ed.), op.cit., p.3.

22   Ibid., p. 5.

23 See Marcuse's account of 'Technological rationality' in ch. 5 of his *One Dimensional Man*, London, Sphere, 1968.
24 See L. Althusser, 'Freud and Lacan', in *Lenin and Philosophy*, trans. B. Brewster, London, New Left Books, 1971. See also references in R. Sharp, *Knowledge, Ideology and the Politics of Schooling*, London, Routledge & Kegan Paul, 1980, pp. 98, 106 and 115.
25 L. Althusser, 'Ideology and Ideological State Apparatuses', in *Lenin and Philosophy*, op.cit., p. 146.
26 K. Harris, *Education and Knowledge*, London, Routledge & Kegan Paul, 1979, p. 164.
27 L. Althusser, op.cit., p. 147.
28 K. Harris, op.cit.; see for example p. 129: 'education, given the circumstances of a liberal democratic society, is concerned to create easily satisfied "pigs"; and it is concerned to promote a pernicious type of ignorance rather than to overthrow ignorance.'
29 See as perhaps a naive example of this: G. Murdock, 'The Politics of Culture', in D. Holly (ed.), *Education or Domination*, London, Arrow, 1974.
30 R. Williams, 'Base and superstructure in Marxist cultural theory', in *New Left Review*, 82, December 1973. Reprinted in R. Dale, G. Esland and M. MacDonald (eds), *Schooling and Capitalism*, London, Routledge & Kegan Paul with the Open University Press, 1976, p. 205 (page refs to Dale et al.).
31 Ibid., p. 205.
32 Ibid., p. 205.
33 Ibid., p. 205.
34 K. Harris, op.cit., p. 154.
35 L. Althusser, op.cit., p. 148.
36 See S. Baron et al. (Education Group: Centre for Contemporary Cultural Studies), *Unpopular Education*, London, Hutchinson in association with the Centre for Contemporary Cultural Studies, University of Birmingham, 1981, pp. 39-40.
37 R. Sharp, *Knowledge, Ideology and the Politics of Schooling*, London, Routledge & Kegan Paul, 1980, p. 158.
38 N. Poulantzas, *Political Power and Social Classes*, trans. T. O'Hagan, London, New Left Books and Sheed & Ward, 1973, p. 215.
39 M.W. Apple, *Ideology and Curriculum*, London, Routledge & Kegan Paul, 1979, p. 128.
40 R. Williams, op.cit., pp. 206-7.
41 D. Reynolds and M. Sullivan, 'Towards a New Socialist Sociology of Education', in L. Barton, R. Meighan and S. Walker (eds), *Schooling, Ideology and the Curriculum*, Barcombe, Lewes, Falmer Press, 1980, p. 178.
42 A. Gramsci, *Selections from Prison Notebooks*, edited and translated by Q. Hoare and G.N. Smith, London, Lawrence & Wishart, 1971, p. 9.
43 N. Poulantzas, op.cit., p. 207.

44 R. Sharp, op.cit., p. 145.
45 Ibid., p. 167.
46 Ibid., p. 167.
47 Ibid., p. 167.
48 H. Entwistle, *Antonio Gramsci: Conservative Schooling and Radical Politics*, London, Routledge & Kegan Paul, 1979, p. 95.
49 N. Keddie, 'Classroom Knowledge', in M.F.D. Young (ed.) op.cit.
50 D. Reynolds and M. Sullivan, op.cit., p. 179.
51 Ibid., p. 187. My emphasis.
52 G. Whitty, *Ideology, Politics and Curriculum*, Unit 8 of Course E353: Society, Education and the State, Milton Keynes, Open University Press, 1981, p. 10.
53 R. Williams, op.cit., pp. 206-7.
54 For a careful consideration of the issue of independent schooling see B. Cohen, *Education and the Individual*, London, Allen & Unwin, 1981, ch. 4. See also A.N. Gilkes, *Independent Education*, London, Victor Gollancz, 1957. For the de-schooling arguments see the useful collection of articles made by Ian Lister, *Deschooling: A Reader*, Cambridge University Press, 1974. See also I.D. Illich, *Deschooling Society*, Harmondsworth, Penguin, 1973; E. Reimer, *School is Dead*, Harmondsworth, Penguin, 1971; and P. Goodman, *Compulsory Miseducation*, Harmondsworth, Penguin, 1971.
55 B. Ackerman, *Social Justice in the Liberal State*, New Haven and London, Yale University Press, 1980, ch. 5.
56 H. Entwistle, op.cit., pp. 91-2.
57 F.A. Hayek, *The Constitution of Liberty*, London, Routledge & Kegan Paul, 1960, chs. 7: e.g. p. 106:

> The dogmatic democrat feels, in particular, that any current majority ought to have the right to decide what powers it has and how to exercise them, while the liberal regards it as important that the powers of any temporary majority be limited by long term principles.

Chapter 11 Teachers, assessment and accountability

1 As witness the fate of the Schools Council 'N and F' proposals which involved lengthy and thorough study and research, would have widened the curriculum for most 16-18-year-old pupils, but were rejected mainly because of opposition from universities. See Schools Council Working Paper 60: *Examinations at 18+: the N and F Studies*, London, Evans Brothers and Methuen Educational, 1978. As an example of the opposition see University of Cambridge Local Examinations Syndicate, *The N and F Proposals: Comments on The Report to the Schools Council*, May 1978.
2 See, for example, H. Taba, *Curriculum Development*, New York,

Harcourt, Brace & World, 1962, ch. 19; D.K. Wheeler, *Curriculum Process*, University of London Press, 1967, ch. 10; D. Pratt, *Curriculum Design and Development*, New York, Harcourt, Brace, Jovanovich, 1980, part 3.

3 L. Stenhouse, *An Introduction to Curriculum Research and Development*, London, Heinemann, 1975, chs 5, 6 and 7.

4 See, for example, A.N. Oppenheim, *Questionnaire Design and Attitude Measurement*, London, Heinemann, 1966.

5 By discussion, for example.

6 For an extensive bibliography see J. Freeman, H.J. Butcher and T. Christie, *Creativity: A Selective View of Research*, 2nd edition, London, Society for Research in Higher Education, 1971.

7 On criterion-referenced assessment see S. Brown, *What Do They Know? A Review of Criterion-Referenced Assessment*, Edinburgh, HMSO, 1980; and S. Brown, *Introducing Criterion-Referenced Assessment: Teachers' Views*, Stirling Educational Monographs no. 7, Department of Education, University of Stirling, 1980.

8 For reasons why this should be so see C. Bailey, 'Morality, reason and feeling', in *Journal of Moral Education*, vol. 9, no. 2, 1980, pp. 114-21.

9 And for a more detailed treatment of this idea see C. Bailey, *Theories of Moral Development and Moral Education: A Philosophical Critique*, unpublished Ph.D. thesis, University of London, 1974, chs 5 and 9.

10 C. Bailey, 'Education, accountability and the preparation of teachers', in *Cambridge Journal of Education*, vol. 13, no. 2, 1983. Some material in this chapter draws on this article.

Index